HANDBOOK OF
Water and Wastewater Analysis

KANWALJIT KAUR

ATLANTIC
PUBLISHERS & DISTRIBUTORS (P) LTD

ATLANTIC
PUBLISHERS & DISTRIBUTORS (P) LTD

7/22, Ansari Road, Darya Ganj, New Delhi
Tel.: +91-11-4077 5252, 2327 3880
E-mail: orders@atlanticbooks.com
Web: www.atlanticbooks.com

Reprint 2026

Published by Atlantic Publishers & Distributors (P) Ltd.

Printed & bound in India by Atlantic Print Services

PREFACE

This book is about water and wastewater analysis and how the quality of water is ascertained. Ten or fifteen years ago, this topic was considered to be merely an interesting novelty. Since then it has become clear that water analysis is a discipline in itself. A great need is being felt all over the world to permeate environmental education to all levels of the society. All these attempts made at any level seem to have a sectoral approach. With this backdrop evolved the concept of *Sustainable Knowledge Through Partnership* in January 2000 and the project was mobilized thereafter. The present book is mainly based on this project.

It has become clear that the chemistry and water-quality of pristine water systems is a vast and complex field. For these reasons, understanding the unique position of water analysis has gone beyond being a novelty, to being an important component of engineering and management.

But understanding the water quality, and using this understanding to solve practical water quality problems, is not easy or straightforward. Analysts are trained to understand the complexity and diversity of these chemical processes, but seldom have training in environmental science. Thus, it is often difficult for them to appreciate how various factors mould and shape the quality of water in the environment. It is also difficult for them to appreciate how chemical processes affect the water quality and in turn the environment. This book is specifically designed to bridge this gap between applied chemistry and applied environmental science.

The book covers a wide spectrum of water and wastewater analysis and treatment. It puts together the methods of sampling, testing and analyzing the results along with various water-related standards. It also contains information about waste minimization in laboratories.

This book is divided into nine chapters. Chapter 1 gives the basic safety instructions to be followed in laboratories. Although not intended as an exhaustive treatise or as a substitute for formal training, Chapter 2 lays the groundwork for various analytical techniques. Chapter 3 focuses on sampling methods and preservation techniques. Chapter 4 gives the methods of estimation of various parameters for establishing the water quality of a particular water sample. Data validation and analysis techniques are spelt out in Chapter 5.

Chapter 6 deals with options for pollution prevention and waste minimization in laboratories. While various factors affecting water quality are outlined in Chapter 7, several water-related standards find mention in Chapter 8. The last chapter serves as a ready reckoner for all those using the book.

This book is intended to be an easy-to-use workbook for analysts, students, researchers and instructors. This is more of a workbook which a reader can build and improve upon as he goes by using it as per his needs.

I owe my gratitude to all those persons who have directly or indirectly helped me in bringing out this book.

This book is dedicated to my father, who taught me that the best kind of knowledge to have is that which is learned for its own sake. It is also dedicated to my mother, who taught me that even the largest task can be accomplished if it is done one step at a time.

I am thankful to my husband who offered me unconditional love and support throughout the course of writing this book. My family and my lovely son have been for me a constant source of motivation and enthusiasm.

Kanwaljit Kaur

CONTENTS

SAFETY IN LABORATORIES AND CHEMICAL HYGIENE

1

LABORATORY RULES

1. Do not leave a hazardous experiment unattended. It is not a good practice.
2. Wear a lab coat, cover feet and confine loose clothing and hair.
3. Wear safety glasses at all times.
4. Do not rub the eyes with your hands. Hands are frequently contaminated.
5. Do not use mouth to fill pipettes.
6. Never attempt to identify an unknown chemical by smelling or tasting it.
7. Do not use chipped or broken glassware.
8. Do not operate electrical equipment with wet hands.
9. Use distilled water from a wash bottle for the final rinse of glassware that has previously been washed or rinsed with tap water. Use distilled water to prepare all solutions requiring water even when in directions, only water is mentioned.
10. Never assume glassware or other materials are clean unless they are so marked.
11. Label all solutions and reagents to avoid mix up. The label should have the name (not the formula) of the material in the container, the date and initials.
12. Chemicals ideally should be stored by compatibility, not by alphabetical arrangement. Oxidizers should be separated from organics, air/water reactives must be kept

dry and cyanides should be stored away from acids. Volatile toxic substances should be stored in volatile storage cabinets adequate for the purpose.

13. Bottle carriers should be used for transporting chemicals in glass containers. Pour chemicals carefully and never add water to concentrated acid. Metal containers and non-conductive containers (e.g. glass or plastic) holding more than five gallons must be grounded when transferring flammable liquids.
14. Integrity of containers should be checked and compatibilities observed. For example, hydrofluoric acid must not be stored in glass and some oxidizers should not be stored in plastic containers.
15. Most experiments should be done in triplicate. Record all data in your lab notebook using the correct number of significant figures. Discard any value(s) appearing superfluous in final report of results. Use the same balance for all weighing.
16. Heat concentrated acids and bases in fume hoods. Dilute concentrated acids before disposal in the sink.
17. Never heat a closed system. It may result in an explosion.
18. Never heat flammable materials with an open flame or near an ignition source.
19. All equipment and materials should be located at least 6" back inside the ventilation hood/fuming chamber.
20. Do not use ventilation as a storage cabinet. Excessive storage can obstruct airflow and cause areas of low air velocity at the face opening.
21. It is essential to keep all common work areas (such as fume hoods, balance areas, etc.) and your work area clean.
22. If something is spilled, wash it off immediately with lots of water, and then report to the instructor. Clean up the spill later according to instructions from the instructor.
23. Do not store reagents near a sink or leave them near the balance where they will be in the way and get knocked over. Return all reagents to their proper location as soon

as possible after use. Be sure everything is returned to its original location before leaving and ensure nothing is left in the balance room, in a fume hood or at some other location.

24. In an emergency, turn off all of the utilities (gas, water, electricity) being used.
25. Exits, aisles and safety equipment must not be obstructed in any way with equipment, furniture, etc. Work areas and floors are not to be used for excessive storage.
26. Disposal of laboratory waste should always be done as per procedures prescribed.
27. Gain thorough familiarity with each experiment before starting it. Get familiarity with all the chemical reactions and the reason for using a reagent. Continuously observe each experiment for reasonable properties and consult instructor if anything looks strange or is unexpected.
28. Read all chemical labels prior to use. Be sure about the chemical being used.
29. Review the hazards of all reagents being used in an experiment before you start, and be prepared to respond to an emergency. Always refer to Material Safety Data Sheets when needed. Ensure that reagent bottle labels possess which relevant safety information is on the reagent labels. Read them before you use the reagent.
30. Get familiar with the placement and method of use of safety equipments.

COMMON ERRORS TO AVOID

1. Incorrect use of the balance.
2. Inadequate mixing of solutions or samples.
3. Reading and/or recording data incorrectly.
4. Using contaminated glassware.
5. Failure to understand what an instrument is doing.
6. Failure to study and understand each experiment and to recognize significant information while performing the experiment.

ANALYTICAL TECHNIQUES

2

WEIGHING TECHNIQUES

For accurate weighing, an analytical balance should be used. Solids and liquids should be weighed in weighing bottles. Do not use weighing paper. Never use fingers to handle the object being weighed. Use tongs, spatula or a paper strip. All weighing should be by difference.

Electronic Balance Rules

- Keep the balance CLEAN!
- Keep the doors closed when weighing.
- At least once each day do a CALIBRATION.
- Never weigh objects when they are hot.
- Do not handle objects with your bare fingers.

When you press Tare, the balance readout is simply set to zero.

When you use Calibrate, a known mass is internally placed on the balance, and the electronics are recalibrated to provide the exact magnetic current to electromagnet to balance the mass as displayed.

Preparing Weighing Bottles for Drying

Proper use of weighing bottles would prevent all spillage inside the balances. Because chemicals would be in a closed container, there would be no problems with moisture pickup and changes in mass during weighing. Far too many analysts still use weighing paper inside these balances which causes mess and inaccuracies.

Another common error is placing heavy beakers and flasks inside the balance and then attempting to weigh chemicals into them. Remember that electronic balances of this type can only weigh a maximum allowed mass of about 100 grams.

Use of Desiccators

Desiccators are designed to provide an environment of standard dryness. The desiccant found inside maintains this. A colour indicator turns pink when it is exhausted. Don't leave the lid off for prolonged periods or the desiccant will soon be exhausted.

A common error is to leave the lid of a freshly dried weighing bottle on when it is first placed into the desiccator. The moisture in the desiccator must be allowed to equilibrate with the solid in the weighing bottle. This will take several hours, and is best done by leaving the weighing bottle top off until the next analysis session.

- Desiccators are used to store the weighing bottles that have dried chemicals in them.
- Desiccators maintain a constant low humidity. It takes overnight for chemicals or glassware to equilibrate to this state of "Standard Dryness".
- When the indicator in the desiccant changes colour it is time to recycle it.

How to Weigh Solids?

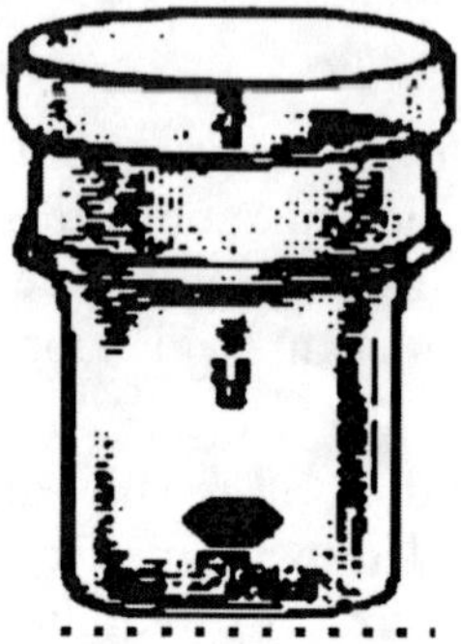

- Clean and dry all your weighing bottles.
- Label each with a distinctive mark using a graphite pencil on a frosted area.
- Weigh each of your bottles and enter its tare (empty) mass in your lab book.

Weighing Solids: Proper Drying

- Transfer the solid into the weighing bottle.
- Place it in a beaker with the cap off as shown, and with a watch glass (ribbed or use glass hooks) covering it.
- Dry at the recommended temperature and for the recommended time.

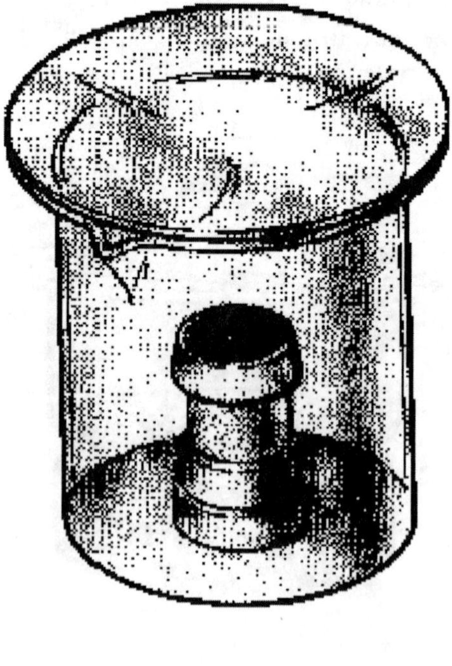

- Place the weighing bottle in the desiccator and allow it to reach standard dryness. This usually takes overnight.
- Note that the top of the weighing bottle is left off while it is equilibrating. Once equilibrated, the weighing bottle top should be put on.

To transfer a known mass to the receiving beaker or flask, first weigh the closed container and contents, then transfer the amount you need, then weigh the closed container again.

Preparing Solutions from Weighed Solids

When a solution of known concentration is to be prepared, the analyst must first determine how much solid is required. This is known as the target value. A common error is to spend an hour in the balance room trying to hit this target value exactly usually by using a spatula to move crystals of solid back and forth between the weighing bottle (WB) and the beaker. This is a big waste of time. If the target value is calculated to be 0.5743 g, the analyst need only hit this value within 10% or so, so any mass between 0.5 and 0.6 g would be okay. Just record the mass to the nearest 0.0001 g.

Making Solutions from Weighed Solutes

1. Weigh WB and solute. Record the mass.

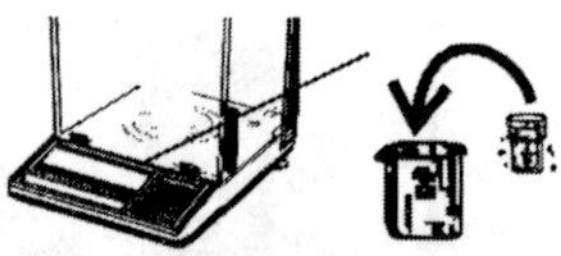

2. Transfer solute to a small beaker.

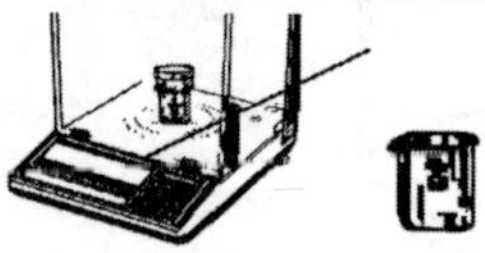

3. Weigh WB and remaining solute. Record the mass compute solute mass.

4. Take the beaker into the lab to make the solution.

Making Solutes from Weighed Solutes

Remember that the weighing bottle (WB) belongs in the balance, and a small beaker to receive the solid is kept outside the balance. Once we are within 10% of the target value it is time to write the final mass down and transfer the contents of the beaker into the volumetric flask.

The transfer must be **quantitative** so use a funnel to prevent missing the small opening of the flask. Use a wash bottle to wash all the solid into the flask. Then rinse down the beaker, the funnel, and the inside neck of the volumetric flask.

Add enough water to the flask to dissolve the solid. After dissolution, add water to just below the calibration line. A dropper should be used to make the final adjustments to the calibration mark itself. Now shake the flask for 10 or 20 minutes to ensure that the solution is completely uniform.

1. Partially dissolve the solute with distilled water, then pour it into the volumetric flask.
2. Repeat this process until all of the solute is dissolved and poured into the flask. Rinse the beaker to ensure quantitative transferral.
3. Rinse the funnel inside and out as you remove it from the volumetric flask.
4. Add more water to the volumetric flask. If any solute is still not dissolved, get it to dissolve now.
5. Add water to the calibration mark. Mix thoroughly.

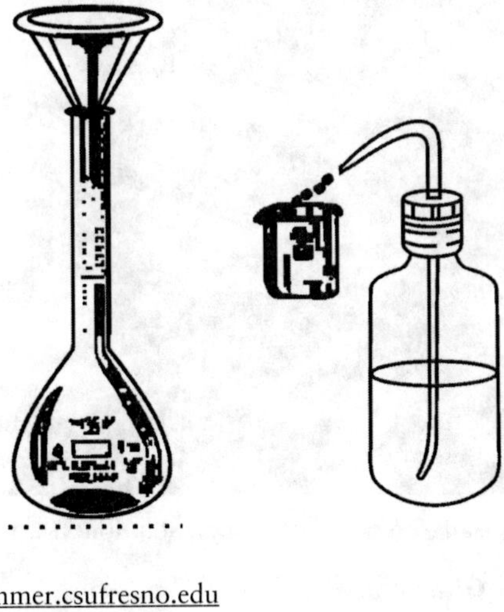

Source: http://zimmer.csufresno.edu

VOLUMETRIC GLASSWARE

Beakers and Flasks

Beakers and flasks are marked to indicate approximate measure only. They should never be used to measure a liquid accurately. They should be calibrated as per IS specifications/ standard methods.

Volumetric Flask

Description

A volumetric flask is used to measure very precisely one specific volume of liquid (100 ml, 250 ml, etc. depending on which flask you use). This flask is used to prepare a solution of known concentration. A volumetric flask should not be used to heat substances or store solutions, and you should pipette directly from the volumetric flask.

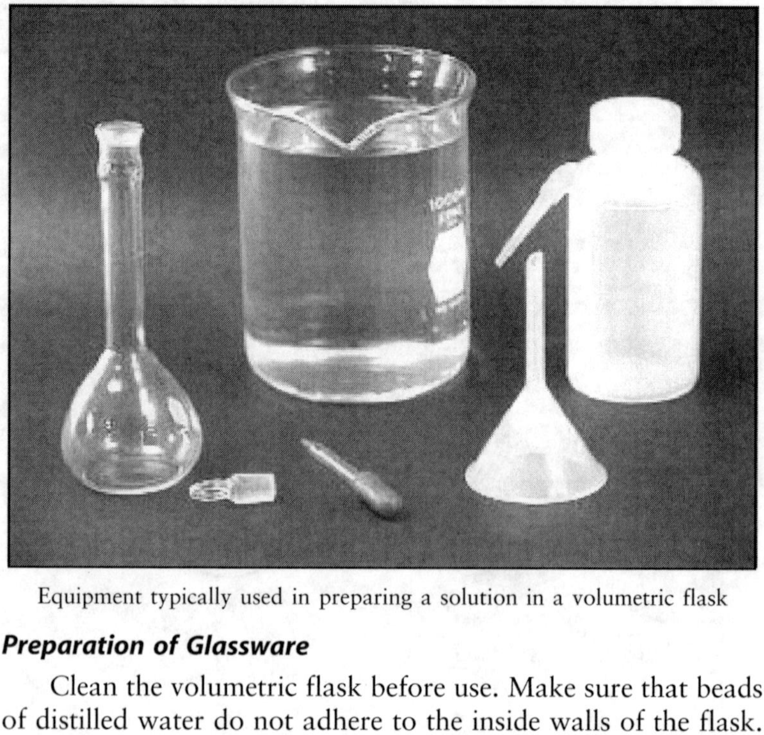

Equipment typically used in preparing a solution in a volumetric flask

Preparation of Glassware

Clean the volumetric flask before use. Make sure that beads of distilled water do not adhere to the inside walls of the flask.

Check especially the region between the volumetric mark and the mouth of the flask.

Dissolving a Solute

When dissolving a solid or liquid, remember to add the chemical to water, rather than *vice versa*, especially when diluting concentrated acids. For solutions of solid in a liquid solvent, first dissolve the solid in a vessel other than the volumetric flask, in case the solid must be heated or crushed in order to be dissolved. After the solid dissolves, pour the liquid into the volumetric flask and use the solvent to rinse all of the solvent and all of the solution from the vessel into the flask. However, if the solid is known to be very soluble, it may be added directly to the flask.

Preparing and Storing a Solution

To make the solution in the volumetric flask, add the liquid solvent to the flask until the solution level is just below the neck of the flask. Stopper the flask, and mix by turning upside down and back. After thorough mixing, slowly add solvent until the meniscus is aligned with the mark when viewed directly at eye level. Transfer the solution to a storage bottle. Once prepared, a solution should never be stored in a volumetric flask.

Finer Points

Mix the solution well when the level of liquid is near the bottom of the neck of the flask. Touch the outside of the flask and verify that your solution is at approximately room temperature before final dilution to the mark. Use a medicine dropper to bring the solution to the mark. Use a stopper when mixing the solution.

Before mixing

After mixing

Graduates (Graduated Cylinders)

The graduate is generally used for a close, approximate measure of volume. Liquids in glass cylinders have a curved surface due to adhesion of the liquid to the walls of the cylinder. This curved surface is called the meniscus. Fill one of your graduates with about half full water and note the meniscus.

If the liquid is clear (transparent) and has a concave meniscus the volume is read by placing your eyes level with the bottom of the meniscus and reading the volume with respect to the graduated scale on the side of the cylinder. When a liquid is turbid or has a convex is meniscus the same procedure is used except that the top of the meniscus is read.

Pipettes

Two types of pipettes are commonly used. The graduated pipette (Mohr pipette) is marked with graduations to enable the user deliver a definite volume of the liquid. The bulb pipette delivers a fixed volume. Solutions are drawn up into both pipettes in the same manner. A special pipette pump or bulb should be used. Both types of pipettes should be calibrated before use.

Description

Pipetting involves drawing a liquid into a pipette and allowing liquid to drain from the pipette in a controlled manner. Pipetting is used to quantitatively transfer exact volumes of a liquid from one container to another.

Mohr Pipette

Preparing a Pipette for Transfer

Before using your pipette, be sure it is free of chips and cracks, is clean, and has been rinsed several times with the solution you will pipette. This will help ensure accurate volume measurements and avoid contamination of the liquid.

Drawing Liquids into the Pipette

Two types of bulbs are commonly used to draw liquid into a pipette: the standard pipette bulb and the three-way safety bulb.

Never use your mouth to draw liquid into a pipette. While drawing up solution, make certain that the pipette tip remains below the surface of the liquid; this will prevent drawing liquid into the pipette bulb.

Reading the Volume

Determine the volume of solution in a pipette by reading the bottom of the meniscus at eye level. Record the volume using all certain digits and one uncertain digit. Certain digits are obtained from calibration marks. Uncertain digits (the last digit in the number) are estimated between calibration marks.

Accurately Transferring a Volume of Liquid

Accurately transferring a specific volume of liquid from one container to another requires a careful attention to detail. Pay special attention to the level of liquid in the pipette and carefully monitor the meniscus.

When transferring solution, do not allow the liquid to drain past 10.00 ml mark. The pipette can accurately deliver up to 10.00 ml, but the liquid below the 10.00 ml mark is not included in this measurement and its volume cannot be specified.

Volumetric Pipette

The volumetric pipette is used in a manner similar to the Mohr pipette. Like the Mohr pipette, the first step in using a volumetric pipette is to prepare the pipette for use. Next, draw liquid into the pipette using either a standard bulb or a three-way safety bulb. Draw liquid past the graduation on the neck of the pipette, and then drain liquid to align the meniscus with the graduation.

Next, transfer the liquid to the receiving vessel. Unlike the Mohr pipette, which should not be completely drained when a liquid is transferred, the liquid in the volumetric pipette should be drained completely into the receiving vessel. However, do not blow out the last little bit of liquid from the pipette tip.

Burettes

Burettes deliver variable volumes of liquids. Burettes consist of a small diameter graduated column, a capillary tip and a valve called a stopcock which controls the flow. The burette, like the pipettes, should be calibrated. The most commonly used burette has a total capacity of 50 ml and is calibrated in 0.1 ml intervals. The burette is supported by a clamp to a support stand.

The burette must be "cleaned" before being used. Make sure that the stopcock is closed, then carefully pour some of the solution to be used in the experiment into the top of the burette, with the aid of a small funnel. Fill the burette only about a quarter of the total volume. The funnel is removed and the burette taken from its support and rotated along its length. The solution is rolled around, wetting the inside walls of the burette. Pour the solution out through the top. Repeat a second time, this time running the solution out through the capillary tip.

The burette, after being lined, is filled over the zero mark. To flush air from the capillary, the stopcock is opened fully for an instant, then closed. If any air bubbles remain the flushing must be repeated. After removal of all air bubbles, the liquid level is adjusted to some mark (it should not be zero) and recorded. When the amount of liquid needed has been released from the burette, the stopcock is closed. Allow drainage along the sides, then touch off any drop which might be hanging from the tip.

The Burette and Volume Delivering

Volumetric methods of analysis depend on the volume of a standard solution. Usually, this solution is delivered from a burette. When writing volume data obtained from using a burette, it should be done in the following manner:

Titration of 25 ml of HCl 0.1 M vs. NaOH

	#1	#2	#3
Final burette reading (ml)	35.8	35.4	35.9
Initial burette reading (ml)	0.7	0.3	0.7
Volume delivered	35.1	35.1	35.2

Helpful Hints on the Use of a Burette

The volumetric analysis exercises will make use of a 50 ml burette. When reading a burette it is important that your line of sight be in a direction perpendicular to the burette column. All burette reading should be done using a burette card.

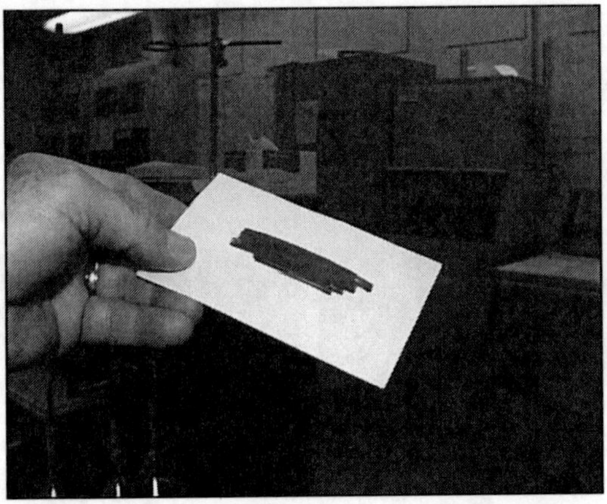

The black streak is produced using a felt tipped pen and offers the analyst a constant dark reflection against a white background of higher precision in determining relative titrant volumes.

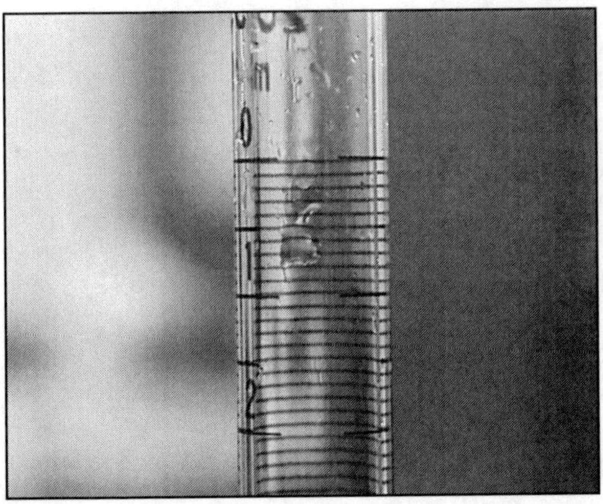

Another problem often encountered by analysts is poor drainage. Note that this burette has droplets which stick to the inner wall. If your burette shows such droplets, use one of the burette brushes and Alconox to wash the inner surface. If that doesn't improve the drainage, draw some dichromate/sulfuric acid cleaning solution into the burette for more thorough cleaning.

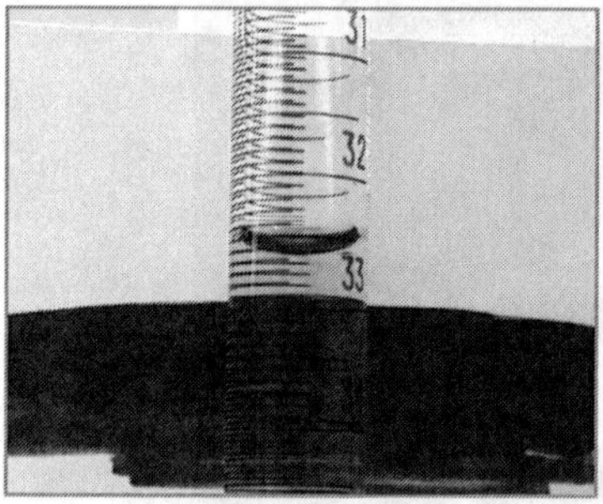

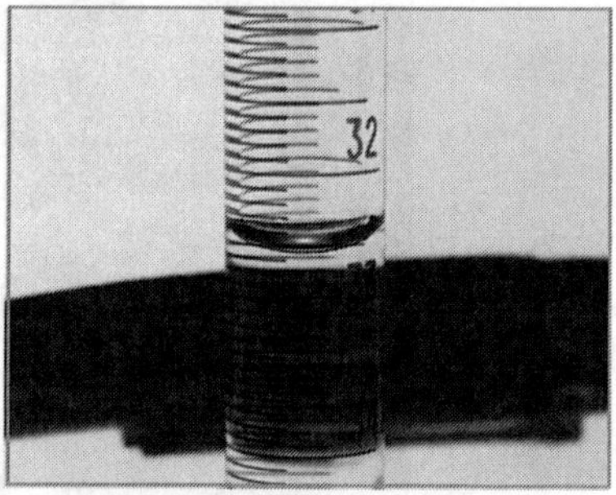

A 50 ml burette can be read to ±0.1 ml, but in order to be able to interpolate to the last digit, the perpendicular line of sight must be followed with meticulous care. Note in these two photographs, one in which the line of sight is slightly upward and the other in which it is downward, that an interpolation is difficult because the calibration lines do not appear to be parallel.

The use of a burette card and a line of sight perpendicular to the burette column are techniques which must be adopted to achieve maximum precision. Note the final photograph in which the level of the meniscus bottom can be determined to within ±0.1 ml.

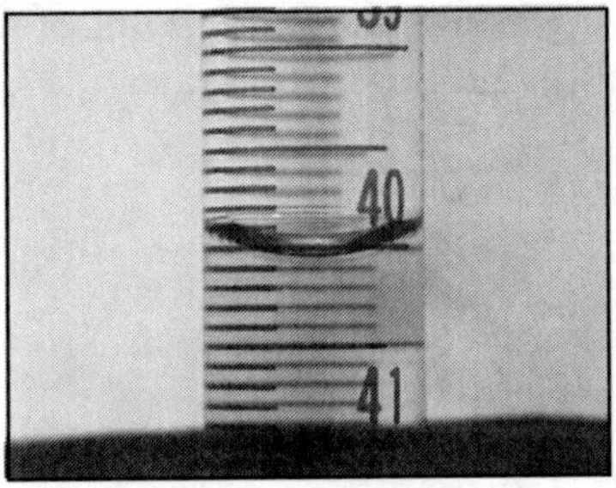

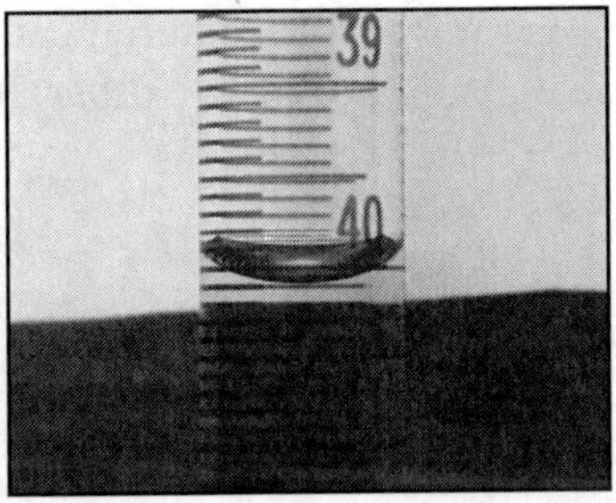

The burette card ought to have a black streak with a distinct horizontal zone of black against white. Moreover, when held behind the burette, the upper limit of the black streak ought to be placed just under the meniscus, so that the bottom of the meniscus can be seen distinctly against a narrow zone of white. Note in the photo on the left that the apparent level of the meniscus is different from that on the right. Since placing the black streak just under the meniscus is more repeatable than at some variable distance, the close placement is recommended. If you are assigned a burette with a white instead of a blue or black scale, a burette card other than white ought to be used.

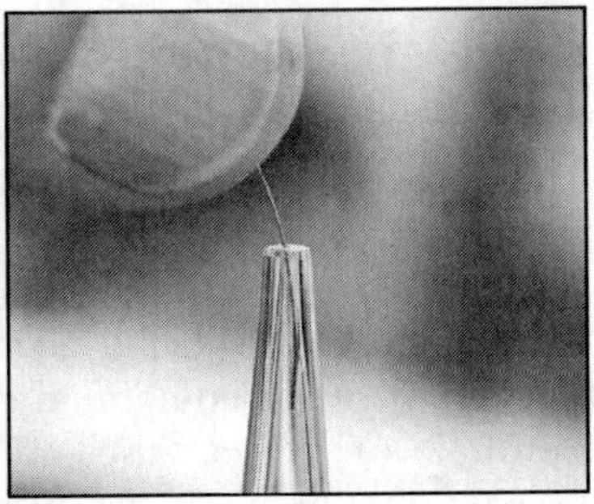

Pipettes and burettes accumulate inert solid material that must be removed from time to time. Here the top photo shows the nozzle of a burette, which will not pass through. You may have to use a wire, available on the lower ledge of the burette case, to clean out this material. It is best to do it with the petcock valve removed so that when you do a reverse wash after poking it free, the material can be washed out at the point of the valve instead of at the other end of the burette cylinder.

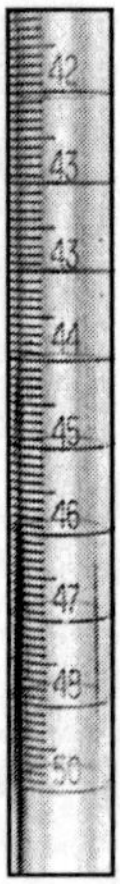

Finally, a brand new burette, just taken out of the box, ought to be examined carefully, as ought a burette returned to service after having been in storage for a long time. Production errors are rare but they do occur. Burettes in storage may be there for reasons not connected with a lack of need.

Source: NT Curriculum Project.

GRAVIMETRIC METHODS OF ANALYSIS

Gravimetric analysis or quantitative analysis by weight is the process of isolation and weighing an element or a definite compound of the element in as pure a form as possible. The element or compound is separated from a weighed portion of the substance being examined. The separation of the element or of the compound containing it may be affected in a number of ways, the most important of which are: (a) precipitation methods; (b) volatisation or evolution methods;

(c) electroanalytical methods; and (d) extraction and chromatographic methods.

Gravimetric Method of Determining Small Amount of Impurities

In many reagent specifications, it is directed that a precipitate or residue be collected and either dried or ignited so as to provide certain information concerning the purity of the reagent. Except where it is directed otherwise in the specific reagent tests, the following directions and precautions may be used in collecting, drying and igniting precipitates.

General Considerations

When the use of a tared container is specified, the container will be carried through a series of operations identical to those used in the procedure, including drying, igniting, cooling in a suitable desiccator and weighing. In general, desiccators should be charged with indicating type silica gel. Stronger desiccants may be required for certain applications. The length of the drying or ignition and the temperature employed must be the same as specified in the procedure in which the tared equipment is to be used. Where it is directed to dry or ignite to constant weight, two successive weighings may not differ by more than ±0.0002 g, the second weighing following a second drying or ignition period.

In those operations wherein a filtering crucible is specified, a fritted glass crucible, a porous porcelain crucible, or a crucible having a sponge platinum mat may be used. Certain solutions may attack the filtering vessel; for example, both fritted glass and porcelain are affected by strongly alkaline solutions. Even platinum sponge mats are attacked by hydrochloric acid unless the crucible is first washed with boiling water to remove oxygen.

Collection of Precipitates and Residues

In many of the tests, the amount of residue or precipitate may be so small as to escape easy direction. Therefore, the absence of a weighable residue or precipitate must never be assumed. However small, it must be properly collected, washed and dried or ignited. The size and type of the filter paper to be used is selected according to the amount of precipitate to be collected or not to be collected, not the volume of solution to be filtered.

Often when barium chloride is added in slight excess to precipitate barium sulfate, the amount of precipitate produced is so small that it is hard to see and collect. If a small amount of a suspension of ashless filter paper pulp is added towards the end of the period of digestion on the steam bath or hot plate, the flocculation and collection of the sulfate are facilitated.

Some precipitates have a strong tendency to "creep", while others, like magnesium ammonium phosphate, stick fast to the walls of the container. The analyst should guard against the possibility of any precipitate escaping beyond the upper rim of the filter paper.

Precipitates, especially if recently produced, may be partially dissolved unless proper precautions are taken with both their formation and subsequent washing. In general, precipitates should not be washed with water alone but with water containing a small amount of common ion to decrease the solubility of the precipitate. It is much better to wash with several small portions. Calcium oxalate precipitates should be washed with a 1% ammonia solution containing 0.1% ammonium oxalate.

Ignition of Precipitates

The proper conditions for obtaining the precipitate are given in the individual test directions. The precipitate is collected on an ashless filter paper of suitable size and porosity, the residue and paper are thoroughly washed with the proper solution, and the moist filter paper is folded about the residue. The filter paper is then placed in a suitable tared, preconditioned crucible, and the paper is dried. The drying may be done by using a 105°C oven, by heating on a plate or by using an infrared lamp. When dry, the gentle ignition, and the crucible is finally ignited at 800 ± 25°C for 15 min. The ignited crucible is cooled in a suitable desiccator and weighed.

Insoluble Matter

The intent of these tests is to determine the amount of insoluble foreign matter (for example filter, fibers and dust particles) present under test conditions designed to dissolve completely the substance being tested. After dissolution and prior to filtration, it is a good practice to check visually (using a white background) for insoluble foreign matter.

Procedure

Prepare a solution of the sample as specified in the individual test direction. Unless otherwise specified, heat to boiling in a covered beaker, and digest on a low-temperature (±100°C) hot plate (or a steam bath) for one hour. Filter the hot solution through a suitable tared, medium-porosity (10-15m) filtering crucible. Unless otherwise specified, wash the beaker and filter thoroughly with hot water, dry at 105°C, cool in a desiccator and weigh.

Residue after Evaporation

This test is designed to determine the amount of any higher-boiling impurities or non-volatile dissolved material that may be present in a reagent chemical. It is used chiefly in testing organic solvents and some acids.

The preferred container for the evaporation of almost all reagents is a platinum dish. However, in many cases other containers (for example, dishes of porcelain, silica, or aluminium) may be found suitable. In a few cases, such as when strong oxidants are evaporated, platinum should not be used.

A low-temperature (100°C) hot plate is usually specified in the test in this book for evaporations. A steam bath may be used, if the steam is generated from deionized or distilled water in a properly maintained apparatus.

The residue is not dried to constant weight in this test because continued heating may slowly volatilize some of the high-boiling impurities. The drying condition specified will, however, yield reproducible and reliable results so that drying to constant weight is not necessary.

Procedure

Place the quantity of reagent specified in the description in a suitable tared container. Evaporate the liquid gently so that boiling does not occur, and do so in a hood, protected from any possibility of contamination. Unless otherwise specified, dry the residue in an oven at 105°C for 30 minutes. Cool the container in a suitable desiccator, and weigh. Calculate the per cent residue and the weight of residue and the weight of the sample.

Loss on Ignition

This test is intended to determine the amount of volatile material due to occluded water or process contamination. The procedure follows directives in the residue after ignition test except that the addition of sulfuric acid is eliminated. Calculate the percentage of material lost in ignition.

Residue after Ignition

These tests are designed and intended to determine the amount of non-volatile inorganic material that may be present in a reagent. They are applied to those inorganic reagents that can be sublimed or volatilized without decomposition; among these are reagents such as ammonium salts, mercury salts and some inorganic acids. Various organic reagents are also tested against this requirement.

The interpretation of the instruction to "ignite" has varied widely. After considerable study of various residues involved, a temperature of 800 ± 25°C for 15 minutes has been adopted. This should assure constant conditions for conversion of the residues to the desired composition without causing appreciable loss of the impurities themselves.

Loss on Drying

This test is designed to determine the amount of volatile material present in a sample due to process contamination, inherent affinity for volatile impurities, or designated moles of hydration. The volatile content must be removable at relatively low temperatures. Accurately weigh the sample in a conditioned and tared vessel compatible with the material being tested. Unless otherwise noted, dry the material to constant weight in an oven at 105°C; care must be taken to avoid sample loss as a result of spattering or crystal fractionation. Cool sample in a desiccator and weigh. Calculate the percentage of material lost on drying.

Substances Not Precipitated

These procedures are designed and intended to determine those soluble impurities that remain after the principal constituent has been removed by precipitation, as prescribed in the reagent specification.

In these tests, a solution of the reagent in question is treated with a particular precipitating agent, the precipitate is removed by filtration, and a specified volume of the filtrate is used for determination. The aliquot portion is transferred to a tared dish on a low-temperature (±100°C) hot plate (or a steam bath), and the liquid is evaporated without boiling or spattering. A moist residue, often an ammonium salt, may remain. When volatilizing this residue, great care must be taken to avoid spattering, which may cause a loss of some of the residue. After the residue has been volatilized, it is ignited as directed in the particular test description, cooled in a suitable desiccator, and weighed.

Weights of Precipitates and Residues

With few exceptions, the weight of the sample used in the test will ensure that at least 0.001 g of the impurity to be determined will be present if the sample fails the test.

The advantages offered by gravimetric analysis are:

1. Determination can be carried out with relatively inexpensive apparatus.
2. It is accurate and precise when using modern analytical balances.
3. It has the important advantage of being an absolute method, i.e. direct measurement without involving any calibration.

The constituent being determined is precipitated from solution in a form which is so slightly soluble that no appreciable loss occurs when the precipitate is separated by filtration and weighed. Applications of the above conceptions are to be found in the following recognized procedures in gravimetric analysis:

1. Precipitation is usually carried out in hot solutions, since the solubility generally increases with rise in temperature.
2. Precipitation is effected in dilute solution and the reagent is added slowly and with thorough stirring. The slow addition results in the first particles precipitated acting as nuclei which grow as further material precipitates.
3. A suitable reagent is often added to increase the solubility of the precipitate and thus lead to larger primary particles.
4. A procedure, which is commonly employed to prevent supersaturation from occurring, is that of precipitation from homogenous solution. This is achieved by generating the precipitating agent within the solution by means of a homogenous reaction at a similar rate to that required for precipitation of the species.

TITRIMETRIC METHODS OF ANALYSIS

The term 'titrimetric analysis' refers to quantitative chemical analysis carried out by determining the volume of a solution of accurately known concentration which is, required to react quantitatively with a measured volume of a solution of the substance to be determined is titrated. The point at which this occurs is called the equivalence point or the theoretical (or stoichiometric) end point. The completion of the titration is detected by some physical change, produced by standard solution itself (e.g. the faint pink colour of potassium permanganate) or, more usually by the addition of an auxiliary reagent, known as an indicator; alternatively some other physical measurement may be used. After the reaction between the substance and the standard solution is practically complete, the indicator should give a clear visual change (either a colour change or the formation of turbidity) in the liquid being titrated. The point at which this occurs is called the end point of the titration. In the ideal titration the visible titration end point will coincide with the stoichiometric or theoretical end point. In practice, however, a very small difference usually occurs. This difference represents the titration error.

For use in titrimetric analysis a reaction must fulfil the following conditions:

1. There must be a simple reaction, which can be expressed by a chemical equation.
2. The reaction must be relatively fast.
3. There must be an alteration in physical or chemical property of the solution.
4. An indicator should be available which by a change in physical properties, should sharply define the end point of the reaction.

Description

A titration is a laboratory procedure for quantitative analysis. In a titration two reagents are mixed, one with a known concentration and one with an unknown concentration. There is some way to indicate when the two reagents have reacted essentially completely, and at the end of the titration the unknown solution's concentration can be calculated.

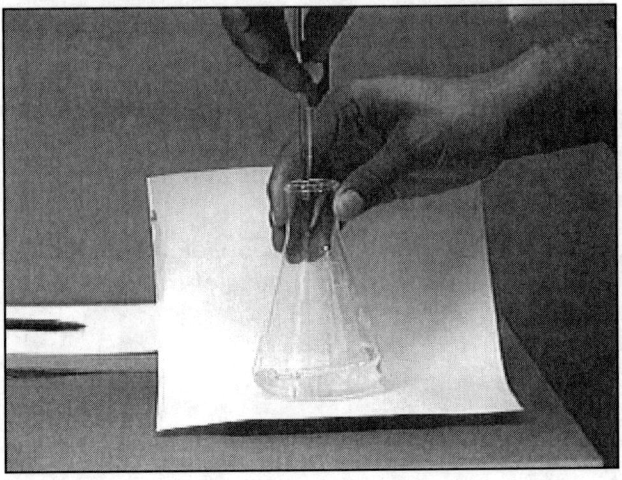

Typically one reagent is a solution and is added from a burette. This solution is called the titrant. The solution from the burette is added to a flask that contains either a measured volume of a solution or a weighed quantity of solid that has been dissolved. The burette has graduations that are used to read the volume of titrant added to the flask.

Preparing the Burette

Rinse a clean burette several times with 5 ml portions of the titrant (the solution that will be added to the flask).

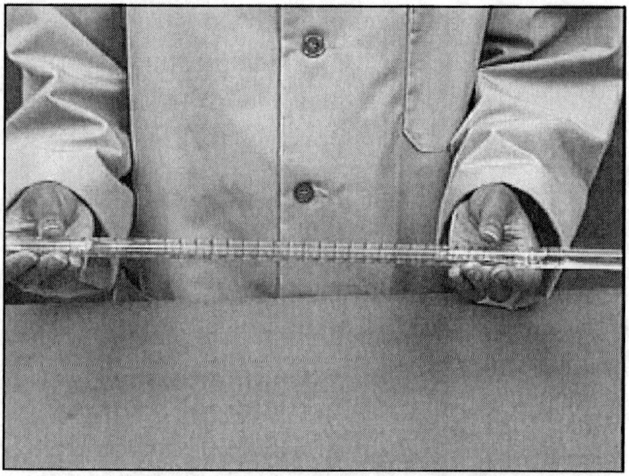

Rinsing burette by rotating between fingers

Allow the titrant to drain through the burette stopcock so that the tip gets rinsed with titrant as well. Discard the rinse solution in a waste beaker. Clamp the burette into place, and fill it with the titrant.

Remove air bubbles from the tip of the burette and the stopcock by draining several milliliters of titrant. Dispose of the drained titrant in a waste beaker.

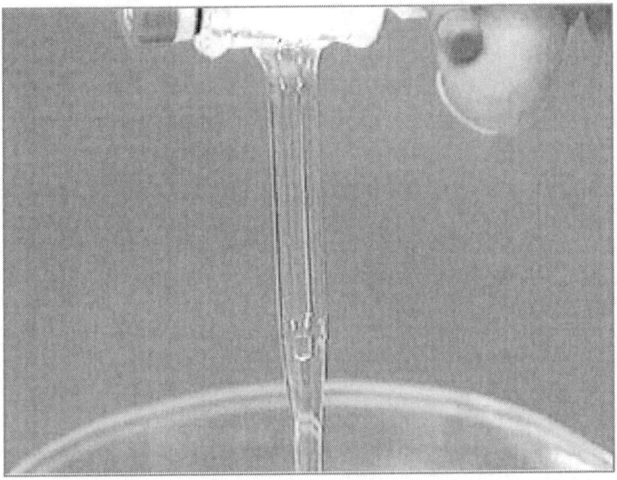

Close-up of the burette tip. Note the large air bubble that must be removed

Make sure the volume reading in the burette is at the 0.00 ml mark or below (the meniscus does not need to be on the 0.00 ml mark to begin the titration). Record the volume reading on the burette. Determine the volume by reading from the bottom of the meniscus at eye level. All certain digits and one uncertain digit should be recorded.

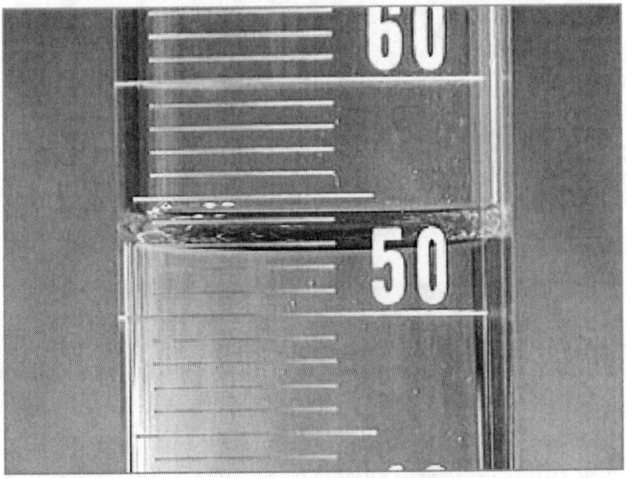

Burette reading of 52.7 ml

Preparing the Sample

If the sample to be titrated is a solution, pipette the desired volume into an Erlenmeyer flask. Record the exact volume transferred. Dilute the sample with a small portion of distilled water (about 10 to 20 ml). If the sample is a solid, weigh the desired mass, add the solid to an Erlenmeyer flask, and dissolve it in distilled water. Be sure to record the exact mass of sample used.

Change in colour of a chemical indicator is usually used to signal the end point of the titration. If necessary, add a few drops of an appropriate indicator to the solution.

Adding the Titrant

The rate of addition of titrant is determined by the rate at which the indicator changes colour. At the beginning of the titration, titrant may be added quickly since the indicator colour disappears rapidly. When the colour persists for longer periods of time, add titrant more slowly (a drop or less at a time).

Be sure to mix the two reactant solutions thoroughly by swirling the flask as the titrant is added. If solution splashes up to the side of the flask, you can use distilled water to wash it back into the solution. Placing the flask on a piece of white paper will often help you observe the first appearance of colour change.

Determining the End point

Overshooting the endpoint of the titration by adding too much titrant is a common error. The end point for this titration is reached when you reach a pale colour that persists throughout the solution for several seconds.

Flask before end point...

...approximately at end point...
(very faint pink tinge)

...after end point

Remember to record the volume reading of the burette when you have reached the end point. The volume added to the flask is equal to the final volume reading minus the initial volume reading.

Source: NT Curriculum Project.

The following terms are used in volumetric calculations:

(a) Normal Solution (N): A normal solution of a substance may be defined as the solution which contains one gram equivalent of a substance per litre. It is shown by symbol

"N". Similarly a solution containing 1/5 g equivalent of a substance per litre is indicated as N/5.

(b) Standard Solution: A standard solution is a solution of definite concentration, the strength of which is known to us. The strength of the solution is generally expressed in terms of normality.

Standard solutions are now commonly expressed in terms of molar concentrations or molarity (M). Such standard solutions are specified in terms of the number of moles of solute dissolved and volume made up to 1 litre.

$$\text{Molarity (M)} = \frac{\text{g moles of solute}}{\text{Volume of solution in liters}}$$

(c) Equivalent Weight: Gram equivalent is that weight in grams which is chemically equivalent to 1.008 g of hydrogen, 8 g of oxygen or 35.46 g of chlorine.

(i) Equivalent weight of an acid: Equivalent weight of an acid is that weight which is obtained by dividing its molecular weight by the number of replaceable hydrogen atoms present in one molecule of acid, i.e. equivalent weight of an acid

$$= \frac{\text{Mol. wt. of salt}}{\text{No. of replaceable hydrogen atoms present in one molecule}}$$

$$\text{i.e. Eq. wt. of acid} = \frac{\text{Mol. wt.}}{\text{Basicity}}$$

Thus Eq. wt. of H_2SO_4 = 98/2 = 49.

(ii) Equivalent weight of base: Equivalent weight of a base is that weight which neutralizes completely one gram equivalent of the acid,

i.e. $HCl + NaOH \rightarrow NaCl + H_2O$

Here one gram equivalent weight (36.5) of HCl reacts completely with 40 g of NaOH, hence equivalent weight of NaOH is 40.

(iii) Equivalent weight of a salt is calculated as follows:

Eq. wt. of a salt

$$= \frac{\text{Mol. wt. of salt}}{\text{Total no. of positive and negative valencies of the radicals}}$$

e.g. Eq. wt. of Na_2CO_3 and $CaCO_3$ are 106/2 = 63 and 100/2 = 50 respectively.

(d) Normality: The fraction of gram equivalent of a substance dissolved in one litre of the solution determines the normality of the solution. The normality of any solution is N/10 means that only one tenth of the gram equivalent weight of that substance is dissolved in one litre of the solvent.

SPECTROSCOPY

Fundamentals of Spectroscopy

Spectroscopy is the use of the absorption, emission, or scattering of electromagnetic radiation by atoms or molecules (or atomic or molecular ions) to qualitatively or quantitatively study the atoms or molecules, or to study physical processes. The interaction of radiation with matter can cause redirection of the radiation and/or transitions between the energy levels of the atoms or molecules. A transition from a lower level to a higher level with transfer of energy from the radiation field to the atom or molecule is called absorption. A transition from a higher level to a lower level is called emission if energy is transferred to the radiation field, or non-radiative decay if no radiation is emitted. Redirection of light due to its interaction with matter is called scattering, and may or may not occur with transfer of energy, i.e. the scattered radiation has a slightly different or the same wavelength.

Absorption

When atoms or molecules absorb light, the incoming energy excites a quantized structure to a higher energy level. The type of excitation depends on the wavelength of the light. Electrons are promoted to higher orbitals by ultraviolet or visible light, vibrations are excited by infrared light, and rotations are excited by microwaves.

An absorption spectrum is the absorption of light as a function of wavelength. The spectrum of an atom or molecule depends on its energy level structure, and absorption spectra are useful for identifying of compounds.

Measuring the concentration of an absorbing species in a sample is accomplished by applying the Beer-Lambert Law.

Emission

Atoms or molecules that are excited to high energy levels can decay to lower levels by emitting radiation (emission or luminescence). For atoms excited by a high-temperature energy source this light emission is commonly called atomic or optical emission (see atomic-emission spectroscopy), and for atoms excited with light it is called atomic fluorescence. For molecules it is called fluorescence if the transition is between states of the same spin, and phosphorescence if the transition occurs between states of different spin.

The emission intensity of an emitting substance is linearly proportional to analyte concentration at low concentrations, and is useful for quantitating emitting species.

Scattering

When electromagnetic radiation passes through matter, most of the radiation continues in its original direction but a small fraction is scattered in other directions. Light that is scattered at the same wavelength as the incoming light is called Rayleigh scattering. Light that is scattered in transparent solids due to vibrations (phonons) is called Brillouin scattering. Brillouin scattering is typically shifted by 0.1 to 1 cm^{-1} from the incident light. Light that is scattered due to vibrations in molecules or optical phonons in solids is called Raman scattering. Raman scattered light is shifted by as much as 4000 cm^{-1} from the incident light.

Beer-Lambert Law

The Beer-Lambert law (or Beer's law) is the linear relationship between absorbance and concentration of an absorbing species.

The general Beer-Lambert law is usually written as: A = a(lambda) * b * c

where A is the measured absorbance, a(lambda) is a wavelength-dependent absorptivity coefficient, b is the path length, and c is the analyte concentration. When working in concentration units of molarity, the Beer-Lambert law is written as: A = *epsilon* * b * c

where *epsilon* is the wavelength-dependent molar absorptivity coefficient with units of M^{-1} cm^{-1}.

Instrumentation

Experimental measurements are usually made in terms of transmittance (T), which is defined as:

$$T = I / I_o$$

where I is the light intensity after it passes through the sample and I_o is the initial light intensity. The relation between A and T is:

$$A = - \log T = - \log (I / I_o).$$

Absorption of light by a sample

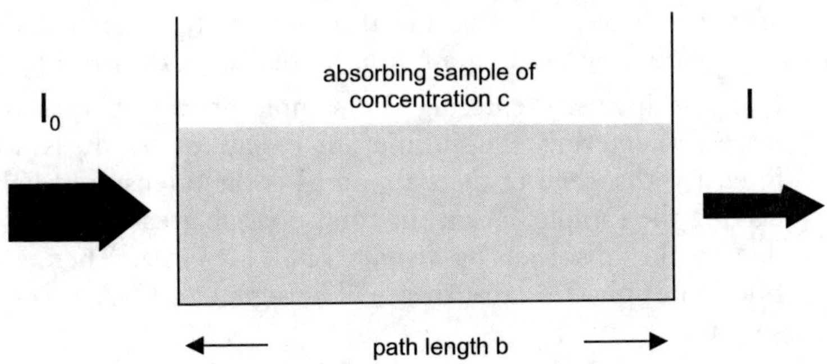

Modern absorption instruments can usually display the data as either transmittance, percentage-transmittance, or absorbance. An unknown concentration of an analyte can be determined by measuring the amount of light that a sample absorbs and applying Beer's law. If the absorptivity coefficient is not known, the unknown concentration can be determined using a working curve of absorbance versus concentration derived from standards.

Derivation of the Beer-Lambert law

The Beer-Lambert law can be derived from an approximation for the absorption coefficient for a molecule by approximating the molecule by an opaque disk whose cross-sectional area, *sigma*, represents the effective area seen by a photon of

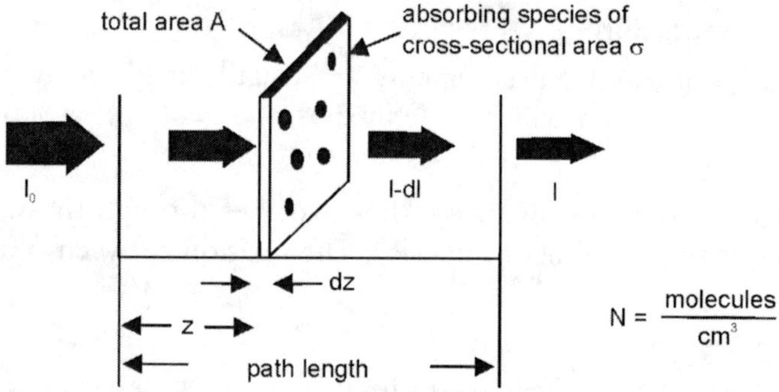

frequency *w*. If the frequency of the light is far from resonance, the area is approximately 0, and if *w* is close to resonance the area is a maximum. Taking an infinitesimal slab, dz, of sample:

I_o is the intensity entering the sample at z = 0, I_z is the intensity entering the infinitesimal slab at z, dI is the intensity absorbed in the slab, and I is the intensity of light leaving the sample. Then, the total opaque area on the slab due to the absorbers is *sigma* * N * A * dz. Then, the fraction of photons absorbed will be *sigma* * N * A * dz / A so,

$dI / I_z = - sigma * N * dz$

Integrating this equation from z = 0 to z = b gives:

$In(I) - In(I_o) = - sigma * N * b$

or $- In(I / I_o) = sigma * N * b$.

Since N (molecules/cm^3) * (1 mole / 6.023×10^{23} molecules) * 1000 cm^3/litre = c (moles/litre).

and 2.303 * log(x) = ln(x)

then – log(I / I_o) = *sigma* * (6.023×10^{20} / 2.303) * c * b

or – log(I / I_o) = A = *epsilon* * b * c

where *epsilon* = *sigma* * (6.023×10^{20} / 2.303) = *sigma* * 2.61×10^{20}.

Typical cross-sections and molar absorptivities are:

		sigma (cm^2)	*epsilon* (M^{-1} cm^{-1})
absorption —	atoms	10^{-12}	3×10^{8}
	molecules	10^{-16}	3×10^{4}
	infrared	10^{-19}	3×10
	Raman scattering	10^{-29}	3×10^{-9}

Limitations of the Beer-Lambert Law

The linearity of the Beer-Lambert law is limited by chemical and instrumental factors. Causes of non-linearity include:

- deviations in absorptivity coefficients at high concentrations (>0.01M) due to electrostatic interactions between molecules in close proximity
- scattering of light due to particulates in the sample
- fluorescence or phosphorescence of the sample
- changes in refractive index at high analyte concentration
- shifts in chemical equilibria as a function of concentration
- non-monochromatic radiation; deviations can be minimized by using a relatively flat part of the absorption spectrum such as the maximum of an absorption band
- stray light.

ATOMIC SPECTROSCOPY FOR METALS

Introduction

Atomic-absorption (AA) spectroscopy uses the absorption of light to measure the concentration of gas-phase atoms. Since samples are usually liquids or solids, the analyte atoms or ions must be vaporized in a flame or graphite furnace. The atoms absorb ultraviolet or visible light and make transitions to higher electronic energy levels. The analyte concentration is determined from the amount of absorption. Applying the Beer-Lambert law directly in AA spectroscopy is difficult due to variations in the atomization efficiency from the sample matrix, and non-uniformity of concentration and path length of analyte atoms (in graphite furnace AA). Concentration measurements are usually determined from a working curve after calibrating the instrument with standards of known concentration.

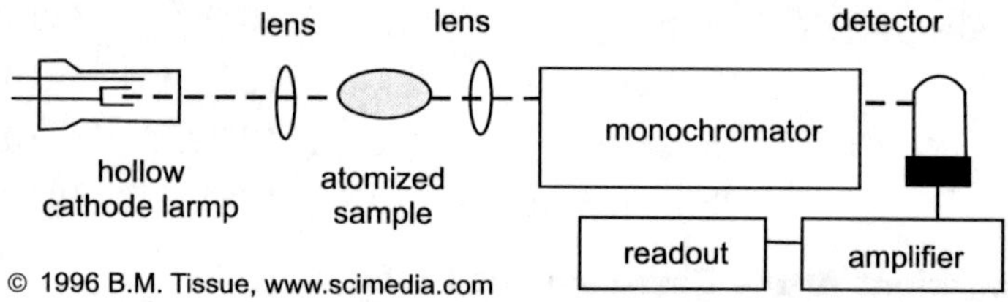

Schematic of an atomic-absorption experiment

Instrumentation

Light Source

The light source is usually a hollow-cathode lamp of the element that is being measured. Lasers are also used in research instruments. Since lasers are intense enough to excite atoms to higher energy levels, they allow AA and atomic fluorescence measurements in a single instrument. The disadvantage of these narrow-band light sources is that only one element is measurable at a time.

Atomizer

AA spectroscopy requires that the analyte atoms be in the gas phase. Ions or atoms in a sample must undergo desolvation and vaporization in a high-temperature source such as a flame or graphite furnace. Flame AA can only analyze solutions, while graphite furnace AA can accept solutions, slurries, or solid samples.

Flame AA uses a slot type burner to increase the path length, and therefore to increase the total absorbance. Sample solutions are usually aspirated with the gas flow into a nebulizing/mixing chamber to form small droplets before entering the flame.

The graphite furnace has several advantages over a flame. It is a much more efficient atomizer than a flame and it can directly accept very small absolute quantities of sample. It also provides a reducing environment for easily oxidized elements. Samples are placed directly in the graphite furnace and the furnace is electrically heated in several steps to dry the sample, ash organic matter, and vaporize the analyte atoms.

Light Separation and Detection

AA spectrometers use monochromators and detectors for UV and visible light. The main purpose of the monochromator is to isolate the absorption line from background light due to interferences. Simple dedicated AA instruments often replace the monochromator with a bandpass interference filter. Photomultiplier tubes are the most common detectors for AA spectroscopy.

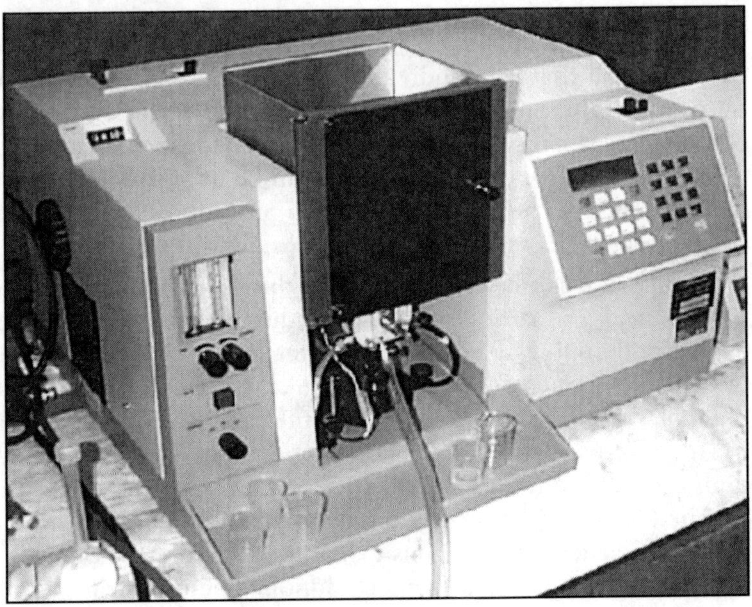

Picture of a flame atomic-absorption spectrometer

Picture of a graphite-furnace atomic-absorption spectrometer

SEPARATION TECHNIQUES

Introduction

A sample that requires analysis is often a mixture of many components in a complex matrix. For samples containing unknown compounds, the components must be separated from each other so that each individual component can be identified by other analytical methods. The separation properties of the components in a mixture are constant under constant conditions, and therefore once determined they can be used to identify and quantify each of the components. Such procedures are typical in chromatographic and electrophoretic analytical separations.

A mixture can be separated using the differences in physical or chemical properties of the individual components. As an example, dumping spaghetti and water in a colander separates the two components because the liquid water can run through the colander but the solid spaghetti cannot (assuming that it is not grossly overcooked as prepared in some university dining halls). Some water will stick to the spaghetti and some spaghetti may go down the drain because the colander is not 100% efficient. An analogous example is the filtering of a solid precipitate to separate it from a solution. These separations are based on the states of matter of the two components, other physical properties that are useful for separations are density and size. Some useful chemical properties by which compounds can be separated are solubility, boiling point, and vapour pressure.

Simple Separation Procedures

- Centrifugation
- Crystallization
- Distillation
- Extraction
- Filtering

Solvent Extraction

Many organic liquids are immiscible with water and so, when such a liquid is added to water, two layers are formed. Whether the organic layer is the upper or lower layer depends upon the relative density of the organic liquid and water. Suppose we have an aqueous solution of two components A and B and add to this an immiscible organic liquid. If we shake the mixture vigorously and then allow the mixture to settle, if one of the components is more soluble in the organic layer than in the aqueous layer then this component will be extracted into the organic layer. Assuming the other component is more soluble in the aqueous layer then we will have separated the two components into the different layers. If we carry out this separation in a separating funnel then we can separate the two layers by simply draining off the lower layer.

An organic liquid used for solvent extraction must be a good solvent for the solute(s) to be extracted. After being shaken with an aqueous solution, the droplets of the organic liquid should coalesce quickly and settle out as a separate layer. To do this, the specific density should be substantially greater or substantially less than 1 g cm^{-3} (the specific density of water). Examples of organic solvents used for solvent extraction include:

Chloroform is a heavy solvent which is widely used for

extracting organic compounds and metal complexes from aqueous solution.

Benzene and ethyl ether are lighter than water solvents. The degree of separation afforded by solvent extraction will be determined by the distribution ratio, that is the relative concentration of the solute in the organic and aqueous phase.

Separation can be improved by increasing the number of extractions, for instance $3 \times 10\ cm^3$ extractions will give a better separation than a single $30\ cm^3$ extraction.

Extraction of Metal-Organic Complexes

A large number of organic compounds form complexes with metal cations. Many of these complexes are more soluble in organic solvents than in water and hence are extractable. For example, the iron(III)-cupferron chelate or the aluminium(III)-oxine complex is extracted by chloroform. The distribution ratio for this type of complex is usually very large, so only one or two extractions of the complex with fresh solvents are needed. The chelating reagents are solids and the metal complexes are insoluble in water. The metal is extracted by adding an aqueous solution of the reagent to an aqueous solution of the sample and extracting the precipitated metal complex with an organic solvent. Alternatively, the chelating reagent may be dissolved in a water-immiscible organic solvent, which is then shaken with the sample solution. Shaking produces a temporary emulsion of the two liquid phases. Metal ions in the sample solution react with the chelating reagent at the interfaces between phases and then are extracted into the organic phase.

CHROMATOGRAPHY

Introduction

Chromatography is a separation method that relies on differences in partitioning behaviour between a flowing mobile phase and a stationary phase to separate the components in a mixture.

A column holds the stationary phase and the mobile phase carries the sample through it. Sample components that partition strongly into the stationary phase spend a greater amount of time in the column and are separated from components that stay predominantly in the mobile phase and pass through the column faster.

As the components elute from the column they can be quantified by a detector and/or collected for further analysis. An analytical instrument can be combined with a separation method for on-line analysis. Examples of such "hyphenated techniques" include gas and liquid chromatography with mass spectrometry (GC-MS and LC-MS), Fourier-transform infrared spectroscopy (GC-FTIR), and diode-array UV-VIS absorption spectroscopy (HPLC-UV-VIS).

Specific Chromatographic Methods

Gas Chromatography (GC)

Applied to volatile organic compounds. The mobile phase is a gas and the stationary phase is usually a liquid on a solid support or sometimes a solid adsorbent.

Introduction

Gas chromatography is a chromatographic technique that can be used to separate volatile organic compounds. A gas chromatograph consists of a flowing mobile phase, an injection port, a separation column containing the stationary phase, and a detector. The organic compounds are separated due to differences in their partitioning behaviour between the mobile gas phase and the stationary phase in the column.

Instrumentation

Mobile phases are generally inert gases such as helium, argon, or nitrogen. The injection port consists of a rubber septum through which a syringe needle is inserted to inject the sample. The injection port is maintained at a higher temperature than the boiling point of the least volatile component in the sample mixture. Since the partitioning behaviour is dependant on temperature, the separation column is usually contained in a thermostat-controlled oven. Separating components with a wide range of boiling points is accomplished by starting at a low oven temperature and increasing the temperature over time to elute the high-boiling point components. Most columns contain a liquid stationary phase on a solid support. Separation of low-molecular weight gases is accomplished with solid adsorbents.

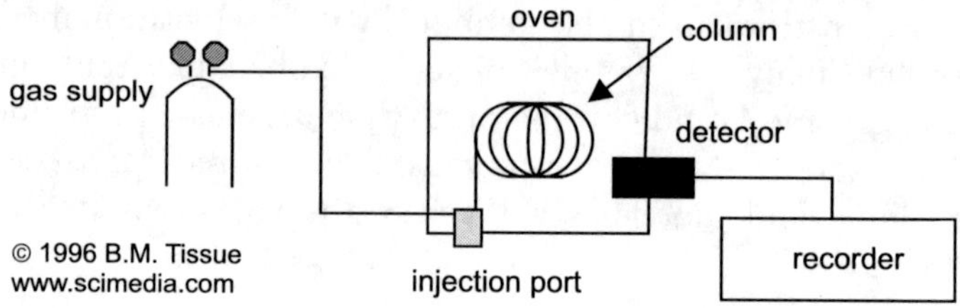

Schematic of a gas chromatograph

High-Performance Liquid Chromatography (HPLC)

A variation of liquid chromatography that utilizes high-pressure pumps to increase the efficiency of the separation.

Introduction

High-performance liquid chromatography (HPLC) is a form of liquid chromatography to separate compounds that are dissolved in solution. HPLC instruments consist of a reservoir of mobile phase, a pump, an injector, a separation column, and a detector. Compounds are separated by injecting a plug of the sample mixture onto the column. The different components in the mixture pass through the column at different rates due to differences in their partitioning behaviour between the mobile liquid phase and the stationary phase.

Instrumentation

Solvents must be degassed to eliminate formation of bubbles. The pumps provide a steady high pressure with no pulsating, and can be programmed to vary the composition of the solvent during the course of the separation. Detectors rely on a change in refractive index, UV-VIS absorption, or fluorescence after excitation with a suitable wavelength. The different types of HPLC columns are described in a separate document.

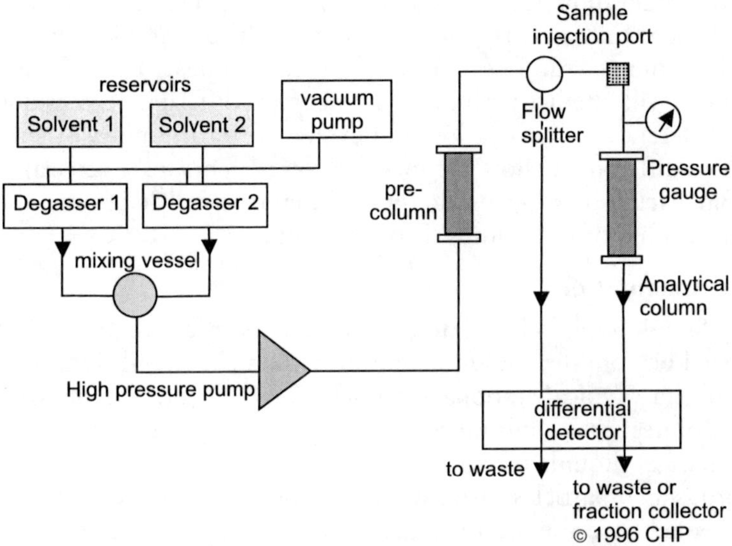

Schematic of an HPLC instrument

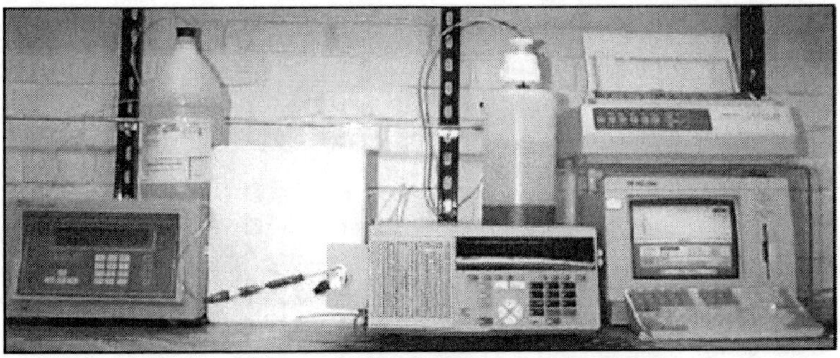

Picture of an HPLC instrument

Liquid Chromatography (LC)

Used to separate analytes in solution including metal ions and organic compounds. The mobile phase is a solvent and the stationary phase is a liquid on a solid support, a solid, or an ion-exchange resin.

Introduction

Liquid chromatography (LC) is an analytical chromatographic technique that is useful for separating ions or molecules that are dissolved in a solvent. If the sample solution is in contact with a second solid or liquid phase, the different solutes will interact with the other phase to differing degrees due to differences in adsorption, ion-exchange, partitioning, or size. These differences allow the mixture components to be separated from each other by using these differences to determine the transit time of the solutes through a column.

Instrumentation

Simple liquid chromatography consists of a column with a fritted bottom that holds a stationary phase in equilibrium with a solvent. Typical stationary phases (and their interactions with the solutes) are: solids (adsorption), ionic groups on a resin (ion-exchange), liquids on an inert solid support (partitioning), and porous inert particles (size-exclusion). The mixture to be separated is loaded onto the top of the column followed by more solvent. The different components in the sample mixture pass through the column at different rates due to differences in their partitioning behaviour between the mobile liquid phase and the stationary phase. The compounds are separated by collecting aliquots of the column effluent as a function of time.

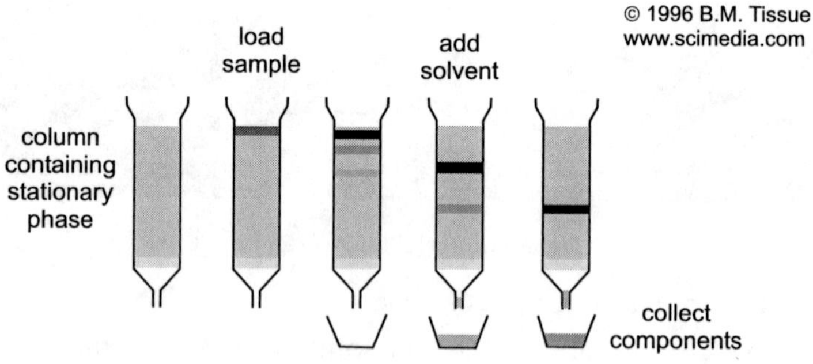

Schematic of a simple liquid chromatography separation

Conventional LC is most commonly used in preparative scale work to purify and isolate some components of a mixture. It is also used in ultratrace separations where small disposable columns are used once and then discarded. Analytical separations of solutions for detection or quantification typically use more sophisticated high-performance liquid chromatography instruments. HPLC instruments use a pump to force the mobile phase through and provide higher resolution and faster analysis time.

Size-Exclusion Chromatography (SEC)

Also called gel-permeation chromatography (GPC), the mobile phase is a solvent and the stationary phase is a packing of porous particles.

Introduction

Size-exculsion chromatography (SEC), also called gel-permeation chromatography (GPC), uses porous particles to separate molecules of different sizes. It is generally used to separate biological molecules and to determine molecular weights and molecular weight distributions of polymers. Molecules that are smaller than the pore size can enter the particles and

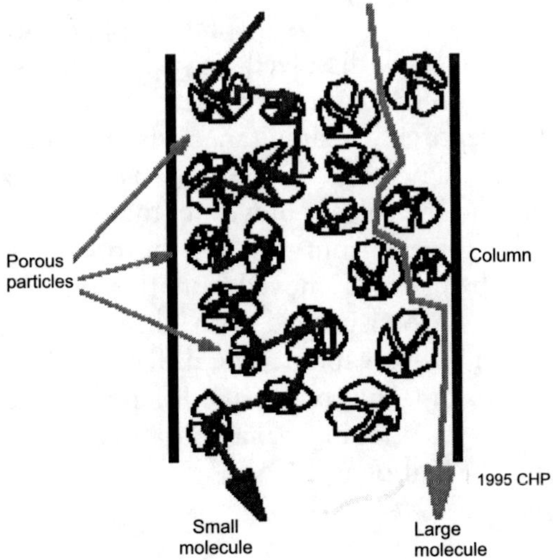

Schematic of a size-exclusion chromatography column

therefore have a longer path and longer transit time than larger molecules that cannot enter the particles.

All molecules larger than the pore size are unretained and elute together. Molecules that can enter the pores will have an average residence time in the particles that depends on the molecules' size and shape. Different molecules therefore have different total transit times through the column.

Thin-Layer Chromatography (TLC)

A simple and rapid method to monitor the extent of a reaction or to check the purity of organic compounds. The mobile phase is a solvent and the stationary phase is a solid adsorbent on a flat support.

Introduction

Thin-layer chromatography (TLC) is a chromatographic technique that is useful for separating organic compounds. Because of the simplicity and rapidity of TLC, it is often used to monitor the progress of organic reactions and to check the purity of products.

Method

Thin-layer chromatography consists of a stationary phase immobilized on a glass or plastic plate and a solvent. The sample, either liquid or dissolved in a volatile solvent, is deposited as a spot on the stationary phase. The constituents of a sample can be identified by simultaneously running standards with the unknown. One edge of the plate is then placed in a solvent reservoir and the solvent moves up the plate by capillary action. When the solvent front reaches the other edge of the stationary phase, the plate is removed from the solvent reservoir. The separated spots are visualized with ultraviolet light or by placing the plate in iodine vapour. The different components in the mixture move up the plate at different rates due to differences in their partitioning behaviour between the mobile liquid phase and the stationary phase.

Source: http://elchem.kaist.ac.kr/vt/chem.ed

BASIC CALCULATIONS

Calculations Involving Amounts

We use two units to describe how much of something we need to use: the gram and the mole. To these we add the prefixes of kilo-(10^3), milli-(10^{-3}), micro-(10^{-6}), and nano-(10^{-9}). If you need to weigh something on the analytical balance, you will need the amount in grams. If you need to do a chemical calculation, the amount will almost always need to be in moles. To convert from one form to the other, just remember that the Gram Formula Weight (GFW) has units of grams/mole.

Example: You are told to weigh out 0.40 millimoles of $MgSO_4$ to use in an EDTA titration. The GFW (found on the label of the reagent bottle) for the solid is 120.37 grams/mole. When solving problems, *always* write the units down.

0.40×10^{-3} units	120.37 grams

= 0.04815 grams

Remember to check your calculation by cancelling out the units. To test yourself, convert the 0.04815 grams back into moles of magnesium sulfate.

Calculations Involving Chemical Reactions

First you must have a balanced chemical reaction. Precipitation, acid-base, and complex formation reactions can be balanced by inspection. Oxidation-Reduction reactions are best balanced by the half-reaction method. All calculations are done with moles. If you are given amounts in grams, convert to moles first. If you are asked for grams, do the calculation with moles, then convert back to grams at the end. The chemical reaction tells you how to convert from moles of one chemical to moles of another.

Example: How many grams of silver chromate can you get by complete precipitation of 0.1273 g of silver nitrate?

$2AgNO_3 + K_2CrO_4 = Ag_2CrO_4(s) + 2KNO_3$

0.1273 g $AgNO_3$	mole $AgNO_3$	1 mole Ag_2CrO_4	331.73 g Ag_2CrO_4
	169.87 g $AgNO_3$	2 mole $AgNO_3$	mole Ag_2CrO_4

= 0.1243 g Ag_2CrO_4.

Working with Concentrations

Concentration is a property of a mixture calculated by dividing one amount by another. Commonly used concentration units include moles/litre, milligrams/litre, milligrams/kilogram, nanograms/gram, and centigrams/gram. When expressed this way, the two amounts are clearly stated. To solve for any concentration, simply figure out Amount A, figure out Amount B, then:

Although current practice is to express all concentrations with the defining units, it is still common to refer to concentrations by name.

Name	Defining units
Molarity (e.g. 0.1200 M)	moles of solute/litre (solutions), or millimoles/millilitre (solutions)
Percent (e.g. 23.45%)	(grams of substance/grams of sample) × 100%, or centigrams/gram (seldom used)
Parts per million (e.g 2.34 ppm, 2.34 mg/L)	milligrams/litre (solutions), or micrograms/millilitre (solutions) milligrams/kilogram (solids), or micrograms/gram (solids)
Parts per billion (e.g. 0.45 ppb, 0.45 μg/L)	micrograms/litre (solutions), or nanograms/gram (solids)

Example 1: 25.00 ml of solution are found to contain 3.45×10^{-8} moles of fluoride ion. What is ppb F for this solution?

We need μg F/litres to get parts per billion. First calculate "Amount A".

3.45×10^{-8} moles F	18.9984 grams F	10^6 micrograms
	mole F	gram

= 0.6554 μg F

Then divide by "Amount B". 0.6554 μg F/0.02500 litres = 26.2 μg/L, or 26.2 ppb.

Example 2: Prepare 200 ml of 6 M ammonia solution from the 15.4 M reagent. This is often called a "dilution problem", but it can be solved from the basic definition of Molarity.

We need 200 ml of 6 M solution. We are told the volume, we need to calculate the amount of ammonia needed.

(6 moles ammonia/litre) × 0.20 litres = 1.20 moles of ammonia.

The source of the ammonia will be the 15.4 M solution. Again using the units:

1.20 moles ammonia	litre of reagent	1000 ml
	15.4 moles ammonia	litre

= 77.9 ml of 15.4 M ammonia reagent needed.

Add 77.9 ml of 15.4 M ammonia reagent to 100 ml of water (for safety), then dilute to 200 ml total volume.

Putting It Together with Titration Calculations

There are two calculations faced in nearly all titrations: the Standardization and the Unknown Run. In either case we have the titrant in a burette (continuous volume measuring device), and the titrate in the flask beneath it. Solution is added until an End Point is reached (usually a colour change). At this point we should have added a Stoichiometrically Equivalent Amount of titrate to the titrant (see the balanced chemical equation for the reaction). The titrant in the burette is given a concentration, usually moles/litre. The titrate in the flask is best expressed as an Amount, usually in moles.

In the examples which follow, we will use the reaction:

$$2AgNO_3 + K_2CrO_4 = Ag_2CrO_4(s) + 2KNO_3$$

Example 1: We have made a solution of about 0.1 M silver nitrate titrant, but need to standardize this to four significant figures. Our standard will be solid K_2CrO_4. How much potassium chromate do we need to weigh out to get a titration near 30 ml?

Since this is a titration, we need potassium chromate that is "equivalent to" 30 ml of 0.1 M $AgNO_3$ ("mmole" is "millimole" in the calculation below):

30 ml $AgNO_3$	0.1 mmole Ag^+	1 mmole K_2CrO_4	194.20 mg
	ml	2 mmole Ag^+	mmole K_2CrO_4

= 291.3 mg K_2CrO_4 (or 0.2913 g).

Example 2: We weigh out 0.2774 g of potassium chromate standard. The titration takes 27.43 ml. What is the concentration of the silver nitrate titrant?

0.2774 g K_2CrO_4	mole K_2CrO_4	2 mole $AgNO_3$	
	194.20 g	1 mole K_2CrO_4	0.02743 L

= 0.1042 moles/litre, or 0.1042 M.

Note how the calculations were done with either ml, mmoles, and mg; or litres, moles, and grams. Use whichever set of units seems most convenient, but remember to be consistent within a calculation.

Example 3: A solid sample weighing 0.2557 g is dissolved and titrated with the 0.1042 M Ag^+ solution. We assume that all chromium in the sample was in the form of chromate ion. If 22.89 ml of titrant was required, compute % Cr in the unknown solid sample.

$$\% \text{ Cr} = (\text{g Cr/g unknown}) \times 100\%$$

We know that g unknown is 0.2557 g, so our problem is half solved already. We can get g of Cr if we know moles of Cr. We can get moles of Cr if we know moles of chromate. We can get moles of chromate if we have moles of silver that reacted with it. We can get moles of silver from titration data. The problem is solved. (This was an example of working backwards.)

22.89 ml	0.1042 mmoles Ag^+	1 mmole K_2CrO_4	1 mmole Cr	51.996 mg Cr
	ml	2 mmole Ag^+	1 mmole K_2CrO_4	mmole Cr

= 62.01 mg Cr

% Cr = (0.06201 g Cr/0.2557 g unknown) × 100%

= 24.25% Cr.

Some Basic Statistical Methods

Other handouts have a more detailed description of what you need to know. Here is a quick summary.

No measurement is perfect. When we read 22.89 ml on our burettes, the measurement error is about ± 0.02 ml. This is called an absolute error, because it has the same units as what we are measuring. Is that a lot? We answer that question by computing a relative error, perhaps in per cent.

Relative error = (0.02 ml/22.89 ml) × 100% = 0.087%

We can now compare this relative error to the relative error allowed for "good work" on a particular titration. For this titration, good work is considered to be 0.2% or less, so it looks OK. Confusion between absolute and relative error produces one of the most common mistakes in statistics exams. If you have figured this out, you are ahead by at least five to ten points on that exam.

The total error in an analytical method is a composite of measurement errors, procedural mistakes, and imperfect chemical conversions. If the number we generate is consistently different from the "true" value, then we have poor accuracy. If we find we cannot get consistent results, then we have poor precision. The only error measurement we can usually make in lab is our precision. We do this by computing some statistics from our results. Statistics are computed by feeding our numbers into a calculator and pushing the button for either the mean (the "average value") and for the standard deviation (a measure of scatter about the mean). From the standard deviation and a t-table, we can calculate the 95% Confidence Limit (CL), a measure of precision accepted by most analytical chemists.

N-1	t for 95%
1	12.7
2	4.30
3	3.18
4	2.78
5	2.57

Example: The following five standardization titrations were performed. How good was the precision? 0.1034 M, 0.1104 M, 0.1087 M, 0.1022 M, and 0.1029 M.

The stat functions on your calculator give you a mean of 0.1055 M, and a standard deviation of 0.00375 M.

This would give a relative error of 4.42%, so the precision is terrible compared to the 0.2% allowed.

The statistics sections of most analytical books also gives you Q tests and t tests for throwing out bad data. With the small data sets, however, you are better off throwing out only those results you know are bad because of procedural errors. If you keep good notes in your laboratory notebook, the suspect data points will already be tagged.

Remember that your overall error in a titration will depend on the combined error from both the standardization runs and the unknown runs. To compute the overall error, first compute the relative errors for these two sets of runs, then

Total Absolute Error Reported = Mean value × Total Relative Error (as a fraction).

Example: Our standardization had a relative error of 4.42%. A similar calculation for our unknown runs gave a mean of 34.55% Cr ±0.14% Cr (95% CL). To compute the total absolute error:

Total Absolute Error = 34.55% Cr × 0.0444 = 1.53% Cr

Report 34.55 ±1.53% Cr (More honest is 35 ±2% Cr from these poor results).

The other important statistical method is Linear Least Squares Analysis (LLS). Other handouts will tell you how to do this using a computer. The important thing to remember, however, is not to put a straight-line through data that is not linear to begin with. Plot your data first. If it looks like a straight-line, then use LLS on it.

The data used in the spreadsheet programme shown above are:

Concentration	Absorbance
1.00×10^{-4}	0.117
3.00×10^{-4}	0.303
5.00×10^{-4}	0.549
8.00×10^{-4}	0.806

The slope and the intercept allow you to compute the Regression Line

$y' = 1.000 \times 10^{3} X + 1.871 \times 10^{-2}$

Where "y" stands for Absorbance values from the spectrophotometry experiment, and X for concentration. y' are values of y calculated from the Regression Line and an X value. This equation can be used to calculate the concentration of an unknown, given its absorbance. Error limits about the regression line are available from the more advanced LLS computer programmes.

Example: The unknown has an absorbance of 0.335. Compute the concentration and estimate the error from the LLS computer results given above.

Solving the Regression Line for concentration, we get: error estimate (from the graph) about $\pm 0.5 \times 10^{-4}$ M.

A more exact calculation of the error is possible from the LLS equations, but probably is not much of an improvement over the estimate shown above. Estimating errors from graphs seems quite mysterious to most students at first. Have your instructor lead you through a few of these until you understand it.

Solubility Equilibria

When you mix chemical compounds together, a precipitate may form. The solubility of this precipitate is of interest to analytical chemists because we often want 99.9+% of an ion to be converted to solid form. Only few simple mathematical relationships are needed to do these calculations.

Consider:

$Ag_2CrO_4(s) = 2Ag^+ + CrO_7^{2-}$ $K_{sp} = [Ag^+]^2[CrO_4^{2-}] = 1.1 \times 10^{-12}$

There are two types of K_{sp} problems for which simple formulas are given:

Type 1: Either Ag^+ or CrO_4^{2-} are in excess (usually called a Common Ion Problem). This is the situation most often encountered, and the easiest to solve.

Example 1: After precipitation of silver nitrate with potassium chromate, the excess chromate is 0.012 M. Calculate the concentration of $[Ag^+]$ in solution.

For other compounds the K_{sp} may have a different form, but solving for the ion what you need is a simple exercise in algebra.

Type 2: If there is no excess silver or chromate, then we have a more complicated situation mathematically. We somewhat misleadingly call this case Simple Solubility.

Example 2: What is the concentration of silver ion if solid silver chromate is allowed to equilibrate with pure water?

Charge Balance tells us that since silver and chromate are the *only ions in solution* (Contrast this with Example 1, where a $[K^+]$ term and a $[NO_3^-]$ would have to be added because of the excess potassium chromate added to the silver nitrate).

$[Ag^+] = 2[CrO_4^{2-}]$

Many students make the mistake of using the methods of Example 2 for all solubility problems, whether there is excess ion present or not. The way to tell which ions may be present in excess after a reaction has taken place is to do some simple bookkeeping. The example below shows the Initial/Final

Spreadsheet Method for following the amounts in chemical reactions.

Example 3: 25.0 ml of 0.10 M $AgNO_3$ is mixed with 36.5 ml of 0.15 M K_2CrO_4. What is the concentration of silver ion after reaction?

$2AgNO_3 + K_2CrO_4 = Ag_2CrO_4(s) + 2KNO_3$

	Ag^+ mmoles	NO_3^- mmoles	K^+ mmoles	CrO_4^{2-} mmoles	$Ag_2CrO_4(s)$ mmoles	Volume ml
Initial	2.50	2.50	10.95	5.475	0	25+36.5
Final	0	2.50	10.95	4.225	1.25	61.5 ml
Molarity				0.0687M		

Work through how these numbers were determined. The Initial millimoles are simply the milliliters (ml) of each solution times the molarities (millimoles/ml). For K^+, there are two potassium ions for each chromate. The Final millimoles are calculated from the chemical reaction between silver and chromate. Remember that two silver ions react with one chromate ion. Nitrate and potassium are Spectator Ions; their millimoles do not change. Silver is (almost) all wiped out, with chromate left in excess. *We are left with a Common Ion problem.* The chromate concentration is obtained by dividing the millimoles of chromate (4.225 mmoles) by the milliliters of solution (61.5 ml).

This may seem pretty complicated, but is just an example of writing everything down that we know, then solving for what we need. Each step is simple. Looking at the information and organizing it into a solution takes thought and practice. It cannot be learned the night before an exam.

More advanced solubility product problems build on these basic ideas. For example, the concentration of excess chromate calculated in Example 3 is not really the Equilibrium Concentration $[CrO_4^{2-}]$ needed in the K_{sp} expression, but is actually the Analytical Concentration $C_{chromate}$ = (mmoles excess chromate/mL of solution), and will be slightly smaller than the equilibrium concentration. In this example, the difference is too small to matter, but in cases where the solubility of the precipitate is fairly high, more advanced methods will be needed based on the use of all the terms in the charge balance expression. The Initial/Final spreadsheet will help in the calculation of many of these terms.

We have also neglected the effect of ionic strength on the activity of the ions, resulting in an apparent increase in the value of the K_{sp}. Ionic strength and activity calculations begin with an Initial/Final spreadsheet to catalog all the ions present.

Acid/Base Equilibria

There are five monoprotic acid/base systems (and one polyprotic) you must be able to solve without fail:

Type	Examples	Approximate formulas
Strong Acid	HCl, HNO_3, H_2SO_4 (first proton), $HClO_4$	$[H^+]$ = C_{SA}, (if $C_{SA} > 10^{-6}$) pH = –log $[H^+]$
Strong Base	NaOH, KOH, $Ba(OH)_2$	$[OH^-] = C_{SB}$, (if $C_{SB} > 10^{-6}$) $[H^+] = K_w/[OH^-]$
Weak Acid	Acids with a K_a, e.g. CH_3COOH, or salts of weak bases, e.g. NH_4Cl.	
Weak Base	Bases with a K_b (mostly amines, e.g. NH_3), or salts of weak acids, e.g. $CH_3COO^-Na^+$.	
Buffer	Mixtures of weak acids and their conjugate bases, e.g. CH_3COOH mixed with $CH_3COO^-Na^+$.	
Amphoteric (polyprotic)	$NaHCO_3$, KHPhthalate.	

Strong acids and bases ionize completely, so there is no equilibrium expression. Only the dissociation of water $H_2O = H^+ + OH^-$, $K_w = [H^+][OH^-] = 10^{-14}$, sometimes expressed as pH = 14 – pOH, needs to be used on occasion to convert between pH and pOH.

Weak acids ionize only partially, and have an equilibrium expression.

Note the distinction between C_{HA}, the molar concentration of the weak acid we think we have placed in the system, and [HA], the equilibrium concentration that *actually exists in solution*.

Weak bases hydrolyze in water, which seems like something different from weak acids. The equations produced are almost identical, however, if you swap H^+ and OH^- as well as K_a and K_b. To confuse students further, the K_b that describes the hydrolysis of a salt of a weak acid is called a K_h in most textbooks. Here K_h and K_b are just called K_b.

The biggest problem students seem to have is recognizing what kind of acid/base system they are solving for. The list of common strong acids and bases is very short and is given in the table on Page 56. Memorize these. Almost everything else will be weak. Buffers are recognized by the presence of both the conjugate acid and the conjugate base of a weak acid or base. In simple problems you will be told what the substances are. In more complicated problems you will be given some chemical that react. In that case you need to use the Initial/Final Spreadsheet Method to determine what is in solution after the reaction is over. Then choose the appropriate acid/base system and solve the equations.

The formulas given above are approximate, but work in so many cases that you would probably be forgiven for misapplying these on occasion. More advanced students will be able to derive these from mass balance, charge balance and the equilibrium expressions, and will know the limitations of the formulas used. Lecture will cover a host of applications not covered here, such as acid/base titration curves and fraction-of-species calculations.

Example 1: What is the pH of 0.0020 M NaOH?

This is a Strong Base. $[OH^-]$ = 0.0020 M.

pOH = –log (0.0020) = 2.70. pH = 14 – 2.70 = 11.30.

Example 2: What is the pH of 0.045 M benzoic acid?

This is not one of the strong acids listed, so it is probably a weak acid. In the back of our analytical book we find that $K_a = 6.3 \times 10^{-5}$. Plugging into the formula:

If you cannot get a stable solution by this means, you must convert this expression into a quadratic equation and solve it by the method you learned in algebra.

Example 3: 3.45 millimoles of acetic acid are mixed with 2.14 millimoles of sodium acetate in 100 ml of distilled water. What is the pH of the solution?

Acetic acid and sodium acetate form a conjugate acid/base pair. That makes this a buffer problem. A look in the back of the book gives us Ka = 1.75×10^{-5}. pKa = $-\log(1.75\times10^{-5})$ = 4.76.

Example 4: 21.3 ml of 0.10 M NH_3 is mixed with 15.6 ml of 0.10 M HCl. What is the pH of the resulting solution?

NH_3 is a weak base. HCl is a strong acid. This mixture seems not to fit into any of the categories above. But wait! Acids and bases REACT with each other (unless they are conjugate acid/base pairs). This calls for an **Initial/Final Spreadsheet.**

$H^+ + Cl^- + NH_3 \rightarrow NH_4^+ + Cl^-$

	H^+ mmoles	Cl^- mmoles	NH_3 mmoles	NH_4^+ mmoles	Volume ml
Initial	1.56	1.56	2.13	0	21.3+15.6
Final	0	1.56	0.57	1.56	36.9 ml
Molarity			0.0154M	0.0423M	

We again ignore the spectator ions. What is left is a BUFFER. The K_b of NH_3 is 1.75×10^{-5}. $pK_b = -\log(1.75\times10^{-5})$ = 4.76; $pK_a = 14 - pK_b = 9.24$.

Example 5: In lab we are asked to do a titration curve for potassium hydrogen phthalate. 3.00 millimoles of KHP are dissolved in 50 ml. What is the beginning pH of this titration?

KHP (P stands for phthalate here) is an amphoteric substance.

(HP^- could accept a proton and act like a base; on the other hand it could give up its proton and act like an acid. This substance does not fall into any of our first five categories.) The parent polyprotic acid is o-phthalic acid. The back of the book gives us $K_1 = 1.2\times10^{-3}$, $K_2 = 3.9\times10^{-6}$.

This equation is an approximation. Your textbook will have the longer and more accurate expression.

Complex Formation Equilibria

Complexing agents are used to bind certain classes of metal ions, forming soluble complex ions. An important complexing agent used for titrations is EDTA, called Y^{4-} for short. The equilibrium constant for the formation of the complex ion is called (surprise!) the Formation Constant, K_f. Metals like calcium—which have very little interesting chemistry—will form complexes with EDTA that can be used for titrations.

Example 1: 45.3 ml of 0.0100 M EDTA is added to 0.300 millimoles of Ca^{2+} dissolved in 50.0 ml of distilled water. What is the concentration of Ca^{2+} *if all of the excess EDTA is present as* Y^{4-}?

This calls for the Initial/Final Spreadsheet once again. (In the next example we will add a modification that deals with EDTA that is not all present as Y^{4-} due to pH effects, so stay tuned.)

$Ca^{2+} + Y^{4-} = CaY^{2-}$

	Ca^{2+} mmoles	Y^{4-} mmoles	CaY^{2-} mmoles	Volume ml
Initial	0.300	0.453	0	50 +45.3
Final	0	0.153	0.300	95.3 ml
Molarity		0.00161M	0.00315M	

Solving K_f for Ca^{2+} we get

It was easy enough, but that was not entirely accurate, as the next example will show.

EDTA is a polyprotic acid as well as a complexing agent. This means it can exist as a combination of the species H_4Y, H_3Y^-, H_2Y^{2-}, HY^{3-}, and Y^{4-}. There will be four acid equilibrium constants, K_1, K_2, K_3, and K_4. The fraction of the species that will be the Y^{4-} we need can be calculated from these equilibrium constants and the mass balance relationship:

$$C_T = [H_4Y] + [H_3Y^-] + [H_2Y^{2-}] + [HY^{3-}] + [Y^{4-}]$$

Where C_T is the total concentration of all free EDTA species in solution. In Example 1 above, C_T would be 0.00161M. To calculate the true concentration of Y^{4-}, we need the fraction of species a_4, where although messy, calculating a_4 at any given pH is straightforward. We can now calculate the true value for $[Y^{4-}]$. It is

$$[Y^{4-}] = C_T\, a_4.$$

Example 2: Calculate the concentration of Ca^{2+} from example 1 at pH = 10 and at pH = 6.

At pH 10, $a_4 = 3.5\times10^{-1}$; at pH 6, $a_4 = 2.2\times10^{-5}$.

Spectrophotometry

Most simple calculations done for spectrophotometry involve reading concentrations from working curves followed by dilution calculations (See the Linear Least Squares example in the Statistics sections above). Metals are often measured by determining the absorbance of a coloured complex, so we need to be sure the complexation is complete by controlling the pH and concentration of the complexing agent. The only other things that need to be calculated involve Transmittance and Absorbance.

To do spectrophotometry in the laboratory we must be familiar with the components of a spectrophotometer. These are the light source (will it emit at the wavelength needed?), the monochromator (will it provide good resolution with low stray light?), the sample cell (will it transmit the wavelength selected?), the detector (will it detect the wavelength selected?), and the readout electronics (should we read out in absorbance, transmittance, or something else?).

We shine a band of coloured light of power P_0 through a cell; it comes out with power P. Transmittance is simply

$$T = P/P_0; \text{ or } \%T = (P/P_0) \times 100\%$$

Absorbance and Transmittance can be calculated from each other by:

$A = -\log T$; or $A = \log(100\%/\%T)$; and we can get T from A by $T = 10^{-A}$.

Absorbance is related to concentration through the absorptivity "a", the cell path length "b" (usually in centimeters), and the Concentration "C". The relationship is called Beer's Law and is simply

$A = abC$

If C is in moles/litre, then "a" is called the molar absorptivity with units of $cm^{-1}mole^{-1}$ litres and is often given the symbol [epsilon]. If other concentration units are used, then "a" has whatever units it takes to make Absorbance come out dimensionless.

The optimum absorptivity is obtained by running a spectrum of our compound. This plot of absorbance vs. wavelength is used to find a peak of maximum absorbance that is not near peaks of interfering substances.

To do a spectrophotometric analysis we measure the absorbance of a series of standard solutions, then plot A vs. C. If Beer's Law is obeyed, we will get a straight-line that can be used to measure the concentrations of unknown solutions.

Deviations from Beer's Law can take place if our metal ions are not completely complexed (chemical effects) or if our solution is so highly absorbing that the stray light in our instrument gives false absorbance readings (instrumental effects). At the other extreme, our solution could be so dilute that the instrument cannot "see" the tiny amount of colour formed. Examining sources of instrumental error shows us that our best measurements are between absorbance 0.1 and absorbance 1.0, with a minimum error at absorbance 0.3.

Example: An iron-phenanthroline complex has a concentration of 10.0 μg Fe/ml and gives a %T of 1.3% in a 1.00 cm cell at 520 nm wavelength using an inexpensive Spectronic 20 spectrophotometer. Calculate the absorbance and the absorptivity of this complex, then state if this is a good standard solution to use.

A Spectronic 20 would not give good measurements at 1.89 A, since that is well above 1.0 A. Either lower the concentrations to around or use a more expensive spectrophotometer that can measure above absorbance 1.0. At this high absorbance Beer's Law would probably not be followed on an inexpensive Spectronic 20, so any calculations using it will contain a lot of error. The calculation shown can be used to estimate a better concentration to try next, however.

Electrochemistry

Oxidation/Reduction reactions proceed by the transfer of electrons from a donor of electrons to an acceptor. The charge transfer reactions, the identities of the donors and acceptors, and the relative energies involved are summarized in the table of Standard Reduction Potentials found in the backs of most analytical chemistry books. Two examples are:

$Cr_2O_7^{2-} + 14H^+ + 6e^- = 2Cr^{3+} + 7H_2O$	$E^o = 1.33$ volts
$Fe^{3+} + e^- = Fe^{2+}$	$E^o = 0.771$ volts

Acceptors of electrons are found on the left-hand side of these half-reactions. Donors of electrons are found on the right-hand side. Additional substances, not involved directly in charge transfer, such as H^+ and H_2O are added as needed to balance the half-reactions. When the half-reactions are arranged in descending order of the Standard Reduction Potentials as shown above, the best electron acceptors are found at the upper left, and the best donors are found at the lower right. The best acceptor in our very short table is then $Cr_2O_7^{2-}$, and the best donor is Fe^{2+}. For a balanced, spontaneous complete reaction, we must place a good donor with a good acceptor, and make sure the number of electrons transferred is the same for both reactions. This gives us the complete balanced reaction of:

$$Cr_2O_7^{2-} + 6Fe^{2+} + 14H^+ = 2Cr^{3+} + 6Fe^{3+} + 7H_2O$$

which can be used as a titration reaction for the determination of Fe^{2+} by dichromate. Using more conventional terms, $Cr_2O_7^{2-}$ is called an oxidizing agent, and Fe^{2+} a reducing agent.

It is possible to measure the potential energy difference in these half-reactions directly. Assume we set up the following electrochemical cell:

Pt| 0.10M $Cr_2O_7^{2-}$, 0.5M Cr^{3+}, 0.2M H^+ || Standard Hydrogen Electrode (SHE)

in which "|" stands for the phase boundary between the Pt electrode and the contents of the cell, and "||" stands for a salt bridge between the left-hand side of our cell and the right side which contains a reference electrode. Next attach an electrometer between the Pt of the left side and the electrode of the SHE on the right. The potential we would measure is

$$E_{meas} = E_{dichromate/chromium(III)} - E_{SHE}$$

The SHE is a reference electrode defined as having a potential of 0.000 volts. E_{meas} then depends on the E value of the dichromate/ Cr^{3+} half reaction. We compute this potential from the Nernst Equation.

Our measured potential is then

$$E_{meas} = 1.23 \text{ volts} - 0.000 \text{ volts} = 1.23 \text{ volts.}$$

Many analytical texts go on to confuse the student with talk of anodes (electrodes where oxidation occurs) and cathodes (electrodes where reduction occurs). In our example above, electrons would be attracted to the positive Pt electrode where they can cause reduction, so it would be the cathode. The SHE is the anode.

Applications of electrochemical calculations occur in redox titration curves, and in potentiometry. In potentiometry, we measure a potential and use it to calculate a concentration directly. pH electrodes are a good example of this.

$$E = K + S \log [H^+] \text{ or } E = K - S \text{ pH.}$$

S and K are determined by calibration against known H^+ standards. From then on, a measurement of E will give us pH =(E – K)/-S.

A redox titration curve of E_{meas} vs. ml of titrant can be calculated by using an Initial/Final Spreadsheet to determine solution composition after a known addition of titrant. The appropriate Nerst Equation is used to calculate the potential.

Example: 50.0 ml of solution containing 3.00 millimoles of Fe^{2+} is titrated with 23.5 ml of 0.01667M $Cr_2O_7^{2}$. Compute the potential of the resulting solution against an SCE reference electrode of 0.242 volts. The H^+ concentration may be assumed to be constant at 1.0 M.

$$Cr_2O_7^{2-} + 6Fe^{2+} + 14H^+ = 2Cr^{3+} + 6Fe^{3+} + 7H_2O$$

	$Cr_2O_7^{2-}$ mmoles	Cr^{3+} mmoles	Fe^{2+} mmoles	Fe^{3+} mmoles	Volume ml
Initial	0.392	0	3.00	0	23.5+50
Final	0	0.784	0.650	2.350	73.5 ml
Molarity		0.0107M	0.00884M	0.0320M	

The only half reaction with non-zero values is that for Fe^{3+}/Fe^{2+}, so we use that Nerst Equation.

Source: A Survival Guide to Analytical Chemistry; David L. Zellmer.

SAMPLING

3

PRINCIPLE

- The objective of water sampling is to collect a portion of water small enough in volume to be transported conveniently to the laboratory while still accurately representing the water source being sampled.
- The objective implies that the relative proportion or composition of all pertinent constituents will be the same in the samples as in the water source being sampled, and that the sample will be handled in such a way that no significant changes in composition occur before the tests are made.

OBJECTIVES

Normally samples are taken with one or more of the following in mind:

(a) To meet regulatory requirements.

(b) To build up an overall picture of the aquatic environment thus enabling pollution cause and effect to be judged.

(c) To provide long-term background data against which future changes can be assessed.

(d) To detect trends.

(e) To provide warnings of potentially deleterious changes.

(f) To check for compliance or for charging purposes.

(g) To precisely characterize an effluent or water.

(h) To investigate pollution.

(i) To collect sufficient data to perform in-depth analysis (e.g. mathematical modeling) or to allow research to be carried out.

Different objectives, as mentioned above can be categorized in three groups:

- *Baseline/Trend*: Long-term standard measurements in order to define status or trends (e.g. to provide background data and early tracing of both slow and rapid quality changes and deterioration process).
- *Surveillance*: Continuous specific measurements for the purpose of water quality management and operational activities so as to check for compliance with standards for designated use (e.g. abstraction for use in potable water supply).
- *Survey*: A finite duration, intensive programme to measure for specific purposes (e.g. analysis of water and solution evolution, including evaluation of primary and secondary sources and process. Identification of anomalous concentrations of pollutants etc.).

SITE SELECTION

Ground Water Sampling

The locations of ground water sampling stations are established from the monitoring objectives, and the spatial and temporal variability of the system. It is important to take the sample at exactly the same location each time only if the same location is consistently sampled, can temporal changes in water quality parameter levels be interpreted with confidence. Therefore, accurate location description must be prepared on the first visit to every sampling site, and these must be carefully followed by investigators on subsequent visits.

In addition to locating sampling stations, field investigators are responsible for observing and recording any unusual conditions such as colour or odour of the water which may indicate a need for additional water samples in addition to those required under monitoring programme. This information and additional samples will prove useful during the interpretive aspects of the study.

Surface Water Sampling

The selection of actual sampling location in the water body shall depend upon the character of the water body. In a lake or wide river many sampling sites should be selected at various corners. If the lake is stratified, three vertical samples at one site (surface, middle and bottom) shall be required. In shallow ponds only surface and bottom samples or a sample from 0.5 to 0.7 m depth shall also suffice. In a stream which is narrow and rapidly moving the water shall be thoroughly mixed, laterally and vertically hence only one sampling point need to be selected at each location along the stream.

In an organically polluted river at least one site should be selected above the outfall of wastes and four sites should be selected downstream representing the zone of recent pollution, saprobic zone, recovery zone and clean water. If the river is known to be polluted by inorganic substances, one point above and one below the point of discharge shall be sufficient.

When selecting sites for surface water quality the following considerations are important:

- That the site can be precisely described (as it is likely that more than one person will need to do sampling).
- That the water body is well mixed both horizontally and vertically at the sampling point.
- That the water body at the sampling site is within easy reach of a road (if the sampler is using a vehicle to get to the site).
- That the water is easily accessible at the sampling point.
- That sampling can be carried out away from the bank (on a river, mid-stream or near to it is usually preferred, on a lake it is best to sample away from the bank as near shore points are rarely representative of the bulk of water).
- That the site is inherently safe for sampling.

SAMPLE COLLECTION

General

- At least one day before sampling, make sure that all arrangements are made as per the checklist given in this section.
- Make sure that you know how to reach sampling site(s). Take help of a location map for the site which shows the sample collection point with respect to prominent landmarks in the area. In case there is any deviation in the collection point, record it on the sample identification form giving reason.
- Rinse the sample container three times with the sample before it is filled.
- Leave a small air space in the bottle to allow mixing of sample at the time of analysis.
- Label the sample container properly, preferably by attaching an appropriately inscribed tag or label. The sample code and sampling date should be clearly marked on the sample container or the tag.
- Complete identification form should be filled for each sampling occasion at a monitoring station. Note that if more than one bottle is filled at a site, this is to be registered on the same form.
- Sample identification forms should all be kept in a master file in the laboratory.

Ground Water

- Samples for ground water quality monitoring should be collected from one of the following three types of wells:
  - Open dug wells in use for domestic or irrigation water supply.
  - Tube wells fitted with hand pump or a power driven pump for domestic water supply or irrigation.
  - Piezometers, purpose-built for recording of water level.

- Open dug wells, which are not in use or have not been abandoned, should not be considered as water quality monitoring stations. However, such wells could be considered for water level monitoring.
- Use a weighted sample bottle to collect sample from an open well about 30 cm below the surface of water. Do not use a plastic bucket, which is likely to skim the surface layer only.
- Samples from the production tube wells should be collected after running the well for about 5 minutes.
- Non-production piezometers should be purged using a submersible pump. The purged water volume should equal 4 to 5 times the standing water volume, before the sample is collected.
- For bacteriological samples, when collected from tube wells/hand pump, the spout/outlet of the pump should be sterilized under flame by spirit lamp before collection of sample in container.

Surface Water

- Samples should be collected from well-mixed section of the river (main stream) 30 cm below the water surface.
- Samples from reservoir sites should be collected from the outgoing canal, power channel or water intake structure, in case water is pumped. When there is no discharge in the canal, sample should be collected from the upstream side of the regulator structure, directly from the reservoir.
- Samples for estimating DO should be collected in a DO bottle using a DO sampler. The DO sample must be fixed immediately after collection, using chemical reagents.

USE OF APPROPRIATE CONTAINERS

The choice and the preparation of container can be of major importance. However, it should be remembered that the

Sample Identification Form for Ground Water Samples

<table>
<tr><td colspan="12">Sample code</td></tr>
<tr><td colspan="4">Observer</td><td colspan="4">Agency</td><td colspan="4">Project</td></tr>
<tr><td colspan="2">Date</td><td colspan="2">Time</td><td colspan="8">Station code</td></tr>
<tr><td colspan="12">Source of sample: o Open dug well o Hand pump o Tube well o Piezometer</td></tr>
<tr><td rowspan="2">Parameter Code</td><td colspan="4">Container</td><td colspan="4">Preservation</td><td colspan="3">Treatment</td></tr>
<tr><td>Glass</td><td>PVC</td><td>PE</td><td>Teflon</td><td>None</td><td>Cool</td><td>Acid</td><td>Other</td><td>None</td><td>Decant</td><td>Filter</td></tr>
<tr><td>(1) Gen</td><td colspan="4"></td><td colspan="4"></td><td colspan="3"></td></tr>
<tr><td>(2) Bact</td><td colspan="4"></td><td colspan="4"></td><td colspan="3"></td></tr>
<tr><td>(3) BOD</td><td colspan="4"></td><td colspan="4"></td><td colspan="3"></td></tr>
<tr><td>(4) COD, NH_3, NO_3^-</td><td colspan="4"></td><td colspan="4"></td><td colspan="3"></td></tr>
<tr><td>(5) H. Metals</td><td colspan="4"></td><td colspan="4"></td><td colspan="3"></td></tr>
<tr><td>(6) Tr. Organics</td><td colspan="4"></td><td colspan="4"></td><td colspan="3"></td></tr>
</table>

Field determinations

Temp °C	pH	EC mmho/cm		DO mg/L	
Odour Code	(1) Odour free	(6) Septic	Colour Code	(1) Light brown	(6) Dark green
	(2) Rotten eggs	(7) Aromatic		(2) Brown	(7) Clear
	(3) Burnt sugar	(8) Chlorinous		(3) Dark brown	(8) Other (specify)
	(4) Soapy	(9) Alcoholic		(4) Light green	
	(5) Fishy	(10) Unpleasant		(5) Green	

If the well is purged, complete below:

Office Well Data		
Diameter	ø	cm
Depth	D	m
Static water level (avg)	SWL	m
Water column (D-SWL)	H	m
Initial volume well	V	L
Projected pump discharge	PQ	L/s
Projected time of purging (V/PQ)	PT	min
Field Flow Measurements		
Static water level on arrival	SWL	m
Actual pump setting		m
Purging duration		min
Pump discharge before sampling	Q	L/min
Pump discharge after sampling	Q	L/min
Volume purged	V	L
Dynamic water level	DWL	m

Field Chemical Measurement			
Time at start of sampling	T (°C)	EC(mmho/cm)	pH
+10 min			
+20 min			
+30 min			
+40 min			

Sample Identification Form for Surface Water Samples

<table>
<tr><td colspan="12">Sample code</td></tr>
<tr><td colspan="5">Observer</td><td colspan="3">Agency</td><td colspan="4">Project</td></tr>
<tr><td colspan="3">Date</td><td colspan="2">Time</td><td colspan="7">Station code</td></tr>
<tr><td rowspan="2">Parameter Code</td><td colspan="4">Container</td><td colspan="4">Preservation</td><td colspan="3">Treatment</td></tr>
<tr><td>Glass</td><td>PVC</td><td>PE</td><td>Teflon</td><td>None</td><td>Cool</td><td>Acid</td><td>Other</td><td>None</td><td>Decant</td><td>Filter</td></tr>
<tr><td>(1) Gen</td><td></td><td></td><td></td><td></td><td></td><td></td><td></td><td></td><td></td><td></td><td></td></tr>
<tr><td>(2) Bact</td><td></td><td></td><td></td><td></td><td></td><td></td><td></td><td></td><td></td><td></td><td></td></tr>
<tr><td>(3) BOD</td><td></td><td></td><td></td><td></td><td></td><td></td><td></td><td></td><td></td><td></td><td></td></tr>
<tr><td>(4) COD, NH_3, NO_3^-</td><td></td><td></td><td></td><td></td><td></td><td></td><td></td><td></td><td></td><td></td><td></td></tr>
<tr><td>(5) H. Metals</td><td></td><td></td><td></td><td></td><td></td><td></td><td></td><td></td><td></td><td></td><td></td></tr>
<tr><td>(6) Tr. Organics</td><td></td><td></td><td></td><td></td><td></td><td></td><td></td><td></td><td></td><td></td><td></td></tr>
</table>

Source of Sample				
Water body	*Point*	*Approach*	*Medium*	*Matrix*
o River o Drain o Canal o Reservoir	o Main current o Right bank o Left bank	o Bridge o Boat o Wading	o Water o Susp matter o Biota o Sediment	o Fresh o Brackish o Salt o Effluent
Sample type	o Grab o Time-comp o Flow-comp o Depth-integ o Width-integ			
Sample device	o Weighted bottle o Pump o Depth sampler			
Field Determinations				
Temp °C	pH	**EC** **mmho/cm**	DO mg/L	
Odour Code	(11) Odour free (12) Rotten eggs (13) Burnt sugar (14) Soapy (15) Fishy	(16) Septic (17) Aromatic (18) Chlorinous (19) Alcoholic (20) Unpleasant	**Colour Code**	(8) Light brown (9) Brown (10) Dark brown (11) Light green (12) Green (13) Dark green (14) Clear (15) Other (specify)
Remarks				
Weather	o Sunny o Cloudy o Rainy o Windy			
Water vel. m/s	o High (> 0.5) o Medium (0.1-0.5) o Low (< 0.1) o Standing			
Water use	o None o Cultivation o Bathing and washing o Cattle washing o Melon/vegetable farming in river bed			

container in which the sample is stored and the stopper should not:

(a) be a cause of contamination (e.g. borosilicate or soda-lime glass containers may increase the content of silica or sodium);

(b) absorb or adsorb the constituents to be determined (e.g. hydrocarbons may be absorbed in a polyethylene container, traces of metals may be adsorbed on the surface of a glass container); and

(c) react with certain constituents in the sample (e.g. fluorides reacting with glass).

It should be remembered that the use of opaque containers or brown (non-aclinic) glass containers can reduce the photosensitivite activities to a considerable extent.

Blank samples should be taken, preserved and analyzed as a check on the suitability of the choice and cleaning procedure.

TYPE OF SAMPLES

Grab Sample — A grab sample is an ordinary sample, which is taken from a particular place representing the whole water quality. This type of sample is valid only when it is certain that the water quality is not changing in a short time and effluent discharges, if any, are fairly regular.

Composite Sample — A composite sample is the one taken at various times from a locality undergoing fluctuations and combining that to know average chemical characteristics. However, no idea of maximum or minimum values can be obtained by a composite sample.

Integrated Sample — In some cases the samples may be collected from a number of nearing localities and may be pooled together to avoid minor variation. This can be done for various samples across the width of a river or the surface and bottom samples of a shallow pond. In deep lakes, however, separate grab samples at various depths shall be required.

The simplest form of a water sampling device is a bottle or bucket attached to a string. However, this will not sink easily below the water surface. To lower a plastic or glass bottle in a body of water it is necessary to use a bracket or holder of sufficient weight to overcome the buoyancy of the bottle and allow it to sink rapidly to the required depth, usually 20-30 cm below the water surface. Such a holder designed to contain a one or two litre bottle is shown in Figure 3.1.

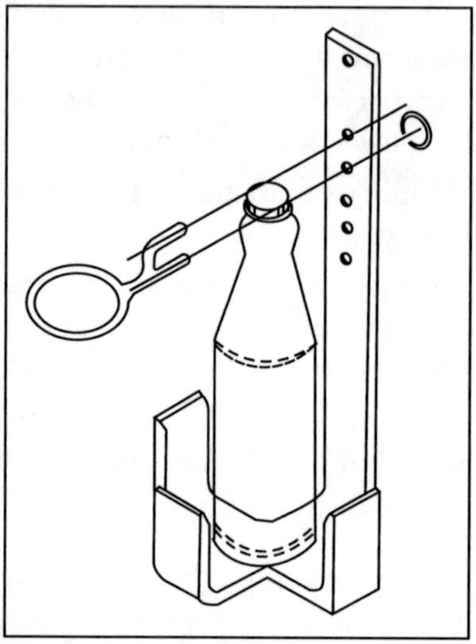

Figure 3.1: Sample bottle holder for sampling

Where feasible a sample may be collected by holding the sample bottle in hand and submerging it. Collect the sample from the well-mixed section of the river, approximately 20-30 cm below the water surface (see Figure 3.2). Care must be taken not to catch any floating material or bed material into the container. If the water is less than 40 cm, the sample should be collected at half the actual water depth. If possible, sampling from shallow waters (less than 40 cm) should be prevented by moving, within the site, to a deeper part of the river or stream.

Samples from reservoir sites will be collected from the outgoing canal, power channel or water intake structure, in case water is pumped. When there is no discharge in the canal, sample will be collected from the upstream side of the regulator structure, directly from the reservoir. Rinse the sample container three times with the sample before it is filled. Leave a small air space in the bottle to allow mixing of sample at the time of analysis.

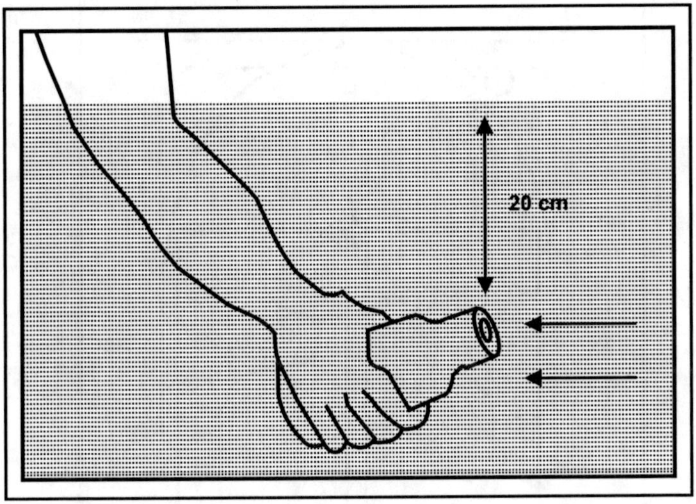

Figure 3.2: Collecting a sample from surface water

Dissolved Oxygen

Collecting a sample for Dissolved Oxygen analysis requires special sampling equipment: a purpose-built dissolved oxygen sampler, for collection of undisturbed samples from surface waters (Figure 3.3). This sampler prevents air bubbles from entering into the sample and changing the dissolved oxygen concentration of the sample.

To collect the sample, insert the special ground glass-stoppered bottle (a 'BOD bottle') into the DO sampler. Submerge the sampler, such that water enters the BOD bottle directly by means of a dip-pipe thus displacing all air from the bottle. Retrieve the sampler after it is full, and then immediately seal the full bottle with a ground glass stopper.

The Dissolved Oxygen sample needs to be 'fixed' immediately after collection.

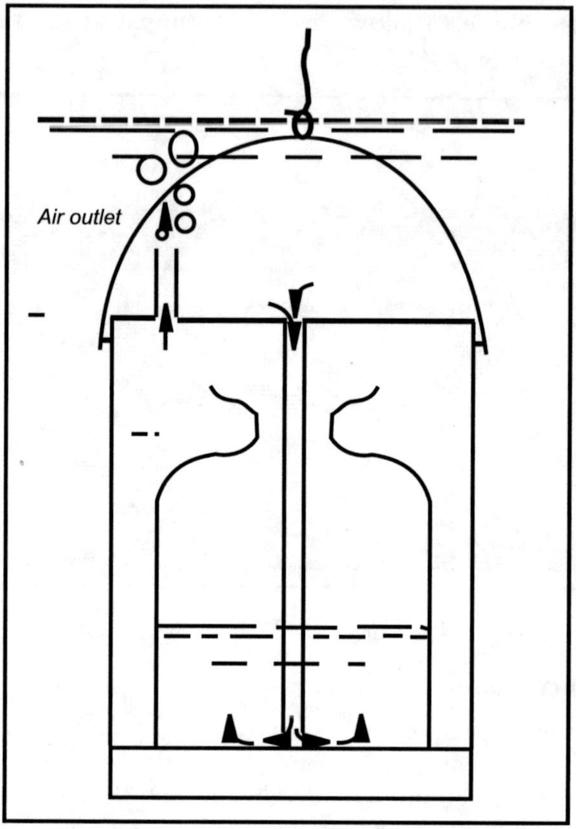

Figure 3.3: Dissolved oxygen sampler (with one BOD-bottle)

REAGENT SOLUTIONS FOR SAMPLING

For some of the field analyses, reagent solutions are necessary for the analysis. All necessary reagent solutions should be prepared in the laboratory and brought to the field by the sample collector. Alternatively, reagent solutions can be kept at a site laboratory, if the 'field analyses' are going to be made there. In all cases, sample preservatives and DO fixing solutions must be brought to the field and added to the samples immediately after collection.

For analysis of pH, buffer solutions are necessary to standardize the pH meter: Buffer solutions should be prepared in the laboratory or purchased, for pH = 2, pH = 7 and pH = 9. For analysis of electrical conductivity, standard potassium chloride solution, KCl (0.01 M) is needed to standardise the conductivity meter.

For analysis of dissolved oxygen, DO fixing chemicals are necessary:

- manganous sulphate solution
- alkaline iodide-azide solution
- concentrated sulphuric acid

DO fixing chemicals should be kept in a glass or PE bottle. If a glass bottle is used, a rubber stopper must be used for the alkaline reagent. A glass pipette or dropper of 2 ml capacity is needed to add the fixing chemicals to the samples.

For preservation of certain samples, concentrated nitric acid and concentrated sulfuric acid are needed. A supply of distilled water is needed for rinsing equipment.

INSTRUMENTS

Some instruments and equipments are necessary to make the field analyses. Instruments and equipments must be brought to the field, or must be available at the site laboratory where the 'field analyses' will be done. Temperature should always be measured in the field:

- For measurement of Temperature, a (mercury) thermometer or thermistor is needed.
- For analysis of Electrical conductivity, a conductivity meter is needed.
- For analysis of pH, a pH meter is needed.
- For analysis of DO, equipment for a DO titration is necessary: Erlenmeyer flask and Burette.

Note: It is possible that instead of separate meters for temperature, pH and conductivity, there is a single instrument with different probes which will measure all three parameters.

A supply of batteries and standard spare parts should also be carried along with the field instruments.

CHECK LIST FOR FIELD VISIT

The table below contains a list of items which should be checked before starting on a sampling mission. At least one day before sampling, make sure that all the arrangements are made as per the check list.

• Itinerary for the trip (route, stations to be covered, start and return time)	• Personnel and sample transport arrangement
• Area map	• Sampling site location map
• Icebox filled with ice or icepacks	• Weighted bottle sampler
• DO sampler	• Rope
• BOD bottles	• Sample containers
• Special sample containers: bacteriological, heavy metals, etc.	• DO fixing and titration chemicals and glassware
• Sample preservatives (e.g. acid solutions)	• Thermometer
• Tissue paper	• Other field measurement kit, as required
• Sample identification forms	• Labels for sample containers
• Field notebook	• Pen/pencil/marker
• Soap and towel	• Match box
• Spirit lamp	• Torch
• Drinking water	• Knife
	• Gloves and eye protection

SAMPLE LABELLING

Label the sample container properly, preferably by attaching an appropriately inscribed tag or label. Alternatively, the bottle can be labelled directly with a water-proof marker. Information on the sample container or the tag should include:

- sample code number (identifying location)
- date and time of sampling
- source and type of sample
- pre-treatment or preservation carried out on the sample
- any special notes for the analyst
- sampler's name.

SAMPLE PRESERVATION AND TRANSPORT

Accurate sampling should be followed by correct handling and preservation of the sample to obtain the reliable results. A few hints are given here:

1. Immediately after collection, clearly label each sample bottle with water-proof ink and record relevant details for each sample.
2. Temperature of water should be immediately recorded.
3. The sample for chemical, biological and bacteriological analyses should preferably be collected separately.
4. The sample should be taken to the laboratory as early as possible; it should be protected from direct sunlight during transportation.

Since most of the parameters change with time, it is imperative to preserve them in a suitable preservative prior to analyses. Dissolved Oxygen, Free CO_2, Alkalinity and pH quickly change with time hence their estimation is to be carried out in the field only.

Preservation techniques of the water samples for chemical analysis

Parameter	Recommended sample volume (ml)	Type of container	Preservation	Allowable holding time
Acidity	100	P, G	Refrigerate -4°C	24 hr
Alkalinity	100	P, G	Refrigerate -4°C	24 hr
BOD	1000	P, G	Refrigerate -4°C	24 hr
COD	50	P, G	H_2SO_4 to pH > 2	7 days
Chlorine, residual	100	P, G	Analyze immediately	—
Chloride	50	P, G	Not required	7 days
Colour	50	P, G	Refrigerate -4°C	24 hr
Cyanide	500	P, G	Refrigerate -4°C; NaOH to pH 12	24 hr
Dissolved oxygen:				
Probe	300	G	Determine at site	—
Winkler	300	G	Fix on site	6 hr
Hardness	100	P, G	Refrigerate -4°C	7 days
Metals	200	P, G	Refrigerate -4°C; HNO_3 to pH < 2	6 months
Ammonia	500	P, G	Refrigerate -4°C, H_2SO_4 to pH < 2	24 hr
Kjeldahl- N	500	P, G	Refrigerate -4°C, H_2SO_4 to pH < 2	7 days
Nitrate	100	P, G	Refrigerate -4°C, H_2SO_4 to pH < 2	24 hr
Nitrite	100	P, G	Refrigerate -4°C	24 hr
Oil and grease	1000	P, G	Add HCl to pH 2	24 hr
pH	100	P, G	Determine at site	—
Phenol	500	G	Refrigerate -4°C, 1.0g $CaSO_4$/lit	24 hr
Phosphate	50	P, G	Refrigerate -4°C	24 hr
Specific conductance	100	P, G	Refrigerate -4°C	24 hr
Solids (total, dissolved)	100	P, G	Refrigerate -4°C	7 days
Sulphate	50	P, G	Refrigerate -4°C	7 days
Sulphide	100	P, G	Analyze immediately	—
Temperature	1000	P, G	Determine on site	—
Turbidity	100	P, G	Refrigerate -4°C	No holding
Radioactivity	1000	P, G	Not required	24 hr

P-Plastics, G-Glass

After labelling and preservation, the samples should be placed in an insulated cool box for transportation (Figure 3.4). Samples should be transported to the laboratory as soon as possible.

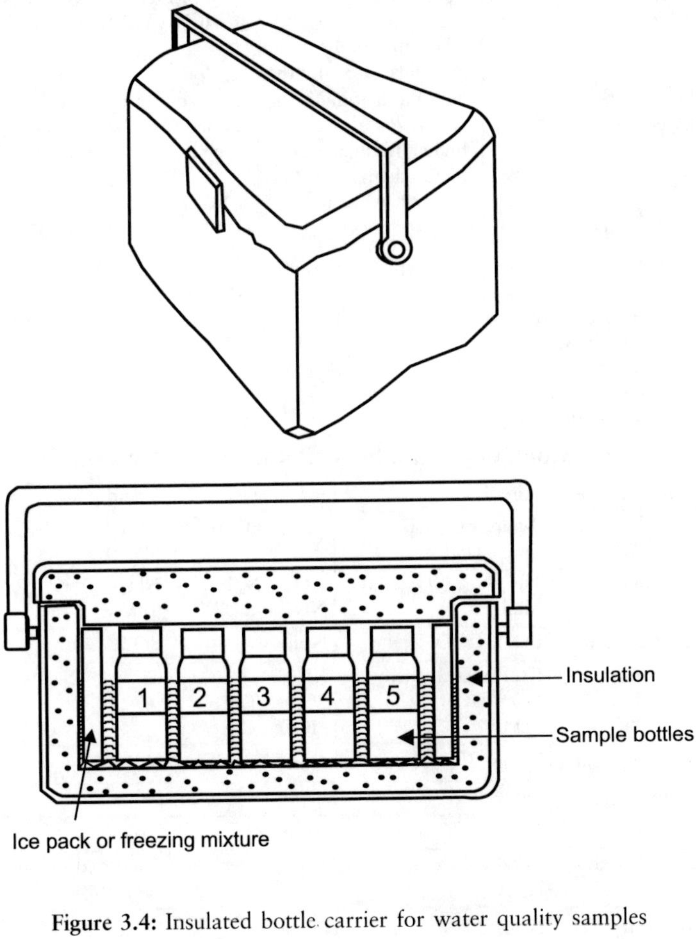

Figure 3.4: Insulated bottle carrier for water quality samples

FREQUENCY AND PARAMETERS

Parameters for analysis of ground water samples

Type of station	Frequency	Parameter
Baseline	Once every year (pre-monsoon, May-June)	Temp, EC, pH, NO_2^- + NO_3^-, total P, K^+, Na^+, Ca^{++}, Mg^{++}, CO_3^-, HCO_3^-, Cl^-, SO_4^-, COD, SiO_2, F, B
Trend	Four times every year, (pre-monsoon, May-June and after intervals of 3 months)	Temp, EC, pH, NO_2^- + NO_3^-, total P, Cl^-, COD
Trend-cum-surveillance	Minimum four times a year (as above), higher frequency if dictated by importance of water use	According to the problem under surveillance (e.g. Heavy metals in mining areas)
• Fluoride		F^-
• Iron		Fe
• Industrial, mining		As, Cd, Hg, Zn
• Salinity due to irrigation, natural contribution or sea water intrusion		K^+, Na^+, Ca^{++}, Mg^{++}, CO_3^-, HCO_3^-, Cl^-, SO_4^-
• Urban pollution		

Parameters for analysis of surface water samples[a]

Parameter group	Initially	Baseline	Trend
General	Temp, EC, pH, DO, TDS	Temp, EC, pH, DO	TDS Temp, EC, pH, DO
Nutrients	NH_3 – N, NO_2 + NO_3, total P	NH_3 – N, NO_2 + NO_3, total P	NH_3 – N, NO_2+ NO_3, total P
Organic matter	BOD, COD	None	BOD, COD
Major ions	K^+, Na^+, Ca^{++}, Mg^{++}, CO_3^-, HCO_3^-, Cl^-, SO_4^-	K^+, Na^+, Ca^{++}, Mg^{++}, CO_3^-, HCO_3^-, Cl^-, SO_4^-	Cl^-
Other inorganics	None	None	None
Metals	None	None	None
Organics	None	None	None
Microbiological[b]	Total coliforms	None	Total and faecal coliforms
Biological	None	None	None

[a] Based on 'surface water quality network design, guidelines and an example', June 1997.

[b] Depending on workload, analysis frequency may be reduced up to 2 samples per year.

Sources:

1. *Standard Methods for the Examination of Water and Wastewater*, 21st Ed., 2005.
2. IS: 3025 (Pt-1)—1987.

METHODS OF ESTIMATION

4

APPEARANCE

- To record general appearance of a sample, use any term that briefly describes its visible characteristics.
- These terms may state the presence of colour, turbidity, suspended solids, sediments, floating material and similar particulate matter detectable by the unaided eye.
- Use numerical values when they are available, as for colour, turbidity and suspended solids.

Observations

Sample No.			
Appearancc			

Source: *Standard Methods for Examination of Water and Wastewater*, 21st Ed., 2005.

COLOUR

- The term colour is used here to mean true colour, that is, the colour of water from which turbidity has been removed.
- Colour in natural waters may occur due to the presence of humic acid, fulvic acid, metallic ions such as iron and manganese, suspended matter, phytoplankton, weeds and industrial wastes, etc. Several industries use artificial colour (e.g. textile), which come out in their wastes.

Method (Platinum Cobalt Method)

Principle

Colour is measured by visual comparison of the sample with platinum-cobalt standards. One unit of colour is that produced by 1 mg of platinum per litre in the form of chloroplatinate ion.

Apparatus

Nessler tubes – 50 ml capacity.

Centrifuge or filter assembly.

Reagents

1. To prepare reference standard of 500 Hazen units on platinum cobalt scale, dissolve 1.246 g potassium chloroplatinate (K_2PtCl_6) and 1.00 g cobaltous chloride ($CoCl_2.6H_2O$) in distilled water containing 100 ml concentrated HCl. Make the final volume 1000 ml with distilled water. This standard solution is equivalent to 500 colour units.
2. Prepare standards having colour units of 5, 10, 15, 20, etc. by using standard chloroplatinate solution.
3. Protect these against evaporation and contamination by use of clean inert stoppers.

Procedure

Representative samples shall be taken in clean glassware, colour should be determined as early as possible after the collection of samples as biological activity or physical changes occurring during storage may affect the colour.

- Observe the apparent colour of the sample by comparison. Compare by looking vertically downward through the cylinders towards a white surface placed at such an angle that light is reflected upwards through the column of liquid. If the colour exceeds 70 units, dilute the sample with distilled water until the colour is in the range of the standards.

- Remove turbidity by centrifuging or filtering sample until supernatant liquid is clear. Compare the centrifuged or filtered water to ensure that turbidity has been removed. If the sample is clear, then compare with standards as given above.

Observations

Sample No.				
Volume of sample taken				
Estimated colour				

Calculation

Calculate the colour units as follows:

Colour units = 50 A/V

where

A = estimated colour of diluted sample, and

V = volume in ml of sample taken for dilution.

Report

Report the results in whole numbers as follows:

Colour units	Record to nearest
1 to 50	1
51 to 100	5
101 to 250	10
251 to 500	20

Source: IS: 3025 (Pt-4)—1983.

TURBIDITY

Turbidity is an expression of the optical property that causes light to be scattered and absorbed rather than transmitted in straight-lines through the sample. Turbidity in water is caused by suspended matter such as clay, silt, finely divided organic compounds and plankton and other microscopic organisms.

Turbidity makes water unfit for domestic purposes, food and beverage industries, and many other industrial uses. Determination of turbidity is an important objective in removal of the turbidity by coagulation, filtration, etc. in drinking water treatment plants. A reduction in turbidity is associated with a reduction in suspended matter and microbial growth. Turbidity in natural waters restricts light penetration for photosynthesis.

Method (Nephelometric Method)

Principle

This method is based on a comparison of the intensity of light scattered by the sample under defined conditions with the intensity of light scattered by standard reference suspension under the same conditions. The higher the intensity of scattered light, the higher the turbidity.

Interference

Turbidity can be determined for any water sample that is free of debris and rapidly settling coarse sediment. Dirty glassware and the presence of air bubbles give false results. Coloured solutes cause low turbidity values.

Apparatus

Sample tubes: The sample tubes should be of clear and colourless glass.

Turbiditymeter

Reagents

1. Turbidity free water: Pass distilled water through membrane filter having a pore size not greater than 0.45 μm. If such filtered water shows a lower turbidity than the distilled water, discard first 200 ml collected. Otherwise use distilled water.

2. Hexamethylene tetramine solution: Dissolve 10.0 g hexamethylene tetramine in demineralised water and dilute to 100 ml.

3. Hydrazine sulphate solution: Dissolve 1.0 g hydrazine sulphate $(NH_2)_2 (H_2SO_4)$ in demineralised water and dilute to 100 ml.

4. Turbidity standard suspension I (Formazin): In a 100 ml volumetric flask mix 5.0 ml hydrazine sulphate solution with 5.0 hexamethylene tetramine solution. After 24 hours standing at 25 ± 3°C, dilute to 100 ml with demineralised water and mix well. Prepare fresh monthly. The turbidity of this solution is 400 Jackson Turbidity Units (JTU).

5. Turbidity standard suspension II: Dilute 10 ml turbidity standard suspension 1 to 100 ml with demineralised water. The turbidity of this solution is defined as 40 JTU. Prepare fresh weekly.

Procedure

- Before each series of turbidity measurements, the instrument span should be standardized on the range settling to be used for measurement.
- Insert the secondary standard for 90% scale value on the approximate range with index mark to the front, and calibrate the instrument with appropriate standards, before inserting the sample into the sample compartment.
- Read the turbidity of the sample in Turbidity Units from the scale corresponding to the range switch selection.
- Report turbidity readings as follows:

Turbidity range in unit	Record to the nearest unit
0 – 1.0	0.05
1 – 10.0	0.1
10 – 40	1
40 – 100.0	5
100 – 400.0	10
400 – 1000.0	50
> 1000.0	100

- *For measurement of turbidity less than 40 units*: Thoroughly shake sample. Wait until air bubbles disappear and pour sample into turbiditymeter tube. Read turbidity directly from instrument scale.

- *Measurement of turbidity above 40 units*: Dilute sample with one or more volumes of turbidity free water until turbidity falls between 30 and 40 units. Compute turbidity of original sample from turbidity of diluted sample and the dilution factor.

Observations

Sample No.				
Standards used for calibration				
Dilution				
Reading				
Turbidity				

Sources:

1. *Standard Methods for the Examination of Water and Wastewater*, 21st Ed., 2005.
2. IS: 3025 (Pt-10)—1984.

ODOUR

Method for determination of true odour is applicable to all types of water and wastewater.

Preparation of Apparatus

Thoroughly clean the required number of wide mouth glass stoppered bottle, prerinsed with HCl to render it completely odourless by repeated washing with odour free distilled water.

Procedure

As soon as possible after collection of sample, fill a bottle half full of sample, insert the stopper, shake vigorously for 2 to 3 seconds and then quickly observe the odour. The sample taken for observation of odour shall be at room temperature.

Report

Report the true odour of the sample at the mouth of the bottle as rotten egg, burnt sugar, soapy, fishy septic, aromatic, chlorinous, alcoholic or any other specific odour. In case it is not possible to specify the exact nature of odour, report as agreeable or disagreeable.

Observations

Sample No.				
Odour				

Sources:

1. *Standard Methods for the Examination of Water and Wastewater*, 21st Ed., 2005.
2. IS: 3025 (Pt-5)—1983.

TASTE

This method is applicable only to water and determine taste threshold for quantitative measurement of detectable taste. For testing, blank and each dilution is transferred to 50 ml beaker and given to observers for testing.

- Make taste tests only on samples known to be safe for ingestion.
- Do not use samples that may be contaminated with bacteria, virus, parasites or toxic chemicals or that derived from unaesthetic source.
- Do not test taste on wastewater or similar untreated effluents.
- Observe all sanitary and aesthetic precautions with regard to apparatus and containers containing the sample. Practice hospital level sanitation of these terms.

Some inorganic chemicals with their threshold limits imparting tastes to the water (After Voznaya 1981):

Salt	Concentration	
	Indefinite, slight, hardly distinguishable taste	Repulsive taste
NaCl	150	500 salty
$MgCl_2$	100	400 bitter
$MgSO_4$	200	500 bitter
$CaSO_4$	70	150 astringent
KCl	350	700 bitter
$FeSO_4$	1.5	5 chalybeate
$MnCl_2$	2	4 stagnant
$FeCl_2$	0.3	0.5 stagnant

Observations

Sample No.				
Taste				

Sources:

1. *Standard Methods for the Examination of Water and Wastewater*, 21st Ed., 2005.
2. IS: 3025 (Pt-7)—1984.

TEMPERATURE

Temperature readings are used in the calculation of various forms of alkalinity, in studies of saturation and stability with respect to calcium carbonate, in the calculation of salinity, and in general laboratory operation.

- Normally temperature measurement may be made with any good mercury filled Celsius thermometer.
- As a minimum, the thermometer should have a scale marked for 0.1°C onward with marking etched on capillary glass.
- Make measurement with the thermometer immersed directly in the water body, after a period of time sufficient to permit contract readings.

- Measure temperature of tap water in a bottle through the water flows until a constant reading is obtained.
- Thermometer should be calibrated using standard thermometer periodically and correction factors to be applied.

Observations

Sample No.				
Temperature				

Sources:

1. *Standard Methods for the Examination of Water and Wastewater*, 21st Ed., 2005.
2. IS: 3025 (Pt-9)—1984.

pH VALUE (POTENTIA HYDROGENII)

pH is the measure of the intensity of acidity or alkalinity and measures the concentration of hydrogen ions in water. It does not measure total acidity or alkalinity. In fact, the normal acidity or alkalinity depends upon excess H+ or HO- ions over the other, and is measured in normality or gram equivalents of acid or alkali. If free H+ are more than HO- ions, the water shall be acidic, or alkaline if it is the other way round.

pH is generally measured on a log scale and equals to negative log 10 of hydrogen ion concentration.

$$pH = -\log_{10} [H^+]$$

$$= \log_{10} \frac{1}{[H^+]}$$

As the ionic product of water is 1×10^{-14} at 25°C, therefore, a neutral solution will have 1×10^{-7} ions of H^+ and OH^- each. pH scale ranges from 0 to 14 with 7 as neutral, below 7 being acid and above 7 alkaline.

Electrometric and colorimetric methods are used for the determination of pH value. Both methods are applicable to all types of water and wastewater.

Electrometric Method

The pH value is determined by measurement of electromotive force of a cell consisting of an indicator electrode.

Interference: Above pH value of 10, high sodium concentrations interfere with the measurement. Sodium errors at pH value levels greater than 10 can be reduced or eliminated by using low sodium error electrodes.

- Oil and grease may interfere by coating the pH electrode and causing a sluggish response. This coating can usually be removed by gentle wiping or detergent washing followed by distilled water rinsing.
- Temperature affects the pH value in two ways, the first is covered by the change in electrode output at various temperatures. This interference can be controlled with instrument system at the temperature of samples. The second source is the change of pH inherent in the sample at various temperatures. The error is sample dependent and cannot be controlled. Therefore, the temperature at the time of analysis should be reported.

Procedure

Sample should be analyzed as soon as possible, preferably in the field at the time of sampling.

- Follow the manufacturer's instructions for operation of pH meter. After required warm up period, standardize the instrument with a buffer solution of pH near that of the sample.
- If field measurements are being made, the electrode may be immersed directly in the sample stream to an adequate depth. If necessary, immerse them into the sample beaker and stir at a constant rate to provide homogeneity and suspension of solids.
- pH meter is to be calibrated for analysis every time a measurement is made, with standard buffer solution (Standard buffer tablets are available commercially).

Observations

Sample No.				
pH				

Colorimetric Method

A series of buffer solutions are used for determination of pH value by visual comparison.

Reagents

Prepare universal indicators by dissolving 0.05 g of methyl orange, 0.15 g methyl red, 0.3 g boromothymol blue and 0.35 g phenolphthalein in 1 litre of alcohol. The colour changes are:

pH	Colour
Upto 3	Red
4	Orange Red
5	Orange
6	Yellow
7	Yellowish Green
8	Yellowish Blue
9	Blue
10	Violet
11	Reddish Violet

Observations

Sample No.				
Colour change				
pH				

Sources:

1. *Standard Methods for the Examination of Water and Wastewater*, 21st Ed., 2005.
2. IS: 3025 (Pt-11)—1987.

SOLIDS

Total Solids

Gravimetric method is prescribed for the determination of total solids. This method is applicable to all types of water and wastewater.

Principle

The sample is evaporated in a weighed dish and dried to a constant mass in an oven either at 103 – 105°C or 179 – 181°C. Total residue is calculated from the increase in mass.

Apparatus

Evaporating dish

Steam bath

Drying oven

Desiccator

Analytical balance

Procedure

- Heat the clean evaporating dish to 180°C for 1 hour. Cool, desiccate, weigh and store in desiccator until ready for use.
- Select volume of sample, which has residue between 25 and 250 mg, preferably between 100 and 200 mg.
- Pipette this volume to a weighed dish placed on the steam bath. Evaporation may also be performed in a drying oven. The temperature should be lowered to approximately 98°C to prevent boiling and spattering of the sample.
- After complete evaporation of water from the residue, transfer the dish to an oven at 103 – 105°C or 179 – 181°C and dry to a constant weight.

Observations

Sample No.				
Initial weight				
Final weight				
Net weight				
Volume of sample taken				
Total solids				

Calculations

Calculate the total solids using following equation:

Total solids, mg/L = 1000M/V

Where, M = mass in mg of total solid and

V = volume in ml of the sample

Report in whole numbers for less than 100 mg/L and above 100 mg/L to three significant figures.

Total Dissolved Solids

Gravimetric method is prescribed for the determination of filterable residue. This method is applicable to all types of water and wastewater.

Principle

The sample is filtered through 0.45 μ filter using appropriate funnel and the filtrate evaporated in a tared dish on a steam bath and dried to a constant mass in an oven either at 103-105°C or 179-181°C.

Apparatus

Filter

- Glass fibre filter disc – (Whatman GF/C or equivalent) 2.1 to 5.5 cm in diameter, pore size 1.2 μm
- Paper – Acid washed, ashless hard filter finish (pore size 2-2.5 μm equivalent to Whatman filter no. 542)

- Gooch crucible – 30 ml capacity with 2.1 or 2.4 cm diameter glass filter disc
- Sintered disc – G-5 or its equivalent with pore size 1 to 2 μm
- Membrane filter – 0.45 μm

Drying oven
Desiccator
Analytical balance

Procedure

- Heat the clean evaporating dish to 180°C for 1 hour. Cool, desiccate, weigh and store in desiccator until ready for use.
- Filter a portion of the sample through any of the above-mentioned filters. Select volume of sample, which has residue between 25 and 250 mg, preferably between 100 and 200 mg.
- Pipette this volume to a weighed dish placed on the steam bath. Evaporation may also be performed in a drying oven. The temperature should be lowered to approximately 98°C to prevent boiling and spattering of the sample.
- After complete evaporation of water from the residue, transfer the dish to an oven at 103 – 105°C or 179 – 181°C and dry to a constant weight.

Observations

Sample No.				
Initial weight				
Final weight				
Net weight				
Volume of sample taken				
Total dissolved solids				

Calculations

Calculate the total dissolved solids using following equation:

Total dissolved solids, mg/L = 1000M/V

Where, M = mass in mg of filterable residue and

V = volume in ml of the sample

Report in whole numbers for less than 100 mg/L and above 100 mg/L to three significant figures.

Total Suspended Solids

Gravimetric method is prescribed for the determination of suspended solids.

Principle

Non-filterable residue is determined by passing the sample through a weighed 0.45 μ filter and drying the filter at 103-105°C or 179-181°C. Total suspended solids is calculated from the increase in mass of the filter.

Apparatus

Filter

- Glass fibre filter disc – (Whatman GF / C or equivalent) 2.1 to 5.5 cm in diameter, pore size 1.2 μm
- Gooch crucible – 30 ml capacity with 2.1, 2.4 or 5.5 cm diameter glass filter disc
- Crucible – Porous – bottom silica, sintered glass, porcelain, stainless steel or
- Alundum crucible with a maximum pore size of 5 μm

Drying oven

Desiccator

Analytical balance

Procedure

- Place the filter on the filter apparatus or insert into the bottom of a suitable Gooch crucible with wrinkled surface up. While vacuum is applied wash the dish with three successive 20 ml volumes of distilled water. Remove filter from filter apparatus (or both crucible and filter, if Gooch crucible is used) and dry in an oven at 103 – 105°C for 1 hour. Transfer to a desiccator and weigh after half an hour. Repeat the drying cycle till a constant weight is attained.

- For deciding the volume of the sample to be taken, turbidity values may be taken into consideration. If turbidity values of a sample is less than 50 units, filter 1 litre sample, if turbidity exceeds 50 units, filter sufficient sample so that non-filterable residue is 50 – 100 mg.
- Assemble the filtering apparatus and begin suction. Wet the filter with a small amount of distilled water. Shake the sample vigorously and quantitatively transfer the predetermined sample volume.
- With suction on, wash the graduated cylinder, filter non-filterable residue with portions of distilled water allowing complete drainage between washings.
- After filtration transfer the filter along with the contents to an oven maintained at either 103 – 105°C or 179 – 181°C for at least 1 hour.
- Transfer to a desiccator and weigh after half an hour. Repeat the drying cycle till a constant weight is attained.

Observations

Sample No.				
Initial weight				
Final weight				
Net weight				
Volume of sample taken				
Total suspended solids				

Calculations

Calculate the non-filterable residue using following equation:

Total solids, mg/L = 1000M/V

Where, M = mass in mg of non-filterable residue and

V = volume in ml of the sample.

Report in whole numbers for less than 100 mg/L and above 100 mg/L to three significant figures.

Volatile and Fixed Solids (Total, Dissolved and Suspended)

Gravimetric method is prescribed for estimation of volatile and fixed portions of total, suspended and dissolved solids. The method is applicable to all types of water and wastewater.

- *Total Fixed Solids*: The dish with residue on completion of test for total residue is heated in a muffle furnace at 550°C for 1 hour. Total, fixed and volatile solids are calculated from loss in mass on ignition.
- *Filterable Fixed Residue*: The dish with residue after completion of test for TDS is heated in a muffle furnace of 550°C for 1 hour. Dissolve fixed and volatile solids are calculated from loss of mass ignition.
- *Suspended Fixed Solids*: The filter with residue after completion of test for TSS is heated in a muffle furnace at 550°C for 1 hour. Suspended fixed and volatile solids are calculated from loss in mass after ignition.

Apparatus

Evaporating dish

Steam bath

Drying oven

Desiccator

Muffle furnace

Analytical balance

Procedure

- Heat the clean evaporating dish to 180°C for 1 hour.

Cool, desiccate, weigh and store in desiccator until ready for use.

- Select volume of sample, which has residue between 25 and 250 mg, preferably between 100 and 200 mg.
- Pipette this volume to a weighed dish placed on the steam bath. Evaporation may also be performed in a drying oven. The temperature should be lowered to approximately 98°C to prevent boiling and spattering of the sample.
- After complete evaporation of water from the residue, transfer the dish to an oven at 103 – 105°C or 179 – 181°C and dry to a constant weight.
- After weighing, ignite the dish in a muffle furnace at 550°C for 1 hour. After ignition, allow the vessel to partially cool in air and transfer to desiccator, cool and weigh.

Observations

Sample No.				
Initial weight (A)				
Final weight (B)				
Net weight (C)				
Volume of sample taken (V)				
Volatile solids Fixed solids				

Calculations

Calculate fixed and volatile solids as follows:

(Total, dissolved and suspended)

$$\text{Volatile Solids, mg/L} = \frac{(A - B) \times 1000}{V}$$

$$\text{Fixed Solids, mg/L} = \frac{(B \quad C) \times 1000}{V}$$

Where, A = mass in mg of residue and dish/filter before ignition

B = mass in mg of residue and dish/filter after ignition

C = mass in mg of dish/filter

V = volume of sample

Report to the nearest whole number for values upto 100 mg/L and to three significant figures for higher values.

Sources:

1 *Standard Methods for the Examination of Water and Wastewater*, 21st Ed., 2005.

2 IS: 3025 (Pt-15 to 18)—1984.

SETTLEABLE MATTER

Two methods are prescribed—one, gravimetric and the other, volumetric, for the determination of settleable matter.

Gravimetric Method

Principle

Settleable matter is determined from the difference in the values of non-filterable residue of the sample, and of suspended matter of the supernatant liquid portion of the sample after it has been allowed to stand for 1 hour. This technique determines matter which will not stay in suspension during settling period and either settles at the bottom or floats to the top.

Apparatus

Filter

- Gooch crucible – 30 ml capacity with 2.1, 2.4 or 5.5 cm diameter glass filter disc.
- Crucible – Porous – bottom silica, sintered glass, porcelain, stainless steel or
- Alundum crucible with a maximum pore size of 5 μm

Drying oven

Desiccator

Analytical balance

Procedure

- Place the filter on the filter apparatus or insert into the bottom of a suitable Gooch crucible with wrinkled surface up. While vacuum is applied wash the dish with three successive 20 ml volumes of distilled water. Remove filter from filter apparatus (or both crucible and filter, if Gooch crucible is used) and dry in an oven at 103 – 105°C for 1 hour. Transfer to a desiccator and weigh after half an hour. Repeat the drying cycle till a constant weight is attained.
- For deciding the volume of the sample to be taken, turbidity values may be taken into consideration. If turbidity values of a sample is less than 50 units, filter 1 litre sample, if turbidity exceeds 50 units, filter sufficient sample so that non-filterable residue is 50 – 100 mg.
- Assemble the filtering apparatus and begin suction. Wet the filter with a small amount of distilled water. Shake the sample vigorously and quantitatively transfer the predetermined sample volume.
- With suction on, wash the graduated cylinder, filter non-filterable residue with portions of distilled water allowing complete drainage between washings.
- After filtration transfer the filter along with the contents to an oven maintained at either 103 – 105°C or 179 – 181°C for at least 1 hour.
- Transfer to a desiccator and weigh after half an hour. Repeat the drying cycle till a constant weight is attained.
- Take a glass vessel of not less than 9 cm diameter and pour well-mixed sample in this vessel in quantity not less than 1 litre and sufficient to have a depth of 20 cm. Allow the sample to stand for 1 hour and without disturbing floating or settled material, siphon 250 ml of sample from center of glass vessel at a point half way between the surface of the settled sludge and liquid surface.
- Determine suspended matter in aliquot of all of this supernatant liquid.

Observations

Sample No.				
M1				
M2				
V1				
V2				
Settleable matter				

Calculations

Calculate the settleable matter from the following equation:

$$\text{Settleable matter, mg/L} - \frac{1000\ M1}{V1} - \frac{1000\ M2}{V2}$$

Where, M1 = mass of non-filterable residue in mg
V1 = volume of sample taken in ml
M2 = mass of non-settleable matter in mg
V2 = volume of supernatant liquid used for determining non-settleable matter in ml.

Report in whole number for less than 100 mg/L and to three significant figures for higher values.

Volumetric Method

Principle

Volume of settleable matter is determined by allowing the sample to stand for 1 hour in an Imhoff cone, suitably calibrated bottom to top and having 1 litre mark.

Apparatus

Standard Imhoff cone.

Procedure

- Mix the sample thoroughly and fill the Imhoff cone upto the 1 litre mark. Let it settle for 45 minutes and gently stir the sides of the cone with a rod by spinning and let it settle for further 15 minutes.

- Record the volume of settleable matter in the cone as ml '1.

Observations

Sample No.				
Volume in cone				
Time for settling				
Settleable matter				

Sources:

1. *Standard Methods for the Examination of Water and Wastewater*, 21st Ed., 2005.
2. IS: 3025 (Pt-19)—1984.

CONDUCTIVITY

Principle

Conductivity is a measure of the ability of an aqueous solution to carry an electric current. This ability depends on the presence of ions, on the total concentration, mobility and the volume and on the measurement.

Apparatus

Conductivity meter.

Calibration

Standard KCl 0.01 M is prepared by dissolving 745.6 mg anhydrous KCl in distilled water. This is the standard reference solution and has a conductivity of 1412 micromhos/cm at 25°C.

Procedure

Calibrate the instrument with 0.01 M KCl before putting sample and adjust temperature to 25.0 ± 0.1°C and calculate cell constant accordingly.

Specific conductance at 25°C, in micromhos/cm = KL

Where, K = Conductivity

L = Cell Constant

Observations

Sample No.				
Standards used for calibration				
Conductivity				

Sources:

1. *Standard Methods for the Examination of Water and Wastewater*, 21st Ed., 2005.
2. IS: 3025 (Pt-14)—1984.

ACIDITY

Principle

Acidity is the quantitative capacity to react with a strong base to a specific pH. It is determined by titrating with a strong base. The equation in its simplest form is as follows:

$$H^+ + NaOH = H_2O + Na^+$$

Mineral acidity is up to pH 4.5 and total acidity is up to pH 8.3

To determine acidity colour change of the indicator is used. In case of coloured water potentiometric method is being used.

Apparatus

pH meter

Burette

Conical flasks

Volumetric flasks

Volumetric pipettes

Reagents

1. Distilled water

2. Sodium hydroxide solution-1 N – Dissolve 4 g NaOH in 1000 ml of distilled water
3. Sodium hydroxide solution-0.02 N – Dilute 20 ml of 1 N NaOH solution to one litre and standardize
4. Phenolphthalein indicator – Dissolve 0.5 g phenolphthalein in 100 ml, 1:1 (v/v) alcohol water mixture and add 0.02 N NaOH solution drop by drop till faint pink colour is observed
5. Methyl orange indicator – Dissolve 0.5 g of methyl orange in distilled water and make up to 100 ml in a volumetric flask.

Procedure

Mineral Acidity (Methyl Orange Acidity)

Determine the pH of water.

Pipette a suitable aliquot of sample into a 100 ml beaker.

The sample is titrated with standard NaOH using methyl orange as indicator. The end point is from orange to yellow colour.

Total Acidity (Phenolphthalein Acidity)

Determine the pH of water.

Pipette a suitable aliquot of sample into a 100 ml conical flask.

The sample is titrated with standard NaOH using phenolphthalein as indicator. The end point is from colourless to faint pink colour.

Observations

Solution by burette	
Solution by pipette	
Indicator used	
End point	

Sample No.	Volume of sample taken	Initial reading	Final reading	Volume of titrant consumed

Calculations

mg/L acidity as $CaCO_3$ =

$$\frac{\text{Vol. of NaOH} \times \text{Normality of NaOH} \times 50 \times 1000}{\text{Vol. of sample taken for titration}}.$$

Sources:

1. IS: 3025 (Part-22)—1986.
2. *Standard Methods for the Examination of Water and Wastewater*, 21st Ed., 2005.

ALKALINITY

Principle

Alkalinity is the quantitative capacity of an aqueous medium to react with hydrogen ions to pH 8.3 (phenolphthalein alkalinity) and then to pH 3.7 (total alkalinity or methyl orange alkalinity). The equation in its simplest form is as follows:

CO_3^{2-} + H+ = HCO^{3-} (pH 8.3)

From pH 8.3 to 3.7, the following reaction may occur:

$HCO^{3-} + H_+ = H_2CO_3$

Phenolphthalein alkalinity is up to pH 8.3 and total alkalinity is up to pH 4.5.

To determine alkalinity colour change of the indicator is used. In case of coloured water potentiometric method is being used.

Apparatus

pH meter

Burette

Conical flaks

Volumetric flasks

Volumetric pipettes

Reagents

1. Distilled water.
2. Sulfuric acid solution-0.1N – Dissolve 2.8 ml in 1000 ml of distilled water.
3. Sulfuric acid solution-0.02 N – Dissolve 200 ml of 0.1 N H_2SO_4 solution in 1000 ml of distilled water.
4. Phenolphthalein indicator – Dissolve 0.5/g phenolphthalein in 100 ml, 1:1 (v/v) alcohol water mixture and add 0.02 N NaOH solution drop by drop till faint pink colour is observed.
5. Methyl orange indicator – Dissolve 0.5 g of methyl orange in distilled water and make up to 100 ml in a volumetric flask.

Procedure

Phenolphthalein Alkalinity

Determine the pH of water.

Pipette a suitable aliquot of sample into a 100 ml conical flask.

The sample is titrated with standard H_2SO_4 using phenolphthalein as indicator. The end point is from faint pink to colourless.

Total Alkalinity (Methyl Orange Alkalinity)

Determine the pH of water.

Pipette a suitable aliquot of sample into a 100 ml beaker.

The sample is titrated with standard H_2SO_4 using Methyl Orange as indicator. The end point is from yellow to orange colour.

Observations

Solution by burette	
Solution by pipette	
Indicator used	
End point	

Sample No.	Volume of sample taken	Initial reading	Final reading	Volume of titrant consumed

Calculations

Mg/L alkalinity as $CaCO_3$ =

$$\frac{\text{Vol. of } H_2SO_4 \times \text{Normality of } H_2SO_4 \times 50 \times 1000}{\text{Vol. of sample taken for titration}}.$$

If the sample does not contain silicates, phosphates, and borates in significant quantities, the following table may be used to calculate bicarbonate, carbonate and hydroxide alkalinities.

ALKALINITY

Alkalinity as $CaCO_3$	Hydroxide alkalinity as $CaCO_3$	Carbonate alkalinity as $CaCO_3$	Bicarbonate alkalinity as $CaCO_3$
P = 0	0	0	T
P = T/2	0	2P	T – 2P
P = T/2	0	2P	0
P > T/2	2P – T	2T – 2P	0
P = T	T	0	0

Sources:

1. IS: 3025 (Part-23)—1986.
2. *Standard Methods for the Examination of Water and Wastewater*, 21st Ed., 2005.

CHLORIDE

Principle

In a neutral or slightly alkaline medium K_2CrO_4 can indicate the end point in chloride titration. AgCl is precipitated quantitatively before red silver chromate is formed.

Apparatus

Burette

Conical flasks

Volumetric flasks

Volumetric pipettes

Spectrophotometer

Nessler's tubes

Measuring cylinders

Reagents

1. K_2CrO_4 indicator solution – 5% w/v.
2. Standard silver nitrate solution – N/35.5 – Dissolve 4.8 g AgNO3 in 1000 ml of distilled water.
3. Aluminium hydroxide suspension – Dissolve 12.5 g of aluminium potassium sulphate or aluminium ammonium sulphate [$AlK(SO_4)_2.12H_2O$ or $AlNH_4(SO_4)_2.12H_2O$] in 1 litre of distilled water. Warm to 60°C and add 55 ml of concentrated ammonium hydroxide slowly with stirring. Let it stand for 1 hour, transfer to a large bottle and wash precipitate by successive additions, with thorough mixing and decanting with distilled water, until free from chloride.
4. Phenolphthalein indicator — Dissolve 0.5 g phenolphthalein in 100 ml, 1:1 (v/v) alcohol water mixture and add 0.02 N

NaOH solution drop by drop till faint pink colour is observed.

5. Sodium hydroxide – 1 N – Dissolve 40 g NaOH in 1000 ml of distilled water.
6. Sulfuric acid – 1 N – Dissolve 28 ml of H_2SO_4 in 1000 ml of distilled water.
7. Hydrogen peroxide – 30%.

Procedure

Pipette a suitable aliquot of sample into a 100 ml conical flask.

To the known volume of the neutralized sample add K_2CrO_4 indicator and titrate with standard $AgNO_3$ to a pinkish yellow end point.

If the sample is coloured, add 3 ml $Al(OH)_3$ suspension, allow to settle and filter.

If sulfide, sulfite or thiosulfate are present, add one ml of H_2O_2 and stir well.

Observations

Solution by burette	
Solution by pipette	
Indicator used	
End point	

Sample No.	Volume of sample taken	Initial reading	Final reading	Volume of titrant consumed

Calculations

Cl^- mg/L =

$$\frac{\text{Vol. of } AgNO_3 \times \text{Normality of } AgNO_3 \times 35.5 \times 1000}{\text{Vol. of sample taken}}.$$

Colorimetric Method (For Low Chloride)

Principle

Solutions of ferric ammonium sulfate and mercuric thiocyanate are added to sample. Chloride reacts with mercuric thiocyanate, which combines with ferric ions to form red ferric thiocyanate. The intensity of the colour is measured at 463 nm.

Apparatus

Volumetric pipettes

Spectrophotometer

Nessler's tubes

Measuring cylinders

Reagents

1. Millipore water.
2. Ferric ammonium sulfate – 5 g ferrous ammonium sulfate in 20 ml water, add 38 ml conc. HNO_3 and boil, cool and make up to 1000 ml.
2. Mercuric thiocyanate solution – 0.30 g mercuric thiocyanate in 100 ml methanol. Keep in amber coloured bottle.
3. Standard chloride solution – 0.014 N – Dissolve 2.395 g of silver nitrate in distilled water and dilute to 1 litre. Standardize against sodium chloride solution (1 ml = 500 µg of chloride).

Procedure

Prepare a series of reference standards by diluting the standard chloride standard solution.

To 25 ml blank, standards and samples, add 5 ml FAS solution, 2.5 ml mercuric thiocyanate solution, mix and allow to stand for 10 minutes.

Measure the intensity of the colour at 463 nm and plot a graph. The concentration can be found out from the graph.

Observations

Sample No.				
Stands used for calibration				
Slope				
Absorbance				
Dilution				
Concentration				

Sources:

1. IS: 3025 (Part-32)—1988.
2. *Standard Methods for the Examination of Water and Wastewater*, 21st Ed., 2005.

TOTAL HARDNESS

Principle

This method depends on ability of ethylene-diamine tetra acetic acid ($C_{10}H_{16}O_8N_2$) or its disodium salt to form stable complex as with calcium and magnesium ions.

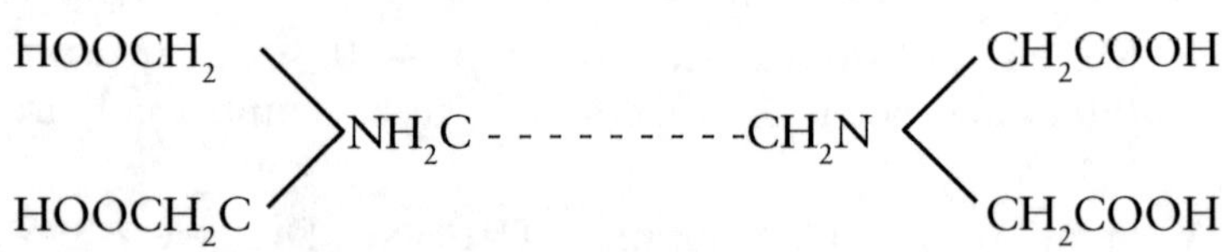

When the dye eriochrome black T (EBT) ($C_2O\ H_{13}N_3O_7S$) is added to a solution containing calcium and magnesium ions at pH 10.0 a wine red complex is formed. This solution is titrated with standard solution of disodium salt of EDTA, which extracts calcium and magnesium from the dye complex and the dye is changed back to its original blue colours. Eriochrome black T is used to indicate the end point for the titration of calcium and magnesium together.

$$Mg^{++} + EBT \rightleftharpoons [Mg - EBT]^{-} + H^{+}$$
(Pink Complex)

$$[Mg - EBT]^{-} + EDTA \rightleftharpoons [Mg - EDTA]^{--} + [EBT]^{--}$$
$$+ [EBT]^{--} \text{ (Blue)} + H^{+}$$

Apparatus

Burette

Conical flasks

Volumetric flasks

Volumetric pipettes

Reagents

1. Buffer solution – Dissolve 16.9 g NH_4Cl and 143 ml conc. NH_4OH, 1.179 EDTA, and 780 mg $MgSO_4.7H_2O$ in 250 ml distilled water.
2. Eriohrome black T indicator – 0.5% in alcohol.
3. EDTA solution – 0.02 N – Dissolve 3.7 g EDTA in 1000 ml of distilled water.

Procedure

To a known quantity of the sample add 2 ml buffer.

Titrate the sample with EDTA solution using the indicator until the last reddish tinge disappears.

Observations

Solution by burette	
Solution by pipette	
Indicator used	
End point	

Sample No.	Volume of sample taken	Initial reading	Final reading	Volume of titrant consumed

Calculations

Total hardness as $CaCO_3$, mg/L =

$$\frac{\text{Vol. of EDTA} \quad \text{Normality of EDTA} \quad 50 \quad 1000}{\text{Vol. of sample taken}}.$$

Sources:

1. IS: 3025 (Part-21)—1988.
2. *Standard Methods for the Examination of Water and Wastewater*, 21st Ed., 2005.

CALCIUM

Principle

In a solution containing both calcium and magnesium, calcium can be determined directly with EDTA (ethylene diamine tetra-acetic acid or its salts) when the pH is made sufficiently high (12 to 13) so that the magnesium is largely precipitated as the hydroxide and an indicator is used which combines, only with calcium.

Apparatus

Burette

Conical flasks

Volumetric flasks

Volumetric pipettes

Reagents

1. NaOH – 1 N – Dissolve 40 g NaOH in 1000 ml of distilled water.

2. Muroxide indicator – Prepare by mixing 200 mg of muroxide with 100 g of NaCl.
3. EDTA solution – 0.02 N – Dissolve 3.7 g EDTA in 1000 ml of distilled water.

Procedure

To a known quantity of the sample add 2 ml NaOH.

Titrate with EDTA using the indicator from pink to purple.

Observations

Solution by burette	
Solution by pipette	
Indicator used	
End point	

Sample No.	Volume of sample taken	Initial reading	Final reading	Volume of titrant consumed

Calculations

Total hardness as $CaCO_3$, mg/L =

$$\frac{\text{Vol. of EDTA} \times \text{Normality of EDTA} \times 50 \times 1000}{\text{Vol. of sample taken}}.$$

Sources:

1. IS: 3025 (Part- 40)—1991.
2. *Standard Methods for the Examination of Water and Wastewater,* 21st Ed., 2005.

SULFIDE

Iodometric Method

Principle

In the alkaline condition, sulfide is precipitated as zinc sulfide. The precipitate is washed and oxidized with excess iodine. The amount of iodine used is determined by titration.

Apparatus

Glass bottles with stoppers

Volumetric pipettes

Burette

Conical flasks

Volumetric flasks

Measuring cylinders

Reagents

1. Zinc acetate solution – 22% w/v.
2. HCl – 1:1.
3. NaOH – 6 N – Dissolve 240 g of NaOH in 1000 ml of distilled water.
4. Standard hypo solution – 0.025 – Dissolve 6.205 g $Na_2S_2O_3.5H_2O$ in 800 ml of distilled water and boil. After cooling add 0.4 g NaOH and make up to 1000 mL.
5. Standard iodine solution – 0.025 N – Dissolve 25 g KI in a little water and add 3.2 g iodine. After iodine has dissolved dilute to 1000 ml and standardize against $Na_2S_2O_3$.
6. Starch indicator.

Procedure

Put 4 drops of zinc acetate solution and 2 drops of 6N NaOH into a 100 ml glass bottle, fill with sample and add 2 drops of 6N NaOH.

Stopper with no air bubbles under stopper and mix by rotating back and forth vigorously about a tranverse axis.

Add enough NaOH to raise pH above 9. Let precipitate settle for 30 mins.

Measure an amount of iodine solution estimated to be an excess over the amount of sulfide present.

Add 2 ml 6 N HCl. Pipette 200 ml sample into flask. If iodine colour disappears add more iodine till colour remains.

Back titrate the excess iodine with standard hypo adding few drops of starch as end point is approached.

Observations

Solution by burette Solution by pipette	
Indicator used	
End point	

Sample No.	Volume of sample taken	Initial reading	Final reading	Volume of titrant consumed

Calculations

Sulfide as S, mg/L =

$$\frac{V1 - V2 \times \text{Normality of hypo} \times 16 \times 1000}{V3}$$

Where V1 = vol. of hypo used for blank

Where V2 = vol. of hypo used for sample

Where V3 = vol. of sample taken for test

Methylene Blue Method

The method is based on reaction of sulfide, $FeCl_3$ and dimethyl-p-phenylene diamine to produce methylene blue. Ammonium phosphate is added after the colour development to remove $FeCl_3$ colour.

Apparatus

Matched test tubes

Droppers

Spectrophotometer

Nessler's tubes

Volumetric pipettes

Reagents

1. Amine sulfuric acid stock – 27 g of N, N Dimethyl-p-phenylene diamine oxalate in cold mixture of 50 ml conc. H_2SO_4 and 20 ml distilled water. Cool and dilute to 100 ml. Dilute 25 ml to 1000 ml.
2. $FeCl_3$ – 100 g in 40 ml water.
3. Diammonium hydrogen phosphate – 400 g in 800 ml distilled water.
4. Methylene blue solution-I – 1.0 g dye in distilled water and standardize using standard sulfide. [1 drop (0.05 ml) = 1.0 mg sulfide]
5. Methylene blue solution-II – Dilute 10 times the MBS-I.

Procedure

Transfer 7.5 ml sample to tube (A).

Add 5 ml amine sulfuric acid and 0.15 ml $FeCl_3$ and mix.

To tube (B) transfer 0.5 ml 1:1 H_2SO_4 and 0.15 ml $FeCl_3$ (3 drops).

Blue colour in (A) indicates the presence of sulfide.

Add 1.6 ml diammonium hydrogen phosphate in each tube. Wait for 10 minutes.

Observations

Sample No.			
Stands used for calibration			
Slope			
Absorbance			
Dilution			
Concentration			

Colour Comparison

(a) Visual

Add methylene blue solution I or II, depending on sulfide concentration dropwise to the second tube and match the colour with methylene blue solution I adjusted so that 0.05 ml (1 drop) = 1.0 mg S^{2-}/L when 7.5 ml of sample are used:

mg S^{2-}/L = No. of drops solution I + 0.1 (no. of drops solution II).

(b) Photometric

Measure the colour using different concentrations of sulfide at 664 nm.

Zero instrument with a portion of treated sample from tube B.

Plot the calibration graph.

Read sulfide concentration from the graph.

Sources:

1. IS: 3025 (Part-29)—1989.
2. *Standard Methods for the Examination of Water and Wastewater*, 21st Ed., 2005.

SULFITE

Principle

Iodine reacts with sulfite. The additional drop of iodine gives blue colour with starch indicator.

Apparatus

Volumetric pipettes

Burette

Conical flasks

Volumetric flasks

Measuring cylinders

Reagents

1. Sulfuric acid – 1:1.
2. Potassium iodate – Iodide titrant – 0.0125 M – Disslove 0.4458 KIO_3, 4.35 g KI and 310 g $NaHCO_3$ in 1000 ml distilled water.
3. Sulfamic acid, crystalline.
4. EDTA reagent – Dissolve 2.5 g in 100 ml distilled water.
5. Starch indicator.

Procedure

Collect fresh sample and immediately add 1 ml EDTA per 100 ml.

Add 1 ml H_2SO_4 and 0.1 g sulfamic acid and titrate with the titrant using starch indicator.

Perform a blank titration also.

Observations

Solution by burette	
Solution by pipette	
Indicator used	
End point	

Sample No.	Volume of sample taken	Initial reading	Final reading	Volume of titrant consumed

Calculations

$$\text{Sulfite as } SO_3 \text{ mg/L} = \frac{(V1 - V2)\quad M \quad 40 \quad 1000}{V3}$$

Where

V1 = ml titrant for sample

V2 = ml titrant for blank

V3 = volume of the sample taken

M = molarity of KI – KIO_3 reagent.

Source: *Standard Methods for the Examination of Water and Wastewater*, 21st Ed., 2005.

SULFATE

Principle

Sulfate is precipitated as $BaSO_4$ in the presence of HCl; the precipitate is washed till free from chloride, ignited and weighed as $BaSO_4$.

The reaction in its simplest form is:

$$SO_4^{2-} + BaCl_2 \text{ - - - - HCl medium - - - - - } BaSO_4 + 2HCl.$$

Apparatus

Muffle furnace

Filter paper – Whatman No. 42 or equivalent

Drying oven

Desiccator

Analytical balance

Crucibles

Reagents

1. HCl – 1+1
2. $BaCl_2$ Solution – 10% w/v.

Procedure

Acidify a known quantity of sample with 1+1 HCl.

Add 10 ml of $BaCl_2$ solution and heat to boil.

Filter through the filter paper. Continue filtration by adding hot water till free from chloride.

Dry the filter paper and ignite in the muffle furnace at about 800°C.

Cool the residue and weigh as $BaSO_4$.

Observations

Sample No.				
Initial weight				
Final weight				
Net weight				
Volume of sample taken				
Sulphate				

Calculations

$$SO_4,\ \text{mg/L} = \frac{\text{mg. } BaSO_4 \quad 96/233 \quad 1000}{\text{Vol. of the sample}}.$$

Turbidimetric Method

Sulfate is precipitated in acetic acid medium. Buffer is added to make the $BaSO_4$ in suspension and measured spectrophotometrically.

Apparatus

Volumetric pipettes

Spectrophotometer

Nessler's tubes

Measuring cylinders

Beakers

Reagents

1. Buffer-A – 30 g $MgCl_2$, 5 g sodium acetate, and 1.0 g KNO_3 and 20 ml acetic acid in 1000 ml.
2. Buffer-B (for very low concentrations of SO_4) – 30 g $MgCl_2$, 5 g sodium acetate, 1.0 g KNO_3, 0.111 g Na_2SO_4 and 20 ml acetic acid in 1000 ml water.
3. $BaCl_2$ crystals.
4. Sulfate standard – 0.1479 g of anhydrous sodium sulfate (Na_2SO_4) in distilled water and dilute to 1 litre.

Procedure

To a known volume of the sample add 20 ml buffer – A and pinch of $BaCl_2$.

Stir thoroughly and take the measurements spectrophotometrically at 420 nm.

Run blank and standards also and plot a graph.

Concentration of sulfate is calculated from the graph.

Observations

Sample No.				
Stands used for calibration				
Slope				
Absorbance				
Dilution				
Concentration				

Sources:

1. IS: 3025 (Part-24)—1989.
2. *Standard Methods for the Examination of Water and Wastewater*, 21st Ed., 2005.

RESIDUAL CHLORINE

O-Tolidine Method

Color developed by o-tolidine is compared with standard colour solutions.

Apparatus

Volumetric pipettes

Spectrophotometer

Nessler's tubes

Measuring cylinders

Beakers

Reagents

1. Dil. HCl – 1:9.
2. O-Tolidine solution – Dissolve 1.35 g o-tolidine dihydrochloride in 1000 ml dil. HCl.
3. $CuSO_4$ solution – Dissolve 1.5 g in 1000 ml water containing 1 ml H_2SO_4.
4. $K_2Cr_2O_7$ solution – Dissolve 0.25 g in 1000 ml water containing 1 ml H_2SO_4.
5. Sodium arsenite solution – Dissolve 0.5 g in 1000 ml water.
6. Standard colour solution – To be prepared as given below. Final volume – 100 ml.

S.No.	Chlorine, mg/L	$CuSO_4$ solution, ml	$K_2Cr_2O_7$ solution, ml
1.	0.01	0.0	0.8
2.	0.02	0.0	2.1
3.	0.03	0.0	3.2
4.	0.04	0.0	4.3
5.	0.05	0.4	5.5
6.	0.06	0.8	6.6
7.	0.07	1.2	7.5

8.	0.08	1.5	8.2
9.	0.09	1.7	9.0
10.	0.10	1.8	10.0
11.	0.15	1.8	15.0
12.	0.20	1.9	20.0
13.	0.25	1.9	25.0
14.	0.30	1.9	30.0
15.	0.35	1.9	34.0
16.	0.40	2.0	38.0
17.	0.50	2.0	45.0
18.	0.60	2.0	51.0
19.	0.70	2.0	58.0
20.	0.80	2.0	63.0
21.	0.90	2.0	67.0
22.	1.00	2.0	72.0

Procedure

To 100 ml of the sample add 1 ml reagent and mix.

Take the measurements after 15 minutes spectrophotometrically with the colour standards at 625 nm.

Iodometric Method

Iodine is liberated by adding KI and is titrated with hypo using starch as indicator.

Apparatus

Volumetric pipettes

Burette

Conical flasks

Volumetric flasks

Measuring cylinders

Reagents

1. Glacial acetic acid.

2. KI crystals.
3. Standard sodium thiosulfate solution (Hypo solution) – 0.0125 N – Dissolve 3.2 g sodium thiosulphate in 1000 ml of distilled water.
4. Starch indicator.

Procedure

Acidify the sample with acetic acid and add few KI crystals.

Titrate with standard hypo using starch indicator until the blue colour is discharged.

Observations

Solution by burette	
Solution by pipette	
Indicator used	
End point	

Sample No.	Volume of sample taken	Initial reading	Final reading	Volume of titrant consumed

Calculations

Residual Chlorine, mg/L =

$$\frac{\text{Vol. of hypo} \times \text{normality of hypo} \times 35.45 \times 1000}{\text{Vol. of sample taken}}.$$

Sources:

1. IS: 3025 (Part-26)—1982.
2. *Standard Methods for the Examination of Water and Wastewater*, 21st Ed., 2005.

CHLORINE DEMAND

Principle

Chlorine demand is the difference between the amount of chlorine applied and the amount of chlorine available after a specific contact period. It varies with the amount of chlorine applied, time of contact and the pH of the water.

Apparatus

Flasks of 1 L capacity

Glass stirring rod

Dropper

Volumetric pipettes

Burette

Conical flasks

Volumetric flasks

Measuring cylinders

Reagents

1. Standard sodium thiosulfate solution (Hypo solution) – 0.0125 N – Dissolve 3.2 g sodium thiosulphate in 1000 ml of distilled water.
2. Standard chlorine solution – prepared from bleaching powder. Standardized by titrating with standard hypo using starch as indicator.

Procedure

Measure at least ten portions of water, equal in quantity.

Add increasing amount of chlorine in each portion.

Carry out the test for residual chlorine at the end of specific contact time such as 15 minutes, 30 minutes, 60 minutes etc.

Calculations

Available chlorine, mg, for each drop = A × N × 35 / 20

Where

A = ml titration for sample

N = normality of standard thiosulphate solution

$$\text{Chlorine Demand, mg/L} = \frac{\text{mg/L chlorine added}}{\text{mg/L available chlorine}}$$

pH and the temperature of contact is also required to be mentioned in the report.

Source: Standard Methods for the Examination of Water and Wastewater, 21st Ed., 2005.

CORROSIVITY

Principle

Corrosivity is a measure of stability of water with respect to calcium carbonate. pH or alkalinity is determined before and after treatment with $CaCO_3$. An increased value after treatment shows the corrosive nature of the water.

Apparatus

pH meter

Volumetric pipettes

Burette

Conical flasks

Volumetric flasks

Measuring cylinders

Reagent

1. Precipitated $CaCO_3$ – 10 g.

Procedure

Determine the pH or alkalinity of the sample initially.

Shake the sample with $CaCO_3$ vigorously at an interval of 4 hours and allow it to keep overnight.

Determine the pH or alkalinity of the filtrate.

If the values are higher in the second case, the water is corrosive. If the values are not increased, the water is non-corrosive.

Observations

Sample No.				
Initial pH				
Final pH				
Inference				

Source: IS: 201—1964.

BORON

Principle

Boron in water forms a complex with mannitol and the pH of the water is reduced. The original pH is brought back by titrating with standard alkali. From the value of the alkali, concentration of boron is estimated.

Apparatus

pH meter

Volumetric pipettes

Burette

Conical flasks

Volumetric flasks

Measuring cylinders

Reagents

1. HCl solution – 1 N – Dissolve 500 ml of 1 + 1 HCl to 1000 ml of distilled water.
2. Standard HCl – 0.02 N – Dilute 20 ml of 1 N HCl to 1000 ml.
3. NaOH solution – 0.1 N – Dissolve 4 g of NaOH in 1000 ml of distilled water.
4. NaOH solution – 0.02 N – Dilute 20 ml of 0.1 N NaOH solution to 100 ml.
5. NaOH solution – 0.005 N – Dilute 5 ml of 0.1 NaOH solution to 100 ml.
6. Boron free mannitol.

Procedure

The water sample is acidified with HCl and boil off CO_2. Cool and bring back the pH of the water sample to 7.0.

Add 5 gm boron free mannitol. A decrease in pH will indicate the presence of boron.

Titrate with 0.005 NaOH to bring back the pH of the sample to 7.0 again. Note the volume of NaOH consumed.

Observations

Solution by burette	
Solution by pipette	
Indicator used	
End point	

Sample No.	Volume of sample taken	Initial reading	Final reading	Volume of titrant consumed

Calculations

Boron, mg/L =

$$\frac{\text{Vol. of NaOH} \times \text{normality of NaOH} \times \text{At.Wt. of Boron} \times 1000}{\text{Vol. of the sample taken}}$$

Source: Potentiometric Water Analysis – by Midgley and Torrece.

FREE CARBON DIOXIDE

Principle

Free carbon dioxide reacts with Na_2CO_3 or NaOH to form $NaHCO_3$. Which is indicative by the pink colour of the phenolphthalein indicator. It is preferable to do this test at site.

Apparatus

pH meter
Burette
Conical flasks
Volumetric flasks
Volumetric pipettes

Reagents

1. Distilled water.
2. Sodium hydroxide solution – 1 N – Dissolve 4 g NaOH in 1000 ml of distilled water.
3. Sodium hydroxide solution – 0.02 N – Dilute 20 ml of 1 N NaOH solution to one litre and standardize.
4. Phenolphthalein indicator – Dissolve 0.5 g phenolphthalein in 100 ml, 1:1 (v/v) alcohol water mixture and add 0.02 N NaOH solution drop by drop till faint pink colour is observed.

Procedure

Determine the pH of water.

Pipette a suitable aliquot of sample into a 100 ml conical flask.

The sample is titrated with NaOH using phenolphthalein as indicator.

The end point is from colourless to faint pink colour (pH – 8.3).

In case of coloured sample the titration needs to be carried using pH meter.

Observations

Solution by burette	
Solution by pipette	
Indicator used	
End point	

Sample No.	Volume of sample taken	Initial reading	Final reading	Volume of titrant consumed

Calculations

Free carbon dioxide as CO_2 (mg/L) =

$$\frac{\text{Vol. of NaOH} \times \text{normality of NaOH} \times 44 \times 1000}{\text{Vol. of the sample used}}.$$

Carbon dioxide and forms of alkalinity by calculation

(a) HCO_3^- as $CaCO_3$ (mg/L) = $\frac{T - 5.0 \times 10^{(pH-10)}}{1 + 0.94 \times 10^{(pH-10)}}$ where T is the total alkalinity as $CaCO_3$.

(b) CO_3^{-2} as $CaCO_3$ (mg/L) = $0.94 \times B \times 10^{(pH-10)}$ where B is the Bicarbonate alkalinity.

(c) OH^- as Ca CO3 (mg/L) = $5.0 \times 10^{(pH-10)}$

(d) CO_2 mg/l = $2.0 \times B \times 10^{(6-pH)}$

(e) Total CO_2 mg/l = A + 0.44 (2B + C).

Source: Standard Methods for the Examination of Water and Wastewater, 21st Ed., 2005.

DISSOLVED OXYGEN

Principle

Dissolved Oxygen (DO) rapidly oxidizes an equivalent amount of the dispersed divalent manganous hydroxide precipitate to hydroxides of higher valency states. In the presence of iodide ions in an acidic solution, the oxidized manganese reverts to the divalent state, with the liberation of iodine equivalent to the original DO content. In alkaline condition, manganese reacts with dissolved oxygen precipitating as higher oxides of manganese, which in the acidic medium liberates iodine from KI. The iodine is estimated by titrating with standard hypo.

Apparatus

DO bottles
Volumetric pipettes
Burette
Conical flasks
Volumetric flasks
Measuring cylinders

Reagents

1. Manganese sulfate solution – Dissolve 91 g $MnSO_4.H_2O$ in 250 ml water.
2. Alkaline iodide azide reagent – Dissolve 175 g KOH or 125 g NaOH and 37.5 g KI dissolved in 960 ml water. 10 g of sodium azide in 40 ml of water. Mix the two solutions.
3. Conc. H_2SO_4.
4. Hypo solution – N/80 – Dissolve 3.2 g sodium thiosulphate in 1000 ml of distilled water.
5. Starch indicator.

Procedure

Collect the sample in DO bottle. Add 2 ml $MnSO_4$ solution and 2 ml Iodide azide solution. Shake well by inverting the bottle. Add 2 ml H_2SO_4 and shake well. Titrate with hypo solution using starch as indicator.

Observations

Solution by burette	
Solution by pipette	
Indicator used	
End point	

Sample No.	Volume of sample taken	Initial reading	Final reading	Volume of titrant consumed

Calculations

$$= \frac{\text{Vol. of hypo} \times \text{normality of hypo} \times 8 \times 1000}{\text{Vol. of sample taken for titration}}$$

Sources

1. IS: 3025 (Part-38)—1989.
2. *Standard Methods for the Examination of Water and Wastewater*, 21st Ed., 2005.

BIOCHEMICAL OXYGEN DEMAND

Principle

BOD is the measurement of the relative oxygen requirements of water and wastewater.

Dissolved oxygen is measured initially and after five days of incubation at 20°C from the difference of measurements indicates the BOD.

Apparatus

DO bottles
pH meter
Volumetric pipettes
Burette
Conical flasks
Volumetric flasks
Measuring cylinders
Incubator

Reagents

1. Phosphate buffer – Dissolve 8.5 g KH_2PO_4, 21.75 g K_2HPO_4, 33.4 g Na_2HPO_4 and 1.4 NH_4Cl in 1000 ml.

2. $MgSO_4$ solution – Dissolve 22.5 g $MgSO_4.7H_2O$ in 1000 ml.
3. $CaCl_2$ solution – Dissolve 27.5 g in 1000 ml.
4. $FeCl_3$ solution – Dissolve 0.25 g $FeCl_3$. $6H_2O$ in 1000 ml.
5. Acid and alkali solution – Dissolve 1N H_2SO_4 and 1N NaOH.
6. Na_2SO_4 solution – Dissolve 1.575 g in 1000 ml. Prepare daily.
7. Glucose – Glutamic acid solution – Dissolve 150 mg glucose and 150 g glutamic acid in 1000 ml.
8. Ammonium Chloride – Dissolve 1.15 g in 500 ml. Adjust to pH 7.2 and make up to 1000 ml.

Procedure

Preparation of Dilution Water

The water is saturated with oxygen by bubbling. Allow it to stabilize overnight in the incubator.

Add one ml each of reagents 1 to 4 shake well. Seed the dilutions water if necessary.

Periodically check the dilution water.

BOD Determination

Make different dilution in duplicate and fill with dilution water in DO bottles. Care must be taken that no air bubble is trapped in the bottle. Determine immediate oxygen (IDOD) in one set of samples. The other set is incubated for 5 days at 20°C or for 3 days at 27°C.

After the incubation again determine the DO.

Observations

Dilutions	IDO		IDOD	DO after incubation		FDO	BDO
	Initial reading	Final reading		Initial reading	Final reading		

Calculations

BOD is calculated as = IDOD – DO after incubation × dilution factor.

Pretreatment of the Sample

1. Adjust the sample pH to neutral.
2. Remove the free chlorine; if present calculate by addition of standard Hypo.

Glucose – Glutamic Acid Check

Glucose – glutamic acid has a specific BOD. The correctness of the analysis can be checked with the solution.

Run a blank also with the dilution water for IDOD and DO after the required incubation.

If the BOD value is greater than 1.5 mg/L, prepare fresh dilution water.

If seeding is done, the correction factor must be applied.

Sources:

1. IS: 3025 (Part-44)—1992.
2. *Standard Methods for the Examination of Water and Wastewater*, 21st Ed., 2005.

CHEMICAL OXYGEN DEMAND

Principle

The organic matter and easily oxidizable matter in the sample are oxidized with chromic acid. The unused chromic acid is determined by titrating with standard FAS. Chemical oxygen demand is calculated from the amount of chromic acid used for oxidation.

Apparatus

Round bottom flask with water cooled condensers

Volumetric pipettes

Burette

Conical flasks

Volumetric flasks

Measuring cylinders

Reagents

1. Mercuric sulfate crystals.
2. Sulfuric acid – silver nitrate reagent – Dissolve 10.1 g Ag_2SO_4 in 1000 ml H_2SO_4.
3. $K_2Cr_2O_7$ reagent – 0.0167 M – Add about 500 ml distilled water, 4.913 g $K_2Cr_2O_7$, 167 ml conc. H_2SO_4 and 33.3 g $HgSO_4$.
4. FAS solution – 0.1 N – Dissolve 39.2 g ferrous ammonium sulphate and 10 ml H_2SO_4 in 1000 ml of distilled water.
5. Ferroin indicator – Dissolve 695 mg $FeSO_4.7H_2O$ and 1.485 g 1-10 phenanthroline in 100 ml water.

Procedure

Take a known quantity of well-shaken sample, add a suitable amount of sulfuric acid reagent, to precipitate chloride, add 1 g mercuric sulfate to complex the chloride. Add a known quantity of $K_2Cr_2O_7$, and reflux for two hours. Run a blank also.

When cooled titrate with standard FAS, using ferroin indicator. The colour change is from red to red.

Observations

Solution by burette	
Solution by pipette	
Indicator used	
End point	

Sample No.	Volume of sample taken	Initial reading	Final reading	Volume of titrant consumed

Calculations

COD, mg/L =

$$\frac{(\text{blank titre value} - \text{sample titre value}) \times \text{normality of FAS} \times 8 \times 1000}{\text{Vol. of the sample}}$$

Interferences

Chloride will interfere – if the chloride content is more than 2000 mg/L, do not do COD.

Nitrate will interfere which can be removed by adding 10 mg sulfamic acid, before the addition of dichromate solution.

Source: *Standard Methods for the Examination of Water and Wastewater*, 21st Ed., 2005.

CYANIDE

Principle

Cyanide is estimated either by calorimetric method or by ion selective electrodes. Sulfide will convert CN to SCN, which can be removed by treating the sample with lead carbonate at pH 10.0. Oxidizing agents destroys most of the cyanide. Distillation of the sample can be a possible solution for the removal of interferences. HCN is liberated from an acidified sample by distillation and purging with air. The HCN gas is collected by passing it through an NaOH scrubbing solution.

Apparatus

Boiling flask – 1 L with inlet tube and provision for water cooled condenser

Heating element

Ground glass joints
Spectrophotometer
Nessler's tubes
Measuring cylinders
Volumetric flask
Volumetric pipettes

Reagents

1. $MgCl_2$ solution – 51% w/v – Dissolve 510 mg $MgCl_2.6H_2O$ in 1000 ml of distilled water.
2. NaOH – 1 N – Dissolve 40 g NaOH in 1000 ml of distilled water.
3. Sulphuric acid – 1+1.
4. Lead carbonate powder.
5. Pyridine – Barbituric acid reagent – to 15 g of barbituric acid add 75 ml of pyridine and mix. Add 15 ml conc. HCl cool and make up to 250 ml.
6. Acetate buffer – 410 GM sodium acetate in 500 ml water. Add glacial acetic acid to pH 4.5.
7. Cyanide Stock Solution – Dissolve 1.6 g NaOH and 2.51 g KCN in 1000 ml distilled water (1 ml = 1 mg CN). Standardize with standard silver nitrate.
8. Make intermediate standard by diluting the stock.

Procedure

Distillation

Add 500 ml sample to boiling flask.

When S^{2-} generation from the distilling flask is anticipated, add 50 or more mg of powdered $PbCO_3$ to absorber solution to precipitate S^{2-}.

Add 50 ml 1+1 H_2SO_4 through the air inlet tube. Rinse tube with distilled water and let air mix flask content for 3 mins.

Add 20 ml $MgCl_2$ reagent through air inlet and wash down with stream of water.

Distil the sample to NaOH solution.

Cool and quantitatively transfer absorption solution to a 250 ml volumetric flask.

Colour Development

Place the sample standards and blank.

Add 1 ml acetate buffer, and 2 ml chloramine -T solution.

After two minutes add 50 ml pyridine barbituric acid reagent. Dilute to fixed volume and take the absorbance at 578 nm.

Plot the calibration graph and calculate the concentration from the graph.

Observations

Sample No.				
Stands used for calibration				
Slope				
Absorbance				
Dilution				
Concentration				

Source: *Standard Methods for the Examination of Water and Wastewater*, 21st Ed., 2005.

FLUORIDE

Principle

The SPADNS calorimetric method is based on the reaction between fluoride and Zirconium Lake. As the fluoride concentration increases, the colour becomes progressively lighter.

Apparatus

Volumetric pipettes

Spectrophotometer

Nessler's tubes

Measuring cylinders

Reagents

1. Standard fluoride solution – Dissolve 221.0 mg NaF in one litre. One ml = 100 µg fluoride.
2. SPADNS reagent – Dissolve 960 mg SPADNS in 500 ml distilled water.
3. Zirconyl acid reagent – Dissolve 133 mg zirconyl chloride octahydrate in 25 ml distilled water. Add 350 ml conc. HCl. Dilute to 500 ml.

   Mix solutions 2 and 3.
4. Sodium arsenite solution – Dissolve 5.0 g Na_2AsO_2 in 1000 ml.

Procedure

Prepare fluoride standards up to 1.4 mg/L.

Add 10 ml of the reagent to standards, blank and the samples.

Read absorbance at 570 nm. And calculate the concentration of fluoride from the calibration graph.

If sample contains residual chlorine, remove it by adding one drop of Na_2ASO_2/0.1 mg chlorine.

Observations

Sample No.				
Stands used for calibration				
Slope				
Absorbance				
Dilution				
Concentration				

Sources:

1. IS: 3025 (Part-32)—1988.
2. *Standard Methods for the Examination of Water and Wastewater*, 21st Ed., 2005.

ALUMINIUM

At pH 6.0 eriochrome cyanine-R produce a pink complex, which can be estimated spectrophotometrically at 535 nm.

Apparatus

Volumetric pipettes

Spectrophotometer

Nessler's tubes

Measuring cylinders

Beakers

Reagents

1. Aluminium standard – 500 mg/L – 8.791 g aluminium potassium sulfate in 1000 ml water.
2. Sulfuric acid – 0.02 N.
3. Ascorbic acid – 0.1% w/v in water.
4. Buffer reagent – 136 g sodium acetate in water and 40 ml 1 N acetic acid, dilute to 1000 ml.
5. Eriohrome cyanine-R – 300 mg dye in 50 ml water. Adjust the pH to 9.0 and dilute to 100 ml.
6. EDTA – 0.01 M.
7. NaOH – 1 N – Dissolve 40 g NaOH in 1000 ml distilled water.
8. NaOH – 0.1 N – Dissolve 4 g NaOH in 1000 ml distilled water.

Procedure

To a series of standards, blank and the sample add 1 ml sulfuric acid, 10 ml buffer solution, and 5 ml working dye by diluting the dye 10 times. After 5 minutes read the absorbance.

Prepare a calibration graph and calculate the concentration of the unknown from the graph.

Observations

Sample No.				
Stands used for calibration				
Slope				
Absorbance				
Dilution				
Concentration				

Source: *Standard Methods for the Examination of Water and Wastewater*, 21st Ed., 2005.

CHROMIUM

Hexavalent chromium produces colour with diphenyl carbazide, which shows an absorbance maximum at 540 nm.

Apparatus

Volumetric pipettes
Spectrophotometer
Nessler's tubes
Measuring cylinders
Beakers

Reagents

1. Stock Chromium solution – 500 mg/L – 141.54 mg $K_2Cr_2O_7$ in 100 ml water
2. Nitric acid – conc.
3. Sulfuric acid – conc.
4. Phosphoric acid – conc.
5. Ammonium hydroxide.
6. Potassium permanganate – 4% w/v.
7. Sodium azide – 0.5% w/v.
8. Diphenyl carbazide – 250 mg in 50 ml acetone.
9. Cuoferon – 5% w/v in distilled water.

Procedure

To a series of standards, blank and sample add 10 ml 0.2 N sulfuric acid, and 2 ml diphenyl carbazide. Take the absorbance at 540 nm.

Cupferon solution is used for removing the interference from Mo, V, Fe and Cu.

Observations

Sample No.				
Stands used for calibration				
Slope				
Absorbance				
Dilution				
Concentration				

Source: *Standard Methods for the Examination of Water and Wastewater*, 21st Ed., 2005.

IRON (PHENANTHROLINE METHOD)

Iron is reduced to ferrous state by adding hydroxilamine and treated with 1-10 phenanthroline, which exhibits a maximum absorbance at 510 nm.

Apparatus

Volumetric pipettes

Spectrophotometer

Nessler's tubes

Measuring cylinders

Beakers

Reagents

1. Hydroxilamine solution – 10% w/v.
2. Ammonium acetate buffer – 250 g in 150 ml water, add 700 ml acetic acid.

3. Phenethroline solution – 0.1% w/v in water.
4. Stock iron solution.

Procedure

For total iron, add 2 ml HCl and 1 ml $NH_2OH.HCl$ and heat to boiling, cool to room temperature add 10 ml buffered 2 ml phenenthroline. Take the absorbance at 510 nm, using a series of standards and blank. Calculate the concentration from the graph.

Observations

Sample No.				
Stands used for calibration				
Slope				
Absorbance				
Dilution				
Concentration				

Source: *Standard Methods for the Examination of Water and Wastewater*, 21st Ed., 2005.

SILICA

Molybdosilicate Method

Principle

In the acidified medium, silica and phosphate reacts with ammonium molybdate producing yellow complexes. Oxalic acid is added to suppress the phosphates. Glassware contributes to silica. Tanin, large amount of iron, turbidity, colour, sulfide, and phosphates interfere.

Apparatus

Platinum or plastic dishes

Water bath

Volumetric pipettes

Spectrophotometer

Nessler's tubes

Measuring cylinders

Reagents

1. Sodium bicarbonate.
2. Sulfuric acid – 1 N – Dissolve 28 ml H_2SO_4 in 1000 ml of distilled water.
3. Hydrochloric acid – 1:1.
4. Ammonium molybdate reagent – Dissolve 10 g in 100 ml water. Adjust the pH to 7-8 with silica free ammonia or NaOH.
5. Reducing reagent – dissolve 500 mg 1-amino 2-naphthol 4-sulfonic acid and 1 g sodium sulfite in 50 ml distilled, silica free water. Add 30 g of $NaHSO_3$ in 50 ml water and mix. Filter and keep in a plastic bottle.
6. Oxalic acid – 7.5% w/v in water.
7. Stock silica solution – Dissolve 4.73 sodium meta silicate in 1000 ml water.
8. Standard silica solution – Dilute 10 ml of stock solution to 1000 ml with distilled water (1 ml = 10 mg of SiO_2).

Procedure

To blank, series of standards, and sample add 1 ml 1:1 HCl, and 2 ml ammonium molybdate solution.

Mix and after 10 minutes add 2 ml oxalic acid solution.

Measure the absorbance at 410 nm.

Unreactive silica

Subtraction of reactive silica from total silica gives unreactive silica.

For estimating total silica, add 200 mg $NaHCO_3$ to 100 ml of the sample and digest for one hour at 100°C.

Cool and add 2.4 ml of sulfuric acid reagent with stirring.

Proceed for the estimation of silica as mentioned above. Calculate the unreactive silica.

Heteropoly Blue Method

Procedure

Method to be followed is same as in the case of the previous method. In addition 2 ml reducing reagent is also added.

The blue colour developed is measured spectrophotometrically at wavelength 650 nm.

Minimum detection level in this method is 0.1 mg/L.

Observations

Sample No.				
Stands used for calibration				
Slope				
Absorbance				
Dilution				
Concentration				

Sources:

1. IS:3025 (Part-35)—1988.
2. *Standard Methods for the Examination of Water and Wastewater*, 21st Ed., 2005.

PHOSPHORUS

Principle

Phosphates are classified as ortho phosphates, condensed phosphates and organically bound phosphates. The method responds to ortho phosphates only.

Apparatus

Heating element

pH meter

Volumetric pipettes

Spectrophotometer

Nessler's tubes

Measuring cylinders

Beakers

Reagents

1. Strong acid solution – Dissolve 300 ml H_2SO_4 in 600 ml water, add 4 ml HNO_3 and dilute to 1000 ml.
2. Ammonium molybdate reagent – Dissolve 25 g ammonium molybdate in 175 ml distilled water. Continuously add 280 ml H_2SO_4 to 400 ml water. Cool, mix and dilute to 1000 ml.
3. Stannous chloride solution – Dissolve 2.5 g $SnCl_2$ in 100 ml glycerol. Heat in a water bath.
4. Standard phosphate solution – Dissolve 219.5 mg K_2PO_4 in 100 ml.

Procedure (Stannous Chloride Method)

Preliminary Digestion

(a) *Acid Hydrolizable Phosphates*

The sample is adjusted to pH 8.3 with H_2SO_4 and add 1 ml more. Boil gently for 90 minutes, neutralize and make up to the original volume.

(b) *Total Phosphate*

Add additional 1 ml of H_2SO_4 and 0.5 gm $K_2S_2O_8$ and boil gently. Neutralize to pH 8.3 and make up the volume.

For coloured sample decolorize it with activated carbon.

To a series of standards, and neutralized sample, add 4 ml ammonium molybdate and 0.5 ml of stannous chloride. Measure the colour at 690 nm.

The concentration is calculated from the graph.

Observations

Sample No.				
Stands used for calibration				
Slope				
Absorbance				
Dilution				
Concentration				

Sources:

1. IS: 3025 (Part-31)—1988.
2. Standard Methods for the Examination of Water and Wastewater, 21st Ed., 2005.

AMMONIACAL NITROGEN

Two methods are prescribed for the determination of ammoniacal nitrogen: Nesslerization method and titrimetric method.

Nesslerization Method

Principle

The sample is buffered and distilled. The distillate or the sample as it is, is treated with Nessler's reagent. The colour is measured spectrophotometrically at wavelength 400 – 425 nm.

Apparatus

Distillation apparatus
pH meter
Spectrophotometer
Nessler's tubes
Burette
Volumetric pipette
Conical flask
Volumetric flask

Reagents

1. Zinc sulfate solution – 10% w/v.
2. Sulfuric acid solution – 0.1 N – Dissolve 2.8 ml in 1000 ml of distilled water.
3. Sulfuric acid solution – 0.02 N – Dissolve 200 ml of 0.1 N H_2SO_4 solution in 1000 ml of distilled water.
4. EDTA – Dissolve 50 g in 100 ml water containing 10 g NaOH.
5. Rochelle salt solution – Dissolve 50 g sodium potassium tarterate in 100 ml water.
6. Borate buffer solution – Dissolve 88 ml of 0.1 N NaOH and 500 ml of 0.025 M sodium tetra borate solution to 1000 ml.
7. Sodium hydroxide – 6 N – Dissolve 240 g NaOH in 100 ml of distilled water.
8. Boric acid solution – 2.0% w/v.
9. Nessler's reagent – Dissolve 100 g mercuric iodide and 70 g of KI in small quantity of water. To it add a cool solution of 160 g NaOH in 500 ml mix and dilute to 1000 ml.
10. Stock ammonia solution – Dissolve 3.819 g NH_4Cl in 1000 ml. One ml = 1 mg NH_3 – N.

Preliminary Distillation

Add 500 ml water and 20 ml of borate solution to a distillation flask and adjust pH to 9.5 with 6 N NaOH solution.

Use 500 ml of dechlorinated sample or a portion diluted to 500 ml with water. Remove residual chlorine by adding, at the time of collection, dechlorinating agent equivalent to chlorine residual. Add 25 ml of borate buffer and adjust pH to 9.5.

Distill the ammonia into 50 ml plain boric acid solution for Nesslerization method.

Procedure

Nesslerization Method

To the untreated sample add zinc sulfate to remove residual chlorine.

Adjust the pH to 9.5 with NaOH.

Allow to stand the treated sample for some time.

To the supernatant add 2 ml of Nessler's reagent and measure the absorbance at 425 nm.

Prepare a series of standards and blank and a calibration graph is plotted. The sample concentration is calculated from the graph.

Titrimetric Method

After distillation the filtrate collected in boric acid is titrated with conc. H_2SO_4 (0.02 N) using the mixed indicator (200 mg methyl red and 100 mg methylene blue in 100 ml ethanol).

A blank is also run as in the case of sample.

Observations

Solution by burette	
Solution by pipette	
Indicator used	
End point	

Sample No.	Volume of sample taken	Initial reading	Final reading	Volume of titrant consumed

Calculations

$$\text{Ammoniacal nitrogen as N, mg/L} = \frac{(A - B) \times 0.02 \times 14 \times 1000}{V}$$

Where

A = vol. of H_2SO_4 used for the sample

B = vol. of H_2SO_4 used for the blank

V = vol. of the sample taken for the test

Sources:

1. IS: 3025 (Part-34)—1988.
2. *Standard Methods for the Examination of Water and Wastewater*, 21st Ed., 2005.

NITRATE

Principle

Nitrate and nitrite are reduced to ammonia under hot alkaline conditions. The ammonia is distilled and determined by Nesslerization.

Nitrite will interfere which can be avoided by estimating nitrite separately and subtracting the value from total nitrate.

Apparatus

Distillation apparatus

pH meter

Spectrophotometer

Nessler's tubes

Burette

Volumetric pipette

Conical flask

Volumetric flask

Reagents

1. Deverdas alloy – Reducing agent (an alloy of 50% Cu, 45% Al and 5% Zn).
2. Borate buffer solution – Dissolve 88 ml of 0.1 N NaOH

and 500 ml of 0.025M sodium tetra borate solution to 1000 ml.

3. Nessler's reagent.
4. Sodium hydroxide – 6 N – Dissolve 240 g NaOH in 1000 ml of distilled water.
5. Sulfuric acid solution – 0.1 N – Dissolve 2.8 ml in 1000 ml of distilled water.
6. Sulfuric acid solution – 0.02 N – Dissolve 200 ml of 0.1 N H_2SO_4 solution in 1000 ml of distilled water.
7. Stock ammonia solution – Dissolve 3.819 g NH_4Cl in 1000 ml. One ml = 1 mg NH_3 – N.

Procedure

Remove ammonia by distillation.

Add one g of Deverdas alloy; distill the ammonia produced by the reduction of Nitrate. Estimate the ammonia concentration and report as Nitrate–Nitrogen.

Sources:

1. IS: 3025 (Part-34)—1988.
2. *Standard Methods for the Examination of Water and Wastewater*, 21st Ed., 2005.

NITRITE

Principle

Nitrite is determined as a reddish-purple azo dye by coupling diazotized sufanilic acid with NEEDA. The maximum colour absorbed at 543 nm.

Apparatus

pH meter

Spectrophotometer

Nessler's tubes

Volumetric pipettes

Measuring cylinders

Reagent

1. Sulfanilamide reagent – Dissolve 5.0 g material in a mixture of 50 ml conc. HCl and 300 ml distilled water. Dilute to 500 ml.
2. NEEDA – Dissolve 500 mg in 500 ml water.
3. Hydrochloric acid – 1:3.
4. Stock nitrite solution – Dissolve 1.232 $NaNO_2$ in 1000 ml. 1 ml = 1.0 mg.

Procedure

Filter the sample if turbid.

Adjust the pH to 7.0 and add 1 ml of sulfanilamide reagent.

After 2 minutes, add 1 ml of NEEDA, mix and allow to stand for 10 minutes.

Measure the absorbance at 543 nm.

Run standards and blank and plot a graph. The concentration is calculated from the graph.

Observations

Sample No.				
Stands used for calibration				
Slope				
Absorbance				
Dilution				
Concentration				

Sources:

1. IS: 3025 (Part-34)—1988.
2. *Standard Methods for the Examination of Water and Wastewater*, 21st Ed., 2005.

ORGANIC NITROGEN

Principle

Organic nitrogen is converted into ammonium sulfate by the addition of H_2SO_4, K_2SO_4, and $HgSO_4$. It is then distilled under alkaline conditions, and the ammonia is collected in boric acid or sulfuric acid. Ammonia is estimated by calorimetric or titrimetric method.

Apparatus

Distillation apparatus
Digestion apparatus
pH meter
Spectrophotometer
Nessler's tubes
Burette
Volumetric pipette
Conical flask
Volumetric flask

Reagents

1. Zinc sulfate solution.
2. EDTA reagent.
3. Nessler's reagent.
4. Stock ammonia solution – Dissolve 3.819 g NH_4Cl in 1000 ml. One ml = 1 mg NH_3 – N.
5. Mercuric sulfate solution – Dissolve 8 g mercuric oxide in 100 ml 6 N – H_2SO_4.
6. Digestion reagent – Dissolve 134 g K_2SO_4 in 650 ml water and 200 ml Conc., H_2SO_4. Add 25 ml mercuric sulfate solution. Dilute to 1000 ml.
7. NaOH – $Na_2S_2O_3$ reagent – Dissolve 500 g NaOH and 25 g $Na_2S_2O_3$ in 1000 ml.
8. Borate buffer solution – Dissolve 88 ml of 0.1 N NaOH and 500 ml of 0.025 M sodium tetra borate solution to 1000 ml.

Procedure

Selection of sample volume is as under:

Organic Nitrogen in the sample, mg/L	Sample volume for digestion, ml
0–1	500
10–10	250
10–20	100
20–50	50
50–100	25

Before digestion, remove ammonia by the addition of NaOH followed by boiling.

Digest the sample by adding digestion mixture. As digestion continues the coloured or turbid sample will become clear or straw coloured.

Add NaOH to make the pH to 9.5 and distilled. The distillate is collected in boric acid or sulfuric acid depending on the method to be used.

Ammonia concentration is determined as given in the ammonia estimation.

Sources:

1. IS: 3025 (Part-34)—1988.
2. *Standard Methods for the Examination of Water and Wastewater*, 21st Ed., 2005.

PHENOLIC COMPOUNDS

Principle

Phenols react with 4-amino antipyrene at pH around 10 in the presence of potassium ferricyanide to form red antipyrene dye having an absorbance maximum at 460 nm.

Samples are distilled with copper sulfate 10% w/v at a pH of below 4 using phosphoric acid.

Apparatus

Separatory funnels
Measuring cylinders
Beakers
Filter paper
Drying oven
Nessler's tubes
Spectrophotometer
Volumetric pipettes
Glass funnels
Volumetric flasks

Reagents

1. Phenol stock solution – Dissolve 100 mg phenol in freshly boiled and cooled distilled water and dilute to 100 ml.
2. Intermediate phenol solution – Dilute 1 ml of stock solution to 100 ml. (1 ml = 10 mg phenol). Prepare daily.
3. Bromide – Bromide solution – Dissolve 2.784 $KBrO_3$ in water and add 10 g KBr, dilute to 1000 ml.
4. HCl – conc.
5. Ammonia – Ammonium chloride buffer – Dissolve 16.9 g NH_4Cl in 143 ml conc. NH_3, dilute to 250 ml.
6. 4-amino antipyrene solution – Dissolve 2 g in 100 ml water.
7. $K_3Fe(CN)_6$ – 8.0% in water.
8. Chloroform.
9. Sodium sulfate.

Procedure

To a series of standards, blank and samples in separating funnels, add 3.0 ml 4 – aminoantipyrene, and 3.0 ml $K_3Fe(CN)_6$ solution and shake.

Allow to stand for 2-3 minutes and extract the colour with chloroform.

Take the absorbance at 460 nm.

Plot a calibration graph, and calculate the concentration in the sample from the calibration graph.

Observations

Sample No.				
Stands used				
for calibration				
Slope				
Absorbance				
Dilution				
Concentration				

Sources:

1. IS: 3025 (Part-43)—1992.
2. *Standard Methods for the Examination of Water and Wastewater*, 21st Ed., 2005.

SURFACTANTS (MBAS)

Principle

Anionic detergents (Surfactants) are absorbed by methylene blue which make the colour darker. The colour is extracted with chloroform and has an absorbance maximum at 650 nm.

Apparatus

Separatory funnels

Measuring cylinders

Beakers

Glass wool

Drying oven

Nessler's tubes

Spectrophotometer

Volumetric pipettes
Glass funnels
Volumetric flasks

Reagents

1. Stock LAS– Weigh an amount of the reference material equal to 1 g LAS. Dissolve in water and dilute to 1000 ml (1 ml = 1 mg LAS).
2. Phenolphthalein indicator solution, alcoholic.
3. NaOH – 1 N – Dissolve 40 g NaOH in 1000 ml distilled water.
4. Sulphuric acid – 1 N – Dissolve 28 ml H_2SO_4 in 1000 ml of distilled water.

Procedure

To a series of standards and sample in separating funnels, adjust the pH to alkaline with alkali to phenolphthalein, discharge the colour with H_2SO_4; add 10 $CHCl_3$ and 25 ml methylene blue. Extract the colour. Continue 2-3 times with fresh quantity of $CHCl_3$.

Take the measurements at 650 nm using chloroform as blank.

Plot a graph and calculate the concentration from the graph.

Observations

Sample No.				
Stands used for calibration				
Slope				
Absorbance				
Dilution				
Concentration				

Source: *Standard Methods for the Examination of Water and Wastewater*, 21st Ed., 2005.

OIL AND GREASE

Partition Gravimetric Method

Principle

Dissolved or emulsified oil is acidified and extracted with organic solvent. The solvent is evaporated and the residue is determined gravimetrically.

Apparatus

Separatory funnels
Measuring cylinders
Beakers
Filter paper
Drying oven
Nessler's tubes
Analytical balance
Volumetric pipettes
Glass funnels
Volumetric flasks
Water bath

Reagent

1. Sodium sulfate
2. Hexane or petroleum ether
3. HCl – 1:3.

Procedure

Samples taken in a separating funnel, acidify and add organic solvent.

Shake well and allow the layers to separate. Continue extraction 2-3 times, and collect the extract together.

Pass through sodium sulfate to remove the traces of water.

Evaporate in a water bath, and finally in an oven maintained about 105°C.

Find the weight of the oil content in the beaker.

Observations

Sample No.				
Initial weight				
Final weight				
Net weight				
Volume of sample taken				
Oil and Grease				

Calculations

$$\text{Oil and Grease, mg/L} = \frac{\text{wt. of the oil} \times 1000}{\text{Vol. of the sample}}.$$

Sources:

1. IS: 3025 (Part-39)—1991.
2. *Standard Methods for the Examination of Water and Wastewater*, 21st Ed., 2005.

METALS (PRELIMINARY TREATMENT)

Procedure

Samples containing particulates or organic material generally require pre-treatment before analysis.

Total metals include all metals, organic or inorganic bound, both dissolved and particulate.

Colourless, transparent samples can be analysed directly without any treatment.

For dissolved metals, filter sample, acidify the filtrate and can be analysed directly.

For total metals, acidify the sample, digest and analyse.

As a general use, HNO_3 is adequate for easily oxidisable matter. HNO_3 – H_2SO_4, HNO_3 – HCl digestion is adequate for readily oxidizable organic matter. HNO_3 – $HClO_4$ or HNO_3 – $HClO_4$ – HF digestion is necessary for difficult to oxidizable organic matter. Dry ashing is helpful if large amount of organic matter is present.

Source: Standard Methods for the Examination of Water and Wastewater, 21st Ed., 2005.

METALS BY FLAME AAS

Direct Air Acetylene Flame Method

This method is applicable to the determination of Sb, Bi, Cd, Ca, Cr, Co, Cu, Fe, Pb, Mg, Mn, Ni, K, Na, Sr and Zn.

Instruction manual of the instrument to be consulted for instrument parameter setting etc.

Select at least three standards for each metal.

Direct Nitrous Oxide-Acetylene Flame Method

This method is used for refractory materials where higher temperature is required for atomization.

Sources:

1. IS: 3025 (Part-40)—1991 for Calcium.
2. IS: 3025 (Part-41)—1991 for Cadmium.
3. IS: 3025 (Part-42)—1992 for Copper.
4. IS: 3025 (Part-45)—1993 for Sodium and Potassium.
5. IS: 3025 (Part-46)—1994 for Magnesium.
6. IS: 3025 (Part-47)—1994 for Lead.
7. IS: 3025 (Part-49)—1994 for Zinc.
8. *Standard Methods for the Examination of Water and Wastewater*, 21st Ed., 2005.

MERCURY BY COLD VAPOR AAS

Principle

Mercury is reduced to mercury atoms which are swept by an inert gas into a quartz absorption cell placed in the optical path of AAS.

Procedure by Digestion Technique

Reagents

1. $KMnO_4$ solution – 5% w/v in water.
2. $K_2S_2O_8$ solution – 5% w/v in water.
3. Hydroxilamine hydrochloride solution – 120 g NaCl and 100 g $NH_2OH.HCl$ in 1000 ml.
4. Stannous chloride solution – 25% w/v in water.

Procedure

To 100 ml sample and blank add 5 ml conc. H_2SO_4 and 2.5 ml HNO_3. Further add 5 ml $KMnO_4$ and 5 ml $K_2S_2O_8$, digest in a water bath, cool to room temperature, decolorize with hydroxilamine hydrochloride solution.

Set the required wavelength and absorption cell. Add stannous chloride and follow the instructions of the manufacturer.

Minimum detection level is 1.0 ppb.

Sources:

1. IS: 3025 (Part-48)—1994.
2. *Standard Methods for the Examination of Water and Wastewater*, 21st Ed., 2005.

METALS BY HYDRIDE GENERATION TECHNIQUE

Principle

Arsenic and selenium are converted into their hydrides by sodium borohydride and estimated by AAS.

Reagents

1. Sodium borohydride – 0.6% $NaBH_4$ w/v and 0.5% NaOH in 10% w/v KI solution.
2. Standard arsenic and selenium solutions.

Procedure

Follow the manufacturer's instructions.

The minimum detection limits are:

For Arsenic – 2 ppb

Selenium – 5 ppb

Source: *Standard Methods for the Examination of Water and Wastewater*, 21st Ed., 2005.

ANALYSIS BY CALCULATION

Percent Sodium

Principle

Per cent sodium is defined as the percentage of sodium to the total cations in water.

Procedure

Calculate Na, K, Ca and Mg in water. Calculate the concentrations in mEq/L.

Calculations

$$\text{Per cent sodium} = \frac{Na/23 \times 100}{Na/23 + k/39 + Ca/20 + Mg/12}$$

Sodium Absorption Ratio

$$\text{SAR can be calculated as } \frac{Na^{+}}{\frac{[Ca^{++} + Mg^{++}]^{1/2}}{2}}$$

Residual Sodium Carbonate

$RSC = (CO_3^{2-} + HCO_3^{2-}) - (Ca^{2+} + Mg^{2+})$

All results are expressed in mEq/L.

DATA VALIDATION

5

Validation of water quality involves checking and assessment of the data to see if there have been any errors made during sampling or analysis of the water quality sample.

PRIMARY VALIDATION OF DATA

The first water quality data collected, within any given sampling and analysis programme, are those obtained by water sampling personnel in the field. As such data can be as important as laboratory derived data, it is vital that they are subject to robust checking procedures to ensure they are as accurate as possible. To guard against the unlikely, but nevertheless possible, risk of field staff not taking samples from the correct place or otherwise fabricating data, all samplers notebooks and laboratory results to which they relate, should be regularly reviewed for discrepancies by suitably experienced senior staff. At a simple level, this can be nothing more than looking over the samplers' measurements and comments, checking them against the analytical results received from the laboratory and, if no discrepancies are apparent, signing them as 'checked and found satisfactory'.

Unexpected Values

The fact that a result differs from that which might have been expected is an indication that there may be a problem with the data. However, this may not be an error but a genuine result which lies outside the normal range of values expected for the sampling point in question. While there is no substitute for experience in detecting unexpected values in data, the process can be considerably aided by displaying the data in a form which makes such datum points easier to spot. Plotting results graphically, or entering them into a table or spreadsheet which can be visually scanned, can considerably aid the process of detecting data outliers.

Illegal Results

When carrying out multiple analyses on a particular sample it is possible to check certain parameters against others to ensure that they are logically possible. A simple general check is that the totals of any variable must be greater than the component parts as in the following examples:

- Total coliforms must be greater than faecal coliforms
- Total iron must be greater than dissolved iron
- Total phosphorus must be greater than dissolved (ortho) phosphorus.

General checks:

Total solids	≥ Total dissolved solids
Total solids	≥ Total settleable solids
COD	≥ BOD
Total coliforms	≥ Faecal coliforms
Total iron	≥ Fe^{+2}, Fe^{+3}
Total P	≥ PO_4^{3-}
EC (μS/cm)	≥ TDS (mg/L)
Total oxidized nitrogen	≥ Nitrate, nitrite
Total oxidized nitrogen	= Nitrate + nitrite
Total hardness	= Ca hardness + Mg hardness

Some conditional checks: correlation parameters:

When there are known correlations between one or more water quality parameters these can be used too. Some of the more well-known correlations between parameters are:

- Total dissolved solids and specific conductance
- pH and carbonate species
- pH and free metal concentrations
- Dissolved oxygen and nitrate

Conditional checks

If pH > 6	then Al_{+3}	< detection limit
If pH > 6	then Mn^{+2}	< detection limit
If pH < 8.3	then CO_3^{2-}	= 0
If DO (mg/L) = 0	then NO_3^-	= 0
If DO (mg/L) > 0	then NO_3^-	= 0
If DO (mg/L) > 7	then Fe^{+2}	= 0

Analytically Unachievable

All analytical methods have a limit of detection and accuracy associated with them. If the results fall outside these ranges for the particular technique employed then it is likely that an analytical or transcription error has corrupted the data.

Significant Figures and Rounding

When analytical data are reported it is important that the number of significant figures quoted reflect the accuracy of the test method used and that any 'rounding off' of the numbers is done correctly and consistently. There are a number of simple rules which should ensure that analytical data are quoted correctly as follows:

- Only report figures which are justified by accuracy of the analytical method used—for example, a result quoted as '9.1267 mg/L' indicates that the method is accurate to four decimal places of milligrams.
- Only report zeros which are justified by the accuracy of the analytical method—for example, if an analytical result is quoted as '8.00 mg/L', the method should be accurate to the two decimal places given; if the method is not so accurate the result should be reported as '8.0 mg/L' (one decimal place) or '8 mg/L' (no decimal place) as appropriate.
- When rounding off numbers, if the digit to be dropped is 5, 6, 7, 8 or 9, the preceding digit should be increased by one unit; if the digit to be dropped is 0, 1, 2, 3 or 4, the preceding digit should not be amended (for example,

2.15 becomes 2.2 but 2.14 becomes 2.1 when rounded to two significant figures).

SECONDARY VALIDATION OF DATA

It is important that data which have been entered onto the computer system are also subject to regular validation. The most effective way to do this is to regularly inspect the data for 'outliers'—that is data points that lie outside the normally expected data range. The list below gives one possible means of analysis these outliers:

- The 'audit trail' of the data point should be investigated to see if any errors have occurred between the original noting of the result and the computer record; it may be necessary, for example, to check the samplers' or analysts' notebooks and any subsequent calculations that have been carried out.
- Any notes which are associated with the sample should be checked as these may give a clue to the reasons why the data point is outside its expected range; for example, the sampler or the analyst may have noted that the sample was different in some way from those normally obtained at a particular sampling point.
- Any other relevant information on the water body, sampling point, time and date of sampling, etc. should also be checked. It may be that the result can be explained by some known local phenomenon; for example, suspended solids concentrations are likely to be high at a river sampling point downstream of temporary construction works.
- Particular attention should be paid to any change in the sampling and analysis regime which may have occurred; results can often be affected because the sampler or analyst is not the regular one, for instance.
- If the above investigations do not reveal any reason for the data point being unusual, the scientist must decide whether the result is likely to be correct or in error and proceed accordingly.

- If the result is thought to be correct, it may mean that there is a need for a further sample or some other investigation of the water quality at the sampling point.
- If the result is thought to be in error, it may be that this sample should be marked so that it is excluded from the subsequent statistical or other analysis—care should be taken here, however, as it is not good practice to exclude data points unless there is strong evidence that they are incorrect.

DATA RECORD, STORAGE AND RETRIEVAL

Data Record

- A recommended format for recording data is given in the following table. It includes all parameters, except heavy metals and trace organics, which may be analyzed in the water quality monitoring programme currently envisaged. Ordinarily, a sample need not be analysed for all the listed parameters.
- Record analyses for heavy metals and trace organics, which will be performed on a limited number of samples, shall be kept in a similar format.
- Columns (2) and (3) are to be filled from the entries in the sample receipt register. Columns (4) to (9) pertain to the field measurements. This information will be available from sample identification forms. Columns (10) to (36) are to be filled in by the analyst(s) to whom the work has been assigned.
- The format also includes primary data validation requirements in columns (37) to (53). The laboratory in-charge shall perform these validation checks as the analysis of a sample is complete. In case the analysis results do not meet any one of the validation checks, whenever possible, the analysis should be repeated. He should also fill in columns (54) and (55).
- The results of the laboratory analyses should be entered from these records in the data entry system.

Data Record and Validation

Data Record

Lab sample no.	Station code	Date of collection	Field determinations						General				Nutrients			Org. matter		Alkalinity		Hardness		Major ions								Other inorganics			Coliforms		Biological
			pH	EC, µ mhos/cm	DC mg/L	Temp, °C	Colour	Odour	pH	EC, µ mhos/cm	TDS, mg/L	TSS, mg/L	NH_3, mg N/L	NO_2^- + NO_3^-, mgN/L	Total P, mg/L	BOD, mg/L	COD, mg/L	Phen, mg $CaCO_3$/L	Total, mg $CaCO_3$/L	Total, mg $CaCO_3$/L	Ca^{++}, mg/L	Ca^{++}, mg/L	Mg^{++}, mg/L	Na^+, mg/L	K^+, mg/L	Cl^-, mg/L	SO_4^{2-}, mg/L	CO_3^{2-}, mg/L	HCO_3^-, mg/L	Si, mg/L	F, mg/L	B, mg/L	Total, MPN/100 mL	Faecal, MPN/100 mL	Chlorophyll A, µg/L
1	2	3	4	5	6	7	8	9	10	11	12	13	14	15	16	17	18	19	20	21	22	23	24	25	26	27	28	29	30	31	32	33	34	35	36

Data Validation

Lab sample no.	Station code	Cations					Anions						Ion balance		EC balance	Carbon balance	CO_2^- balance	Verification certificate	Checked by	Remarks
		Ca^{++}, mEq/L	Mg^{++}, mEq/L	Na^+, mEq/L	K^+, mEq/L	Total cations	Cl^-, mEq/L	SO_4^{2-}, mEq/L	CO_3^{2-}, mEq/L	HCO_3^-, mEq/L	$NO_2^- + NO_3^-$, mEq/L	Total anions	{(41) – (47)}/{(41) + (47)}	(39) / (42)	(12) / (11)	(18) / (17)	If (10) < 8.3 is (19) + 0.7			
1	2	37	38	39	40	41	42	43	44	45	46	47	48	49	50	51	52	53	54	55
																	(48) < 0.1 (49) = 0.8 – 1.2 (50) = 0.55 – 0.9 (51) > 1 (52) = yes			

Data Storage

Normally, nowadays, water quality data are stored on a computer system. It is vital that any such system is not only protected from unauthorized amendment but also adequately backed-up. The back-up file should be regularly updated at a frequency which relates to the importance of the data and how often they are amended.

Data Retrieval

It is preferable if the data retrieval system is designed to allow data to be output in a number of forms as follows:

- As tables, often incorporating simple statistical information (i.e. maximum, minimum, mean, etc.), the content of which in respect of date, time, sample locations, water quality parameters, etc. can be selected by the user.
- As graphs the type of which (i.e., line graph, histogram, pie chart, etc.) is user selectable.
- As maps or charts – if sufficient geographical information is kept on the database printing results on a map often facilitates data analysis.
- As various computer files which can be then exported into other computer packages for further processing (e.g. more sophisticated graphics, more complex statistical analysis or for purposes such as mathematical modeling).

DATA ANALYSIS

Before the collected and stored data can be effectively used, they often need to undergo some form of analysis. Such analysis may be simple, for example, the calculation of elementary statistics or the production of graphical output, or may be more complex involving advanced statistics or mathematical modeling.

Basic Statistics

Basic statistical methods can essentially be divided into two classes as follows:

- Parametric methods – that is, methods which rely on the

data conforming to a certain distribution (often the so-called 'normal' or a related, distribution) which can be described by its 'parameters' (the 'mean' and the 'standard deviation' are examples of parametric statistics).

- Non-parametric methods – that is methods which do not rely on any assumptions about the distribution of the data (the 'median' and 'range' are examples of non-parametric statistics).

The Normal Distribution

There are a number of methods of varying levels of sophistication for assessing whether or not data are normally distributed including the following:

- Visual assessment – that is, arranging the data into classes and then plotting the number of values in each class ('y' axis) against the range of each class ('x' axis).
- Graphical assessment – plotting the data's 'cumulative frequency distribution' on probability graph paper; the data are normally distributed if a straight-line plot is achieved.
- Statistical methods – a number of statistical tests can be used to judge normality—the most well-known being the 'Chi square' (χ^2) test.

The Mean

The mean is the most commonly used descriptive, parametric statistic and is calculated as follows:

$$\text{Mean } (\bar{x}) = (\Sigma x_i)/n$$

(where Σx_i means the summation of all the values in the data set and n is the number of points in the data set).

The mean gives some indication of the central tendency of the data set. However, it can be affected, sometimes quite severely, by extreme or outlying values in the data set with the result that it may not, in such circumstances, be the best way of representing the central tendency of the data. If such a distortion is suspected, it may be preferable to use non-parametric statistics, such as the median and the mode, to describe the data's central tendency.

The Standard Deviation

The standard deviation (σ), another commonly used descriptive, parametric statistic, is calculated as follows:

$$\text{Standard Deviation } (\sigma) = \sqrt{[\Sigma (x_i - \bar{x})^2 / (n - 1)}$$

(where x_i = the ith value in the data set, $\bar{x}$ = the mean of the data set, n = the number of points in the data set and Σ is the symbol for summation).

The standard deviation gives a good indication of the range of values over which the data set is spread. Assuming the data is normally distributed, approximately:

- 68.3% of values will be in the range $\bar{x} \pm \sigma$
- 95.5% of values will be in the range $\bar{x} \pm 2\sigma$
- 99.7% of values will be in the range $\bar{x} \pm 3\sigma$.

It is good practice to quote the standard deviation whenever the mean is quoted. This not only provides a measure of the spread of the data but also gives some indication of the possible distortion of the mean by outlying values.

The Median

The median, like the mean also provides an indication of the central tendency of the data set, and is that value which has an equal number of data points on each side of it. That is, if there are for example, twenty-five values in a data set, then the thirteenth (i.e. the central) data point in numerical order is defined as the median.

The Mode

The mode, yet another measure of central tendency, is the value which occurs most frequently in the data set. It is used more often than the median for describing the central tendency of non-parametric data.

The Range

The range is a measure of the spread of the data. It is simply the arithmetical difference between the highest and the lowest value in the data set.

Percentiles

Any given percentile is that value which has the same percentage of samples which are less than it. For example, the 60th percentile is the data point at which 60% of the data values are less than its value and 40% of samples are more than its value. The median is also the 50th percentile—that is, half of the data set has greater values, and half have lower values, than the median.

Graphical Methods

There are a number of advantages associated with the data analysis using graphical techniques as follows:

- trends in the data are often easier to spot
- outlying data points are normally obvious
- many people find visually presented data more acceptable and more readily understandable.

Time Series Graph

A graph in which water quality data (on the 'y' axis) is plotted against time (on the 'x' axis) in units which will depend on the frequency of sampling. This type of plot helps to identify trends or cyclic patterns in the data and is also a good way of identifying outlying data points. Time series graphs are also useful for spotting connections between two or more water quality variables. If it is suspected, for example, that the biochemical oxygen demand in a river reach increases when the suspended solids load increases, an effective way of checking this can be to plot both of these variables on a time series graph. Visual inspection can then be used to see if peaks and troughs for the two variables coincide.

Histograms

Histograms are effective at displaying the relative differences in data. That is, it is easy to show that a sampling point has twice the pollutant concentration of its neighbour by means of a histogram. Histograms are also useful for displaying data for a non-technical audience as they are easily understood by the majority of people.

Pie Charts

Pie charts, which are circular diagrams divided into a number of segments, are less frequently used for water quality data. They are used when it is necessary to present information about the relative proportions of a particular parameter, however. For example, the relative proportions of a particular pesticide dissolved in water, bound to suspended solid particles or present in the bottom sediments of a river could be represented using a pie chart.

Profile Plots

A plot of water quality data down the length of a river (longitudinal profile) can be useful for observing changes which occur as the river flows downstream. Often such plots are annotated with the positions of major discharges and river tributaries so that the effect of these inputs is clearly visible on the graph. If samples have been collected at various depths, a vertical profile of the data can be plotted. Such plots are often used to analyse how lake water or ground water varies with increasing depth.

Geographical Plots

It is often useful to plot water quality data on a map base to show local and regional variations in water quality. Such a technique can be used to attempt to pinpoint a pollution source from ground water data or merely to show how one river or catchment compares to another in terms of its water quality or pollution load.

Advanced Techniques

In addition to those methods of data analysis given above there are also a number of more advanced techniques which can be used. A brief outline of some of these methods is given below:

- Trend analysis – although this can be done simply by plotting data on a time series graph, it is also possible to analyse trends through the use of sophisticated statistical analyses; trend analysis can be important for the analysis of water quality data as it can aid understanding of variability of data and also allow predictions to be made of likely future water quality.

- Regression and correlation analysis – regression and correlation analysis are related techniques which are used to assess the association between two or more variables; both can be useful techniques for establishing the factors which regulate the variability of a particular water quality parameter.
- Mathematical modeling – a technique for representing and predicting, by means of mathematics, the behaviour of a system; mathematical models can be useful predictive and policy testing tools in that they allow operators to forecast the behaviour of a water body which will occur following some future change to the system.

POLLUTION PREVENTION AND WASTE MINIMIZATION IN LABORATORIES

6

INTRODUCTION

Pollution prevention means not generating waste in the first place by reducing it at the source. Waste minimization is a broader term that also includes recycling and other means to reduce the amount of waste which must be treated/disposed of. A waste chemical is a chemical that has no further use. A hazardous waste is a chemical that presents a danger to people or the environment. Regulatory agencies determine which chemicals are considered hazardous.

Pollution Prevention Hierarchy

- The preferred approach is to eliminate or reduce the amount of waste generated.
- The next option is to recycle and/or recover the by-products for reuse.
- The third alternative is to treat the by-products to make it less hazardous for disposal.
- The final option is to properly dispose the waste.

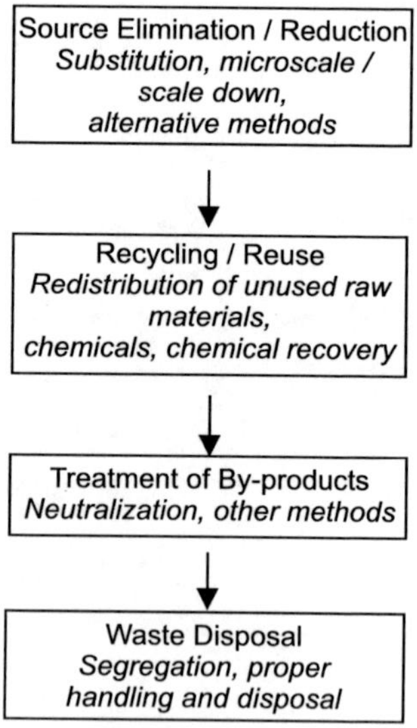

The hierarchy above shows methods of dealing with hazardous waste, in order of preference. The most preferable option on the hierarchy is to reduce the amount of waste that is produced in the first place. This approach—known as source reduction—means that no one has to deal with the waste at all. This is the cornerstone of pollution prevention.

Unfortunately, not all waste can be eliminated, and the waste that is generated must be dealt with. The second best option for managing this waste includes recycling, refining, or recovering the waste for reuse so that new raw materials are not required and so that waste pollutants never reach the land (e.g. a landfill), the water, or the atmosphere, and resources are conserved.

If that is not possible, the next best option would be to treat the waste to reduce its toxicity and its potential for harming the environment. The least preferred management method for hazardous wastes (and non-hazardous wastes) is disposal by landfilling or incineration with proper disposal of the residual ash.

PLANNING FOR WASTE MINIMIZATION

Setting up a waste minimization programme is similar to managing any other aspect of the laboratory. It requires planning and coordinated effort. Steps involved in waste minimization programme include:

- Step 1: Getting everyone involved
- Step 2: Taking a look at waste and waste management practices
- Step 3: Developing a waste minimization plan
- Step 4: Implementing the programme
- Step 5: Keeping at it.

Success of a waste minimization programme relies on the involvement and support of the staff. Everyone has a role to play. Everyone in the laboratory should be made aware of the importance of waste minimization and be encouraged to participate. Upper management support is crucial. Many laboratories have adopted waste minimization policies or guiding principles endorsed or signed by management.

The waste management methodology includes:

- Select team, define objectives and strategy
- Determine criteria to evaluate alternatives
- List the possible pollution prevention alternatives
- Select alternative(s)
- If necessary, quantitative evaluation of alternatives
- Pilot test
- Implementation and optimization

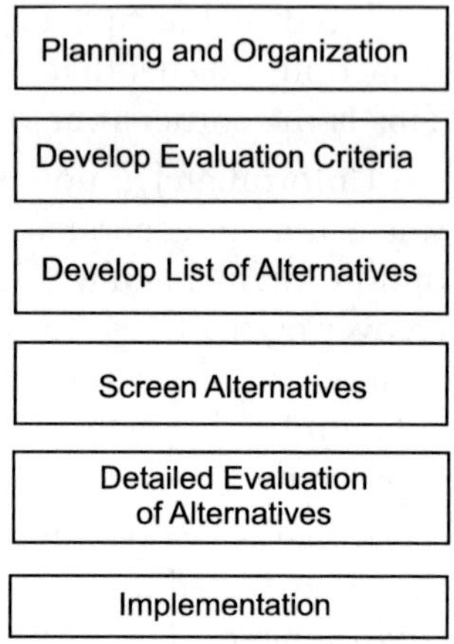

If you know what a chemical is and can safely and legally dispose of it yourself, it may be done. However, if a chemical is hazardous or not known, one cannot throw it in trash or pour it down the drain. By reducing wastes at the source, you are taking the most effective step towards eliminating wastes that would otherwise be released to the environment. Waste minimization and pollution prevention encourage safety in the laboratory. If you reduce the quantity of hazardous substances handled, you reduce the hazard. Waste minimization and pollution prevention save money. One effective waste minimization practice is to reduce the quantity of chemicals purchased, which in turn reduces the amount of money that is tied up in chemical inventory. Waste minimization and pollution prevention alone ensure that laboratory meets legal requirements.

STEPS IN WASTE MINIMIZATION

Purchasing and Inventory

One of the first steps in reducing excess consumption and wastage of material and products is to review the purchasing and inventory practices.

- Materials with recycled content should be purchased where possible.
- A centralized purchasing programme should be implemented, and a person designated to be responsible for the inventory. This person should monitor requests for chemicals and ensure that duplicate chemicals are not ordered by different departments or for different projects if stock already exists.
- Order what is needed. This will prevent storing large quantities of chemicals that may expire before they can be used.
- For chemicals and reagents that are used infrequently or expire quickly, the smallest quantity practicable should be ordered to avoid wasting.
- An up-to-date inventory of chemicals and reagents should be kept.
- Unopened and unused chemicals should be returned to the supplier.
- Labels on all chemicals should be maintained to prevent the generation of unknown wastes, which are harder and more expensive to dispose of. Label should contain information whether the chemical is time or temperature sensitive, or requires special handling.

Office Activities

Office and administrative staff at laboratories waste. Following waste minimization opportunities may be considered:

- Double sided photocopies should be used.
- Backside of single copies can be used for scrap paper.
- Reusable/refillable toner cartridges could be used for photocopies and printers.
- Office supplies such as file folders, binders and envelopes could be reused.
- There should be regular servicing of office equipment to maintain efficiency and prevent wasting materials.

Laboratory Activities

Waste from analytical labs is generally more diverse in composition the waste from other industries. Labs typically generate a number of different, small quantity waste streams, many of which are hazardous or potentially hazardous.

Types of wastes generated by analytical labs

Waste category	Examples of wastes	Hazardous or potentially hazardous
Halogenated solvents	Methylene chloride, Freon, carbon tetrachloride, chloroform	Yes
Non-halogenated solvents	Xylene, acetone, toluene, methanol, isopropyl alcohol	Yes
Unused/expired chemicals	Chemicals and reagents required for sample preparation, analysis, experiments or standards	Possibly
Inorganic acids and bases	Nitric acid, sulphuric acid, acetic acid, sodium hydroxide, potassium hydroxide	Yes—if concentrated No—if dilute
Samples	Solid, liquid, soils, water, hydrocarbons	Possibly
Waste chemicals/ reagents and reaction products	For sample preparation, analysis and experiments; may be toxic (heavy metals, cyanide)	Possibly
Used oil	Lubricating oil from rotating equipment or vacuum pumps	Yes
Radioactive waste	Radioactive ore samples	Yes
Biohazardous waste	Tissue samples, cultures	Yes—unless sterilized
Lab supplies and equipment	Disposable gloves, pipettes, broken glassware	Possibly—if contaminated
Paper	Office paper, computer paper, mixed paper, newsprint	No
Cardboard	Corrugated boxes and inserts from packaging	No
Plastic	Sample containers, moduled and chipped Styrofoam	Possibly—if contaminated
Glass	Sample container, chemical and reagent containers and glassware	Possibly—if contaminated
Wastewater (to sanitary sewer)	Water from washing and rinsing, cooling water, water samples, chemical reaction products	Generally not
Air emissions	Air samples, gas samples, volatile emissions from fume hoods	Possibly

(*Source*: *Waste Minimization Manual*—Analytical Laboratories, Alberta Environmental Protection, Edmonton.)

Reduction Opportunities

Because reduction is the preferred waste minimization alternative, these opportunities should be considered first:

- Alternative analytical methods that use less hazardous chemicals or no chemicals and therefore, produce less waste should be considered. Because most labs are required to follow standard methods, opportunities for method substitution may be limited. However, one should keep abreast with new standard methods that are being developed and tested.
- Less hazardous or less toxic chemicals could be substituted for hazardous chemicals where possible.
- Labels on reagent and reaction products should be maintained properly to prevent the generation of unknown waste, which is expensive to manage and dispose of.
- Where possible scale of experiments should be reduced (e.g. microscale) or tests run on smaller samples.
- The use of solvent and acid in cleaning operations should be reduced.

An Example Microscale Experiment: Redox Titration of Manganese

Using a graduated or volumetric pipette, place 1.00 (± 0.01) ml of 0.0100M $KMnO_4$ solution into each of three 10 mL flasks. Label as A, B and C.

Acid Solution Titration — Add 1.0 ml of 1 M H_2SO_4 to flask A. Charge a microburet with 0.0200M $NaHSO_3$ solution and slowly titrate the permanganate solution drop by drop until the purple colour of the solution disappears. Record the volume of $NaHSO_3$ added.

Neutral Solution Titration — Recharge the microburet with 0.0200M $NaHSO_3$ solution. Record initial volume and titrate the $KMnO_4$ solution in flask B. The purple colour of permanganate will change to brown suspension of MnO_2 at the end point. Record the final volume.

Basic Solution Titration — Add 1.0 ml of 1 M NaOH to the

permanganate solution in flask C. Recharge the microburet with $NaHSO_3$ solution. Record initial volume. Titrate to dark green-coloured end point of MnO_4^{2-}.

(*Source*: *Laboratory Waste Minimization and Pollution Prevention – A Guide for Teachers*, Battelle Research Centre, 1996.)

Reuse Opportunities

There are many opportunities in analytical labs to reuse labware, lab supplies, and in some cases, lab chemicals.

- Sample containers wherever feasible should be reused. This may be feasible for repeat or routine analysis. This may also be feasible for glass containers that can be properly cleaned.
- Possibilities of returning unused chemicals to the suppliers should be explored.
- Chemical and reagent containers should be reused where possible, such as for collecting and storing waste or for storing other chemicals that are purchase in bulk. It should be ensured that they are compatible with the contents and are properly labeled.

Recycling Opportunities

After reduction and reuse, recycling is the next waste minimization measure to consider for the laboratory.

- A key to successful recycling is proper segregation as recyclable materials should be free of contamination from non-recyclable materials.
- Paper and cardboard are commonly recycled by analytical labs.
- Glass and plastic recycling should be considered.
- Used oil from lab equipment (e.g. vacuum pumps or rotating equipment) can be recycled.
- A vermicompost bin for organic food waste from lunch rooms may be considered.

Recovery Opportunities

- Used oil should be collected for recycling or fuel blending.
- If spent solvents are generated regularly, recovery can be very cost-effective. Many solvents are excellent candidates for distillation, including xylene, methanol, acetone and toluene.
- For solvents generated from high performance liquid chromatography, automated, in-line solvent recovery systems are available.
- Many heavy metals have been largely phased out of chemistry experiments, although mercury, silver and other may still be used. Even small amounts of these metals can be recovered in laboratory, possibly as an educational exercise.

An Example Experiment: Recovery of Silver

$$Ag^{+} + NaCl \rightarrow AgCl + Na^{+}$$

$$AgCl \xrightarrow{Zn,\ H_2SO_4} Ag + \text{soluble Zn salts}$$

1. Acidify the salt solution with 6 M nitric acid (to pH paper of about 2).
2. Treat with a 10% excess of 20% aqueous sodium chloride solution.
3. Collect the precipitate (AgCl) in a filtered funnel and wash twice with warm 4 M sulfuric acid and twice with distilled water.
4. Dry the AgCl and grind to a fine powder.

   CAUTION: *Because of the hydrogen, perform the following in a hood away from any source of ignition:*
5. In a fume hood, thoroughly mix 100 g of dry AgCl with 50 g pure granulated zinc metal and stir with 500 ml of 4 N H_2SO_4.
6. When the zinc has dissolved, decant the supernatant solution and mix the crude silver with another 50 g of pure granulated zinc and treat with 500 ml of concentrated 4 N H_2SO_4.

7. After the zinc has dissolved, carefully add about 5 ml of concentrated H_2SO_4 and heat the mixture to 90° Celsius and stir for several minutes.
8. Separate the silver by filtration and wash with distilled water until the washings are free of sulfate. A sample of the resulting silver should give a clear solution in concentrated nitric acid.
9. If AgCl is still present, the solution will appear turbid and treatment with zinc and 4 N H_2SO_4 should be repeated.
10. The zinc salt solutions can be precipitated for disposal.

    (*Note*: These solutions—and other chemical solutions—should not be flushed down the drain without careful consideration of alternatives and review of local regulations.)

(*Reference*: Prudent Practices for Disposal of Chemicals from Laboratories, National Research Council, Washington DC, 1983.)

On-site Treatment of Hazardous Waste

Certain wastes can be less hazardous by simple treatments in the lab. These treatment methods are often specific to the particular compounds or chemicals involved and are based on their chemistry.

- Biohazardous waste can be autoclaved to sterilize it. The sterilized waste can then be disposed of in the regular trash.
- Corrosive and reactive waste can be neutralized before disposal. Neutralization can be done by a simple treatment method requiring a fume hood, personal protective equipment and corrosion resistant containers and equipment. Waste or surplus dilute acid and bases can be used for neutralizing.
- Reducing the volume of dilute solutions of inorganic salts can simplify disposal.
- Strong oxidizing agents such as potassium permanganate, sodium chlorate and calcium hypochloride can be reduced

before discarding to the sanitary sewer. This may be done with an aqueous solution of sodium bisulfite.

- Make sure that you understand the chemistry involved in the particular treatment reaction to avoid an unsafe situation. Also, check the reference materials for details on treatment processes.

Handling and Storing Hazardous Wastes

Hazardous wastes that cannot be further treated or eliminated must be stored and managed in a way that ensures the safety of lab workers and meets the requirements of all applicable regulations and guidelines.

- Familiarize yourself with applicable legislation and regulations and be aware of handling and storage requirements for specific materials, e.g. corrosives, flammables, reactive materials, toxic compounds, etc.
- Segregate hazardous wastes based on compatibility, particularly ignitables from oxidizers or sources of ignition.
- Store hazardous wastes in compatible containers.
- Keep containers closed to prevent spills and vapour releases.
- Properly identify and label wastes according to proper waste management practices.
- Provide an appropriate storage area for hazardous wastes.
- Prevent hazardous wastes from entering storm drains or drains to the sanitary sewer.
- Avoid accumulating hazardous wastes for extended periods.
- Provide appropriate training for the lab staff.

Wastewater Disposal

- Drain disposal should only be to the sanitary sewer not to the storm sewer.
- Familiarize yourself with the municipal sewer by-laws. This is your best resource for determining if a chemical is suitable for drain disposal.

- The quantity of chemicals disposed of down the drain should be relatively small and highly diluted with water.
- In addition to being compatible with the sewer system and treatment plant, there is a need for compatibility with other chemicals entering the drain system.

Landfill Disposal

Conventional landfill disposal is only appropriate for non-hazardous waste. The disposal by landfilling of suitable solid hazardous waste requires strict compliance with specific design requirements.

Waste Minimization Opportunities Summary Table

Waste category	Examples	Characteristics	Minimization opportunities
Halogenated solvents	Methylene chloride Chloroform Freon Carbon tetrachloride Tetrachlorothylene 1,1,1 – trichloroethane chlorobenzene	• Many halogenated solvents and hydrocarbons are toxic • Generally low solubility in water • Special handling required	• Properly segregate halogenated solvents from non-halogenated solvents • Provide appropriate storage for waste solvents (e.g. proper containers, away from ignition sources, segregated from oxidizers) • Consider recovering and recycling (on-site or off-site) • Lab pack and dispose of using a licensed waste management firm • Bulk and dispose of using a licensed waste management firm • Avoid disposal down the drain
Non-halogenated solvents	Toluene Acetone Methanol Isopropyl alcohol Xylene	• Many non-halogenated solvents and hydrocarbons are toxic • Solvents may be ignitable • Special handling required	• Properly segregated halogenated solvents from non-halogenated solvents • Provide appropriate storage for waste solvents (e.g. proper containers, away from ignition sources, segregated from oxidizers) • Consider recovering and recycling non-halogenated solvents (on-site and off-site distillation)

(Contd...)

Waste category	Examples	Characteristics	Minimization opportunities
			• Consider reusing solvents where possible (if high purity not a concern) • Lab pack and dispose of using a licensed waste management firm • Bulk and dispose of using a licensed waste management firm • Avoid disposal down the drain • Consider sending off-site for fuel blending and burn for heat recovery • Reduce the amount of solvent used for rinsing
Unused/expired chemicals	Chemicals and reagents used for sample preparation, analyses, experiments or standards	• May or may not be hazardous depending on nature of chemical	• Only purchase chemicals that are needed • Check current inventories before purchasing • Purchase the smallest amount practicable: work with suppliers to take back unused chemicals • Properly maintain labels to avoid generating unknown wastes • Participate in chemical or waste exchanges
Inorganic acids and bases	Nitric acid Sulphuric acid Hydrochloric acid Acetic acid	• Hazardous in concentrated form • Non-hazardous in dilute form	• Dilute weak acids and bases before disposing down the drain • Neutralize strong acids and bases before disposing down the drain

(Contd...)

Waste category	Examples	Characteristics	Minimization opportunities
	Potassium hydroxide Sodium hydroxide		• Properly manage concentrated acid and base wastes; manage as hazardous waste
Samples	May be solid or liquid hazardous or non-hazardous	• May be hazardous or non-hazardous • Some constituents or characteristics may be unknown	• Determine to the extent possible the characteristics of the sample • Properly store and manage hazardous samples • Dispose of non-hazardous samples down the drain (liquid) or in the trash (solid) • Consider returning samples to your clients (particularly hazardous samples) • Consider charging clients for hazardous waste disposal • Give away fertilizer samples to employees
Waste chemicals, reagents and reaction products	From sample preparation, analyses and experiments	• May be hazardous or non-hazardous depending on nature of chemical • Reaction products may be unknown	• Purchase non-hazardous or less hazardous chemicals where possible • Properly store chemicals to prevent spills and breakage of containers • Use opened containers of chemicals before opening new ones • Consider method substitution to replace hazardous chemicals • Use reaction products from one experiment as a feed material for another

(Contd...)

Waste category	Examples	Characteristics	Minimization opportunities
Used oil	Lubricating oil from rotating equipment and vacuum pumps	• May be hazardous	• Segregate from other wastes • Send off-site for recycling • Send off-site for fuel blending and burning for heat recovery
Lab equipment and supplies	Disposable gloves, pipettes, wipes, broken glassware	• May be hazardous if contaminated but generally non-hazardous	• Avoid use of disposable supplies where practical • Wash and reuse supplies and containers where possible • Avoid contamination where possible
Paper	From office activities and report generation; computer paper, office paper, newsprint	• Non-hazardous	• Use e-mail internally or to send analytical reports to reduce paper waste • Reuse paper where possible • Recycle paper
Cardboard	Corrugated boxes and inserts from packaging	• Non-hazardous	• Reuse cardboard boxes and inserts for shipping sample containers • Recycle cardboard
Plastic	Sample containers, molded and chipped Styrofoam	• Non-hazardous unless contaminated	• Reuse Styrofoam chips where possible • Return Styrofoam to your chemical supplier • Consider reusing plastic containers from chemicals and samples • Recycle plastic containers (provide proper cleaning)

(Contd...)

Waste category	Examples	Characteristics	Minimization opportunities
Glass	Sample containers, chemical and reagent containers and glassware	• Non-hazardous unless contaminated	• Repair and reuse expensive and intricate glassware • Reuse chemical and reagent containers; proper washing required • Recycle glass where possible (provide proper cleaning)
Biohazardous waste	Tissue samples, mocrobiological cultures	• Hazardous unless sterilized	• Sterilize in an auto clave • Dispose of sterilized waste in the trash
Radioactive waste	Radioactive ore samples (uranium)	• Hazardous	• Segregate from other wastes • Properly store and dispose of • Return samples to client
Wastewater	Water from washing and rinsing, cooling water, water samples, chemical reaction products	• Generally non-hazardous but may contain hazardous constituents (toxic metals, organics, etc.)	• Be aware of applicable regulations and by-laws • Neutralize acids and bases before disposing of down the drain • Reduce strong oxidizing agents before disposing down the drain • If in doubt, assume a waste is potentially hazardous and do not dispose of down the drain

(*Source*: *Waste Minimization Manual—Analytical Laboratories*, Alberta Environmental Protection, Edmonton.)

ENVIRONMENTAL EFFECTS AND WATER QUALITY

7

FACTORS AFFECTING WATER QUALITY

PHYSICAL PARAMETERS

Suspended Solids

Sources: Natural—inorganic particles (e.g. clay, silt, soil, soil constituents) and organic (plants fibers, biological solids, algal cells, protein, etc.).

Anthropogenic—domestic wastewater: large quantities of suspended solids especially organic. Industrial wastewater: both inorganic and organic.

Impact: Aesthetics.

Adsorption sites for chemical and biological agents

Organic solids degrade and result in objectionable by-products.

Turbidity

Sources: Surface water—Colloidal material (clay, silt, rock fragments, soil, metals/organics). Ground water—not a problem because of the natural filtering effect.

Household and industrial wastewater, e.g. soap, detergents, emulsifying agents.

Impact: Aesthetically objectionable.

Adsorption sites for chemicals, harmful and undesirable taste and odour.

Disinfection—adsorption and shielding effect. Light penetration and hence photosynthetic reactions in lakes and streams. Sediment deposits that can affect flora and fauna of the stream.

Colour

Sources: Organic debris—e.g. leaves, weeds, wood, etc. water picks tannins, humic acids etc.—yellowish-brown colour.

Iron oxides—reddish colour and manganese oxides—brownish, brackish water.

Industrial wastewater, e.g. textile and dyeing, pulp and paper, food processing, chemical production can add substantial colours.

Impact: Aesthetically objectionable.

Clear non-coloured, poor quality versus potable, objectionable coloured water.

Suitability for both domestic and industrial uses.

Exert a chlorine demand—reduce the effectiveness of chlorination as a disinfectant.

Taste and odour problems and some may even be carcinogenic.

Taste and Odour

Sources: Natural and anthropogenic—e.g. minerals, metals, salts from soil, end products of biological reactions.

Inorganic—produce taste unaccompanied by odour.

Organic substances likely to produce both taste and odour.

Biological decomposition of organics—both taste and odour problems.

Impact: Aesthetics.

Preference for tasteless and odourless water that might actually pose more health risk.

Odour from organics may be more than aesthetics, since some are carcinogenic.

Temperature

Sources: Domestic and industrial sources—heated water in receiving streams.

Impacts: Affects biological activities—rate doubles for every 10° Celsius rise.

Accelerated algal growth in warm water can give rise to algal mats. Secretion of oils and toxins and decay products of dead algal cause taste and odour problems and also exert demand on oxygen. Solubility of oxygen decreases with increase on temperature.

Speciation of fish and other forms of aquatic life are dramatically affected by temperature.

CHEMICAL PARAMETERS

pH

pH is used universally to express the intensity of the alkaline condition of a solution.

Impact: Affects aquatic forms of life—are sensitive to pH.

Affects metal speciation and hence toxicity, e.g. Al^{+3}.

Affects reaction equilibrium, e.g. air stripping of ammonia.

Affects treatment process, e.g. coagulation, precipitation.

Total Dissolved Solids

Sources: Salvation action of water on solids, liquids and gases.

May be organic or inorganic.

Water contact with substances in the atmosphere, on surfaces and within the soil.

Impact: Many dissolved substances are undesirable in water.

Dissolved minerals, gases and organic constituents may produce aesthetically displeasing colour, taste and odour. Some may be toxic and carcinogenic.

Metals

Sources: Natural deposits and discharges of industrial, agricultural and domestic wastewaters.

Impact: Non-toxic-sodium: health hazard to cardiac and kidney patients, corrosive to metal surfaces. Iron and manganese (frequently occurring together): colour problem.

Toxic, e.g. arsenic, cadmium, mercury, chromium and silver. Effect depends on the metals in question, metal speciation of the metals (pH), adsorption onto particles and possible metal interactions.

Organics

Biodegradable: Utilized as food by microorganisms.

Colour, taste and odour problems.

Oxidation of the organics—BOD: anaerobic conditions and products may develop.

Non-biodegradable: Toxicity to microorganisms

Refractory COD, TOC.

Nutrients: Essential for growth

N: Protein and other biological compounds including fertilizers.

Oxidation of NH_3 or NH_4^+ exert oxygen demand.

Nitrate poisoning in infant animals and humans.

Eutrophication.

P: Principally orthophosphates.

Constituents of soils, fertilizers and body and food waste.

Non-toxic, no direct health effect to humans or other organisms.

Serious indirect effect on water quality.

Eutrophication.

Alkalinity

Sources: Include CO_3^{2-}, HCO_3^-, OH^-, HPO_4^{2-}, H_2PO_{4-}, HS^- and

NH_3 (resulting from the dissolution of mineral substances in the soil and atmosphere).

Phosphate from detergents and fertilizers and insecticides.

Hydrogen sulphide, ammonia and bicarbonate from microbial decomposition of organic materials and biological reactions. pH dependent.

Impacts: In large quantity, alkalinity imparts a bitter taste.

Principle objection—reactions that occur between alkalinity and certain cations, with the resultant precipitate fouling pipes and other water system appurtenances.

Hardness

Sources: Calcium, magnesium, iron, manganese, strontium and aluminium.

Impact: Precipitate leaving stains.

Boiler scale causes fouling in water heaters and pipes and hence economic losses.

Magnesium hardness (particularly associated with sulphates) has a laxative effect.

FEW WATER TREATMENT TECHNIQUES

Adsorption

Definition

Adsorption is the physical adhesion of molecules—particularly organic molecule—or colloids to the surfaces of a solid, an adsorbent, without chemical reaction. In some respects, adsorption is similar to coagulation and flocculation. One distinction is that adsorption occurs on an adsorbent solid processed, especially for water treatment, whereas in coagulation and flocculation, the adsorbent is produced *in situ* by the reaction of a chemical, such as alum, with water.

Adsorbents may be either finely powdered materials, applied to water in a clarifier or ahead of the filter, or 0.5 to 1.0 mm granules contained in a vessel similar to a pressure filter. By far the most common adsorbent used in water treatment is activated carbon, used both in powdered and granular forms. Other adsorbers include a variety of clay, magnesium oxide, bone char and activated aluminium. Special ion exchange resins are also used sometimes as adsorbent.

Principle

Since adsorption is a surface reaction, a measure of the effectiveness of adsorbent is its surface area. For carbon, the total surface area is usually 600 to 1000 m^2/g. This surface is negatively charged. In spite of this, the negative charge of most colloids in water does not deter adsorption of high molecular weight materials, since the molecular structure itself becomes the controlling factor as molecular weight increases. Adsorbents are porous and the size of the pores is important. This is measured by iodine number, methylene blue number, or molasses number. The iodine number, a simple titration most commonly used, measures pores passing colloids larger than 1 nm. For activated carbon, this number has a range of 650 to 1000.

Mechanism

Adsorption is a process by which molecules of impurities adhere to the surface of activated carbon. The adherence is an electrochemical attraction. Activated carbon is prepared from a variety of materials such as coal, wood, nutshell and petroleum. The carbon becomes activated by being heated to a high temperature (800°C) in absence of oxygen. This results in creation of microscopic pores on the surface of carbon. This vast amount of surface area provides a great opportunity for adsorption. The activated carbon has a strong adsorptive attraction for other carbon based organic molecules and is outstanding in firmly retaining heavier molecules such as aromatic compounds.

$$C + Cl_2 + 2H_2O \Leftrightarrow CO_2 + 4HCl$$

Aeration

Definition

Aeration is necessary to promote the exchange of gases

between the water and the atmosphere. In water treatment, aeration is practiced for three purposes:

- To add oxygen to water for imparting freshness, e.g. water from underground sources devoid of or deficient in oxygen.
- Expulsion of carbon dioxide, hydrogen sulphide and other volatile substances causing taste and odour, e.g. water from deeper layers of an impounding reservoir.
- To precipitate impurities like iron and manganese in certain forms, e.g. water from some underground sources.

Aeration Mechanism

Gases are dissolved in or liberated from water until the concentration of the gas in the water has reached its saturation value. As a gas, oxygen is slightly soluble in water. At 20°C and sea level saturation concentration is only 9.5 ppm. At this concentration it represents only 0.00095% of the weight of water. Solubility of oxygen in water is inversely proportional to temperature, elevation (pressure) and salinity.

Principle of Gas Transfer

The concentration of gases in a liquid generally obeys Henry's law, which states that the concentration of each gas in water is directly proportional to the partial pressure (product of the volume per cent of the gas and the total pressure of the atmosphere) or concentration of a gas decreases with temperature and dissolved salts in water. Aeration tends to accelerate the gas exchange. The rate of exchange of a gas is governed by the area of interface between the gas and the liquid, the thickness of the interlayers, time of contact, the partial pressure of the gas in the overlying atmosphere and the degree of under-saturation or over-saturation of the gas in the liquid.

To insure proper aeration, it is necessary

- To increase the area of water in contact with the air, i.e. if the water is sprayed, the smaller the droplets produced, the greater will be the area available. Similarly, if water is being made to fall as a film over packing material in a tower, the smaller the size of the packing material, the greater will be the area available;

- To keep the surface of the liquid constantly agitated so as to reduce the thickness of the liquid film, which would govern the resistance offered to the rate of exchange of the gas; and
- To increase the time of contact of water droplets with air or to increase the time of flow, which can be achieved by increasing the height of jet in spray aerator and increasing the height of bed in the case of packed media.

Chemical Precipitation

Definition

The precipitation process makes use of the solubility product of a compound containing an ion or radical that is considered detrimental, and that should therefore be removed before the water is put to use. The reduction of calcium ion concentration by precipitation of calcium carbonate is one such example.

Temperature is an important factor in both precipitation and adsorption reactions. The solubility product is affected by temperature; knowing the solubility characteristics of the desired precipitate will influence the selection of treatment equipment. One of the fundamental principles of precipitation is that the size of a precipitate increases if the chemical reaction is encouraged to occur on previously precipitated particles. If a small crystal and a large crystal of the same substance is placed in a saturated solution of the substance in a beaker, the small crystal will slowly disappear as the larger one grows; if a crystal of salt is introduced into supersaturated, clear salt solution, it will grow as salt comes out of solution on the surface of the seed crystal in preference to forming individual crystal nuclei. Because of these reactions, most precipitation processes in water treatment are conducted by introducing precipitating chemicals into the water in the presence of previously precipitated sludge.

Chemical reactions taking place during lime soda treatment are rather slow. The precipitate formed particularly $CaCO_3$ and

$Mg(OH)_2$ are fine and they tend to produce a supersaturated solution. This eventually results in deposition layer in pipes and boiler tubes producing sludges. This in turn decreases the effective diameter of pipes, clogs the valves, causes corrosion, etc. To prevent these, the following arrangements have to be made:

- Thorough mixing of the chemicals and water is carried out.
- Proper time for completion of reaction to proceed is given.
- Substances that will bring down the fine particle of precipitates, called accelerators, like activated carbon, are to be mixed.
- Coagulants are to be added.
- Suitable sedimentation chambers are provided before filtration.

Chemical Oxidation

The objective of chemical oxidation is to detoxify waste by adding and oxidizing agent to chemically transform the waste. For example, an organic molecule can be converted to CO_2 and water, or an intermediate product that is less toxic than the original and can be amenable to further treatment (e.g. biological methods). The technique is capable of destroying a wide range of organic molecules including chlorinated VOCs, mercaptans, phenols and inorganics such as cyanide. Oxidizing agents commonly used include ozone, hydrogen peroxide and chlorine.

Oxidation and reduction reactions occur in pairs to comprise an overall redox reaction. Oxidizing agents are non-specific and will react with any reducing agent present in the waste stream. Therefore, the processes are most economical when organics other than the ones of concern are in low concentration. Also, reactions between some oxidizing agents (e.g. chlorine) and some organics (e.g. hydrocarbons) may result in chlorine substitution rather than the destruction of the organic. The resulting chlorinated hydrocarbon may be more toxic than the original waste.

Typical Oxidation and Reduction Reactions

	Reagent	Contaminant	Reaction	Comments
Oxidation	Ozone	Cyanide	$NaCN + O_3 \rightarrow NaCNO + O_2$	
	Hydrogen Peroxide	Cyanide Sulphide	$NaCN + H_2O_2 \rightarrow NaCNO + H_2O$ $H_2O_2 + H_2S \rightarrow 2H_2O + S$. $H_2O_2 + S^- \rightarrow SO_4^- + 4H_2O$	pH 8.5 – 10.5
	Chlorine	Ferrous to Ferric	$2Fe^{2+} + HOCl + 6H_2O \rightarrow 2Fe(OH)_3 + Cl^- + 6H^+$	
	Chlorine	Cyanide to Cyanate Cyanate to CO_2	$NaCN + Cl_2 \rightarrow CNCl + NaCl$ $CNCl + CHOOH \rightarrow NaCnO + H_2O + NaCl$ $2NaCNO + 3Cl_2 + 4NaOH \rightarrow N_2 + 2CO_2 + 6NaCl + 2H_2O$	CNCl is a toxic gas
	Chlorine	Manganous Ion to Manganous Dioxide	$Mn(NO_3)_2 + 2e^- \rightarrow MnO_3 + 2NO_3^-$	
	Potassium Permanganate	Sulphide	$4KMnO_4 + 3H_2S \rightarrow 2K_2SO_4 + S + 3MnO + MnO_2 + 3H_2O$	
	Ozone /UV	Organics	$CH_3CHO + O_3 \rightarrow CH_3COOH + O_2$	Forms H_2O_2
	UV/Peroxide	Organics	$CH_2Cl + 2H_2O_2 \rightarrow CO_0 + 2H_2O + 2HCl$	
	Oxygen	Cyanide	$2CN_- + O_2 \rightarrow 2CNO_-$ $CNO_- + 2H_2O + 2H_{2-} \rightarrow CO_2 + NH_4 + H_2O$	Requires activated C and Cu catalyst
Reduction	Sulphur Dioxide	Chromium(VI)	$3SO_2 + 3H_2O \rightarrow 3H_2SO_3$. $2CrO_3 + H_2SO_3 \rightarrow Cr_2(SO_4)_3 + 3H_2O$	It is then precipitated as $Cr(OH)_3$
	Ferrous Sulphate	Chromium(VI)	$2CrO_3 + 6FeSO_4 + 6H_2SO_4 \rightarrow 3Fe_2(SO_4)_3 + Cr_2(SO_4)_3 + 6H_2O$	
	Sodium Borohydride	Copper	$NaBH_4 + 8Cu + 2H_2O \rightarrow 8Cu + NaBO_2 + 8H^-$	

Chlorination

Definition

Chlorine is a greenish-yellow gas with a molecular weight of 70.91. Moist chlorine gas can destroy all ferrous metals, including stainless steel. In its 'dry' gas or liquid form it cannot attack ferrous metals; therefore, it is compressed and shipped in steel cylinders containers and tank cars. Liquid chlorine attacks PVC and most rubber elastomers. Chlorine has a long history of use for preventing microbiological fouling in cooling water systems, for bleaching purposes in the textile and the pulp and paper industries, as a disinfectant for treating potable water and as a chemical reactant in the manufacture of many products.

Chemistry

Chlorine hydrolyzes when dissolved in water to form hypochlorous acid and hydrochloric acid as shown:

$$Cl_2 + H_2O \Leftrightarrow HOCl + HCl$$

Under alkaline conditions, hypochlorous acid dissociates to form hypochlorite ion.

$$HOCl \Leftrightarrow OCl^- + H^+$$

While hypochlorous acid is a very effective microbiocide in industrial water treatment, hypochlorite ion is much less effective. Higher concentrations and longer contact time are necessary for control. The solubility of chlorine in water at 68°F and 1 atm is 7.29 g/L. Usually, the upper limit of chlorine concentration in commercially available chlorinator streams is 3500 mg/L. The specific gravity at 32°F and 1 atm is 2.482, meaning that it weighs 2.482 times the weight of air.

Environmental Considerations

Many of the traditional uses of chlorine are being studied, and tighter restrictions on the use of chlorine are being implemented. Because of the low use levels of chlorine that have been imposed for many applications, dechlorination before final discharge has added to overall cost and complexity of using chlorine. The formation of chlorinated organics and trihalomethane has become a serious environmental health concern.

Coagulation and Flocculation

Definition

Coagulation describes the effect produced by addition of a chemical to a colloidal dispersion, resulting in particle destabilization. Operationally, this is achieved by the addition of appropriate chemical and rapid intense mixing for obtaining uniform dispersion of the chemical. Flocculation is the second stage of the formation of settable particles (or flocs) from destabilized sized particles and is achieved by gentle and prolonged mixing.

Although there is some relation between turbidity of raw water and the proper coagulant dosage, the exact quantity can be determined only by trial. Addition of coagulants in excess of the determined minimum quantity may increase bactericidal efficiency.

In case of the case of coagulation with alum, the control over the alkalinity is very important. Not only should the water contain sufficient alkalinity to completely react with aluminium sulphate but there should be sufficient residual to ensure that the treated water is not corrosive. When ferrous sulphates is used as a coagulant, the pH should be maintained above 9.5 to ensure complete precipitation of the iron. This is done by the addition of hydrated lime. For this reason, the process is sometimes known as 'iron and lime process'.

Distillation

Definition

Distillation is the process of heating a mixture and condensing the resulting vapour to produce a pure substance. Distillation is a process that relies on evaporation to purify water. Contaminated water is heated to form steam. Inorganic compounds and large non-volatile organic molecules do not evaporate with the water and are left behind. The steam then cools and condenses to form purified water. Distillation is one of the oldest methods of water treatment and is still in use today though not commonly as a home treatment method. It can effectively remove many contaminants from drinking water, including bacteria, inorganic and many organic compounds.

Chemistry

Water distillation is an effective process for producing highly treated drinking water. Water distillation can significantly reduce levels of sediment, metals, and biological contaminants, which are unable to travel out of the boiling chamber with the steam. When combined with effective activated carbon filtration, contaminants like VOCs and radon can also be controlled. Water distillation when combined with activated carbon filtration, can be used to effectively treat such contaminants as arsenic, asbestos, benzene, fluoride, lead, mercury, biological contaminants, etc. Distillation is most effective in removing inorganic compounds such as metals, hardness and particulates from a contaminated water supply.

Reverse Osmosis

Whenever two solutions are separated by a cell wall (membrane), a natural transport mechanism takes place called osmosis. During osmosis, the solution of lower concentration tends to migrate through the membrane wall, which allows the solution to pass, while rejecting the total dissolved solids into the solution of higher concentration until the two solutions are in equilibrium. The time-tested practice of gargling with salt water for sore throat relief is a practical deployment of osmotic principles. The concentrated salt solution draws fluids out of the membranes in your throat, thus reducing inflammation. In reverse osmosis, artificial pressure is applied on the concentrated solution side of the membrane, thus forcing water to migrate through the membrane wall into the less concentrated solution. The resulting solution, called permeate, is of very high quality.

Because RO employs cross-flow filtration method, one remaining solids are rinsed off the membrane surface in the concentrate (waste) stream. The concentrate is usually sent to the drain, but in designs where water conservation is a priority, the concentrate may be recirculated or as in a series of configuration, used to feed the next membrane. Because the membrane separates most (typically 95–99%) of the solids from the feed stream, it follows that the waste stream contains a significantly higher TDS concentration.

Ion Exchange

Definition

The process of ion exchange is the ability of the ions, incorporated within a solid material—the ion exchange resin—to be exchanged with ions in solution. This can be used to purify or remove unwanted chemicals from the solution. Synthetic cation and anion exchange resins were developed during the 1930s using certain types of coal treated with sulphuric acid. The resin has the appearance of smooth, spherical beads usually between 0.5 and 1 mm in diameter. However, at the molecular level, each bead has a skeleton-like structure. The resin beads are contained in a suitable vessel called resin bed through which water is passed allowing the chemical reactions to take place.

Mechanism

When a mineral substance dissolves in water, it dissociates into electrically charged particles termed ions. The particles carrying a positive charge are known as cations and those with a negative charge are known as anions. If such a solution is passed through a resin bed filled with a suitable ion-exchange resin, ions are exchanged so that some part from the solution are taken up by resin and an equivalent number are transferred from the resin to the solution. Ion exchange is basically a simple process based on reversible interchange of ions between a liquid and a solid (i.e. the resin), no radical change being involved in the structure of the resin. Positive ions exchange only with positive ions and negative ions with negative ions.

WATER-RELATED STANDARDS

8

BIS STANDARDS FOR DRINKING WATER

Sl. No.	Characteristic	Drinking Water IS: 10500, 1991		Bottled Mineral Water IS: 13428, 1998
		Desirable limit	Max. limit	
1	Colour, Hazen unit, Max	5	25	5
2	Odour	Unobjectionable	-	Agreeable
3	Taste	Agreeable	-	Agreeable
4	Turbidity, NTU, Max	5	10	5
5	pH value	6.5 – 8.5	No relaxation	6.5 – 8.5
6	Dissolved solids mg/L, Max	500	2000	1500
7	Total hardness (as CaCO3), mg/L, Max	300	600	
8	Iron (as Fe) mg/L, Max	0.3	1.0	0.3
9	Chloride (as Cl) mg/L, Max	250	1000	200
10	Free chlorine mg/L, Min	0.2	-	0.2
11	Calcium (as Ca) mg/L, Max	75	200	
12	Copper (as Cu) mg/L, Max	0.05	1.5	1.0
13	Manganese (as Mn) mg/L, Max	0.1	0.3	0.5
14	Magnesium (as Mg) mg/L, Max	30	100	
15	Sulphate (as SO_4) mg/L, Max	200	400 [if Mg is 30 mg/L]	250
16	Nitrate (as NO_3) mg/L, Max	45	100	45
17	Fluoride (as F) mg/L, Max	1.0	1.5	1.5
18	Phenolic compounds (as C_6H_5OH) mg/L, Max	0.001	-	Absent
19	Mercury (as Hg) mg/L, Max	0.001	No relaxation	0.001
20	Cadmium (as Cd) mg/L, Max	0.01	No relaxation	0.01

(Contd...)

Sl. No.	Characteristic	Drinking Water IS: 10500, 1991		Bottled Mineral Water IS: 13428, 1998
		Desirable limit	Max. limit	
21	Selenium (as Se) mg/L, Max	0.01	No relaxation	0.01
22	Arsenic (as As) mg/L, Max	0.05	No relaxation	0.05
23	Cyanide (as CN) mg/L, Max	0.05	No relaxation	0.01
24	Lead (as Pb) mg/L, Max	0.05	No relaxation	0.05
25	Zinc (as Zn) mg/L, Max	5	-	
26	Anionic detergents (as MBAS) mg/L, Max	0.2	1.0	
27	Chromium (as Cr^{+6}) mg/L, Max	0.05	No relaxation	0.05
28	Mineral oil mg/L, Max	0.01	-	Absent
29	Pesticides mg/L, Max	Absent	0.001	
30	Alkalinity mg/L, Max	200	600	600 [as HCO_3]
31	Aluminium (as Al) mg/L, Max	0.03	0.1	0.03
32	Boron (as B) mg/L, Max	1	-	1
33	Barium (as Ba) mg/L, Max	-	-	1.0
34	Silver (as Ag) mg/L, Max	-	-	0.01
35	Alpha emitters Bq/L, Max	10^{-8}	-	10^{-8}
36	Beta emitters pci/L, Max	10^{-7}	-	10^{-7}

QUALITY TOLERANCES FOR WATER FOR INDUSTRIAL AND OTHER USES

Sl. No.	Characteristic	General laboratory use IS: 1070, 1977		
		Grade 1	Grade 2	Grade 3
1	Specific conductivity μmohs/cm at 25°C, Max	0.1	1.0	5.0
2	pH at 25°C	-	-	5.0 – 8.0
3	Total solids or non-volatile residue at 105°C, mg/L, Max	-	1.0	2.0
4	Silica (as SiO_2) mg/L, Max	0.01	0.1	1.0
5	Colour retention of $KMnO_4$ at 27° × 2°C, min	60	10	10

Grade 1: For use in test methods requiring minimum interference and maximum precision and accuracy such as trace analysis. Reagent water may be prepared by distillation of feed water having maximum conductivity of 20 μmohs/cm at 25°C followed by polishing with mixed bed deionizers and passage through 0.45 μm membrane filter.

Grade 2: For use in the general laboratory analytical procedures where freedom from organic impurities is of more significance. It is not applicable for biological or medical analysis and organic trace analysis.

Grade 3: For use in washing of glassware, preliminary rinsing of glassware and feed water for production of higher grade waters or where large quantity of water is required of low purity synthetic test solutions.

Sl. No.	Characteristic	Tolerance limit for inland surface water IS: 2296, 1974		
		For use as raw water for public water supply and bathing ghats	For fish culture	For irrigation
1	Coliform organisms (monthly average MPN/100 ml)	See note 1		
2	pH value	6.0 – 9.0	6.0 – 9.0	5.5 – 9.0
3	Elec. conductance at 25°C, Max		1000$\times$ 10^{-6} mhos	3000 $\times$ 10^{-6} mhos
4	Total diss. solids (inorg) mg/L, Max			2100
5	Fluorides (as F), mg/L, Max	1.5		
6	Chlorides (as Cl), mg/L, Max	600		600
7	Sulphates (as SO_4), mg/L, Max			1000
8	Cyanides (as CN), mg/L, Max	0.01		
9	Selenium (as Se), mg/L, Max	0.05		
10	Lead (as Pb), mg/L, Max	0.1		
11	Total chromium (as Cr), mg/L, Max	0.05		
12	Arsenic (as As), mg/L, Max	0.2		

(Contd...)

Sl. No.	Characteristic	Tolerance limit for inland surface water IS: 2296, 1974		
		For use as raw water for public water supply and bathing ghats	For fish culture	For irrigation
13	Dissolved oxygen, Max	*See* note 2	*See* note 2	
14	Free carbon dioxide (as CO_2), mg/L, Max		6	
15	Free ammonia (as N), mg/L, Max		1.6	
16	Biochemical oxygen demand (5 days at 20°C), mg/L, Max	3		
17	Phen compds (as C_6H_5OH), mg/L, Max	0.005		
18	Alpha emitters, µc/mL, Max	10^{-9}	10^{-9}	10^{-9}
19	Beta emitters, µc/mL, Max	10^{-8}	10^{-8}	10^{-8}
20	Nitrates (as NO_3), mg/L, Max	50		
21	Boron (as B), mg/L, Max			2.0
22	Per cent sodium, Max			60
23	Oil and grease, mg/L, Max	0.1	0.1	
24	Insecticides	Absent		

Note 1: Not more than 5000, with less than 5% samples with values $\geq$ 20,000 and less than 20% of samples with values $\geq$ 5000.

Note 2: 40% saturation value or 3 mg/L whichever is higher.

Sl. No.	Characteristic	Textile Industry IS: 201, 1992			Rayon Manufac-turing industry IS: 2725, 1964
		General purpose	Bleaching, dyeing and subsequent processing	Wool scouring	
1	Colour, Hazen unit, Max	20	5 (note 1)	70	5
2	Turbidity, NTU, Max	2	2	2	1 (Silica scale unit)
3	Total hardness, mg/L, Max	50 (note 2)	2	2	5
4	Iron (as Fe), mg/L, Max	0.25	0.1	0.2	0.05
5	Manganese (as Mn), mg/L, Max	0.10	0.10	0.10	0.03
6	Iron and Manganese added together, Max	0.25	0.1	0.1	0.05
7	Aluminium (as Al), mg/L, v	0.1	0.1	0.1	
8	Sulphate (as SO_4), mg/L, Max	100	-	-	
9	Chloride (as Cl), mg/L, Max	100	-	-	
10	Total alkalinity, mg/L, Max	150	150	150	75
11	Total dissolved solids, mg/L, Max				200
12	Silica (as SiO_2), mg/L, Max				10
13	Heavy metals (as Pb), mg/L, Max				0.01

Note 1: When dark and medium dark dyeing is done, a relaxed maximum limit 20 may be permissible, but for whites and delicate the limit shall not be relaxed.

Note 2: For processes which are not sensitive to hardness salts or internal sequestering agents are used, a maximum limit of 2 permissible.

Sl. No.	Characteristic	Fermen-tation industry IS: 4700, 1968	Ice manu-facture IS: 3957, 1966	Processed food industry IS: 4251, 1967
1	Turbidity, NTU, Max	10	5	10
2	Colour, Hazen unit, Max	20	5	20
3	Odour	None	None	None
4	Total solids, mg/L, Max	1000		1000
5	Total dissolved solids, mg/L, Max		1000 [(a)]	

(Contd...)

Sl. No.	Characteristic	Fermentation industry IS: 4700, 1968	Ice manufacture IS: 3957, 1966	Processed food industry IS: 4251, 1967
6	Total hardness (as $CaCO_3$), mg/L, Max	500	600	600
7	Alkalinity (as $CaCO_3$), mg/L, Max		100	
8	Chloride (as Cl), mg/L, Max	250	250	250
9	Sulphate (as SO_4), mg/L, Max	200	200	200
10	Iron (as Fe), mg/L, Max	0.3	0.3	0.3
11	Manganese (as Mn), mg/L, Max	0.2	0.2	0.2
12	Copper (as Cu), mg/L, Max	1.0	1.0	1.0
13	Zinc (as Zn), mg/L, Max	15.0	15.0	15.0
14	Magnesium (as Mg), mg/L, Max	125	125	75
15	pH value	6.0 – 9.2	6.5 – 9.2	6.5 – 9.2
16	Fluoride (as F), mg/L, Max	1.5	1.5	1.5
17	Nitrates (as N), mg/L, Max	20		20
18	Phen compds (as C_6H_5OH), mg/L, Max	0.001	0.001	0.001
19	Arsenic (as As), mg/L, Max	0.2	0.2	0.2
20	Chromium (as Cr^{+6}), mg/L, Max	0.05	0.05	0.05
21	Cyanide (as CN), mg/L, Max	0.01	0.01	0.01
22	Lead (as Pb), mg/L, Max	0.1	0.1	0.1
23	Cadmium (as Cd), mg/L, Max		0.01	0.01
24	Mercury (as Hg), mg/L, Max		0.01	0.001
25	Selenium (as Se), mg/L, Max	0.05	0.05	0.05
26	Coliform bac MPN index/ 100 ml, Max	Zero	Less than 1	
27	Std. plate count/ml, Max	100	100	50[(b)]
28	Proteolytic and lipolytic organisms, combined count per ml, Max			50[(c)]
29	Alpha emitters Bq/L, Max	10^{-9}	10^{-9}	10^{-9}
30	Beta emitters pci/L, Max	10^{-8}	10^{-6}	10^{-8}

(a) For clear transparent ice, TDS content should not exceed 300 mg/L.

(b) Not applicable in case of cooling water and of hot water used in dairy industry.

(c) Not applicable in case of cooling water, hot water and for water used for general purposes in dairy industry.

Sl. No.	Characteristic	Storage batteries IS: 1069, 1993	Vitreous enamel industry IS: 8914, 1978	Plain & reinforced concrete IS: 456, 1978
1	Non-volatile residue mg/L, Max	1		
2	Chloride (as Cl) mg/L, Max	1	13	2000 (1) 1000 (2)
3	Calcium (as Ca) mg/L, Max		30	
4	Magnesium (as Mg) mg/L, Max		8	
5	Sulphate (as SO_4) mg/L, Max		25	500 (as SO_3)
6	pH value	6.5 – 7.5	7.6	Not less than 6
7	Heavy metals (as Pb) mg/L, Max	0.1		
8	Hardness (as $CaCO_3$) mg/L Max	Not detectable	39	
9	Bicarbonate (as HCO_3) mg/L, Max		117	
10	Iron (as Fe) mg/L, Max		0.3	
11	Manganese (as Mn) mg/L, Max		0.005	
12	Iron (Fe) and Manganese (Mn) mg/L, Max	0.1		
13	Oxidizable matter	To pass the test		
14	Sp. elec. conductivity at 25° C in dionic units (or μmhos/cm) Max	5		
15	Total dissolved solids mg/L, Max	2	147	
16	Organic solids, mg/L, Max			200
17	Inorganic solids, mg/L, Max			300
18	Suspended matter, mg/L, Max			2000

(1) For plain concrete work.

(2) For reinforced concrete work.

Sl. No.	Characteristic	Swimming pools IS: 3328, 1993
1	pH value	7.5 - 8.5*
2	Total alkalinity (as $CaCO_3$), mg/L, Max	50 – 500*
3	Aluminium (as Al), mg/L, Max	0.1
4	Total residual chlorine, mg/L, Max	
(a)	At inlet, Max	0.5

(Contd...)

Sl. No.	Characteristic	Swimming pools IS: 3328, 1993
(b)	At outlet, Min	0.2
5	Oxygen absorbed in 4 hours at 27°C, mg/L, Max	1.0
6	Total dissolved solids, mg/L, Max	1500
7	Chloride (as Cl), mg/L, Max	500
8	Iron (as Fe), mg/L, Max	0.1
9	Heavy metals (as Pb), mg/L, Max	0.1
10	Colour, Hazen unit, Max	10
11	Turbidity, NTU, Max	10
12	Odour	Odourless
13	Taste	Palatable

* Too low an alkalinity and low pH are the most common causes of complaints of taste, odour and eye irritation. At pH lower than 7.5, there is an increased tendency for formation of dichloramine and nitrogen chlorides or similar compounds.

Coliform organisms: If any Most Probable Number (MPN) result is more than 10 per 100 ml, a fresh sample shall be tested within 24 hours. The two consecutive results shall not show MPN index of Coliform organism of more than 10 per 100 ml.

Sl. No.	Characteristic	Pulp and paper industry IS: 2724, 1964				
		Ground wood paper	Kraft paper bleached	Kraft paper & pulp unbleached	Soda and sulphite paper	High grade paper
1	Colour, Hazen unit, Max	20	15	100	10	5
2	Turbidity, Silica scale unit, Max	50	25	100	15	10
3	Total dissolved solids, mg/L, Max	500	300	500	300	300
4	Total hardness, mg/L, Max	200	100	200	100	100
5	Iron (as Fe), mg/L, Max	1.0	0.25	1.0	0.25	0.25
6	Manganese (as Mn), mg/L, Max	0.5	0.1	0.5	0.05	0.05
7	Iron and Manganese together, mg/L, Max	1.0	0.25	-	0.25	0.25
8	Total residual chlorine, mg/L, Max	2.0	2.0	-	2.0	2.0

CLASSIFICATION AS PER CPCB

Designated Best Use

Nomenclature

Drinking water source without conventional treatment but after disinfection	Class A
Outdoor bathing	Class B
Drinking water source with conventional treatment followed by disinfection	Class C
Propagation of wildlife and fisheries	Class D
Irrigation, industrial cooling and controlled waste disposal	Class E

Sl. No.	Parameters	Class A	Class B	Class C	Class D	Class E
1	Dissolved oxygen, mg/L Min	6	5	4	4	-
2	Biochemical oxygen demand, mg/L, Max	2	3	3	-	-
3	Total Coliform organism, MPN/100 ml, Max *	50	500	5000	-	-
4	Total dissolved solids, mg/L, Max	500	-	1500	-	1200
5	Chloride (as Cl), mg/L, Max	250	-	600	-	600
6	Colour, Hazen unit, Max	10	300	300	-	-
7	Sodium absorption ratio, Max	-	-	-	-	26
8	Boron (as B), mg/L, Max	-	-	-	-	2
9	Sulphates (as SO_4), mg/L, Max	400	-	400	-	1000
10	Nitrates (as NO_3), mg/L, Max	20	-	50	-	-
11	Free ammonia (as N), mg/L, Max	-	-	-	1.2	-
12	Conductivity at 25° C, μmhos/cm, Max	-	-	-	1.0	2.25
13	pH value	6.5 – 8.5	6.5 – 8.5	6.5 – 8.5	6.5 – 8.5	6.0 – 8.0
14	Arsenic (as As), mg/L, Max	0.05	0.2	0.2	-	-
15	Iron (as Fe), mg/L, Max	0.3	-	50	-	-
16	Fluorides (as F), mg/L, Max	1.5	1.5	1.5	-	-
17	Lead (as Pb), mg/L, Max	0.1	-	0.1	-	-

(Contd...)

Sl. No.	Parameters	Class A	Class B	Class C	Class D	Class E
18	Copper (as Cu), mg/L, Max	1.5	-	1.5	-	-
19	Zinc (as Zn), mg/L, Max	15	-	15	-	-

* If the coliforms are found to be more than the prescribed tolerance limits, the criteria for coliforms shall be satisfied if not more than 20% of the samples exceed the tolerance limits, the criteria for coliforms shall be satisfied if not more than 50% samples have values more than 4 times the tolerance limits.

GENERAL DISCHARGE LIMITS

S. No.	Parameter	Standards as per Environment (Protection) Rules, 1993[1]			
		Inland surface water	Public sewers	Land for irriga-tion	Marine coastal areas
1	Colour and odour	*See* note	*See* note	*See* note	*See* note
2	Suspended solids, mg/L, Max	100	600	200	a) For process wastewater 100 b) For cooling water effluent 10% above total suspended matter of influent
3	Particle size of suspended solids	Shall pass 850μ ISI sieve	–	–	a) Floatable solids, Max 3 mm b) Settleable solids, Max 850 μ
4[2]	–	–	–	–	–
5	pH value	5.5 – 9.0	5.5 – 9.0	5.5 – 9.0	5.5 – 9.0
6	Temperature, °C, Max	Shall not exceed 5°C above the receiving water temperature	–	–	Shall not exceed 5°C above the receiving water temperature

(Contd...)

Sl. No.	Parameter	Standards as per Environment (Protection) Rules, 1993			
		Inland surface water	Public sewers	Land for irrigation	Marine coastal areas
7	Oil and grease, mg/L, Max	10	20	10	20
8	Total residual chlorine, mg/L, Max	1.0	–	–	1.0
9	Ammonical nitrogen (as N), Max	50	50	–	50
10	Total Kjeldahl nitrogen (as N), mg/L, Max	100	–	–	100
11	Free ammonia (as NH_3), mg/L, Max	5.0	–	–	5.0
12	Biochemical oxygen demand (5 days at 20°C), Max	30	350	100	100
13	Chemical oxygen demand, mg/L, Max	250	–	–	250
14	Arsenic (as As), mg/L, Max	0.2	0.2	0.2	0.2
15	Mercury (as Hg), mg/L. Max	0.01	0.01	–	0.01
16	Lead (as Pb), mg/L	0.1	1.0	–	2.0
17	Cadmium (as Cd), mg/L, Max	2.0	1.0	–	2.0
18	Hexavalent chromium (as Cr^{+6}), mg/L, Max	0.1	2.0	–	1.0
19	Total chromium (as Cr), mg/L, Max	2.0	2.0	–	2.0
20	Copper (as Cu), mg/L, Max	3.0	3.0	–	3.0
21	Zinc (as Zn), mg/L, Max	5.0	15	–	15
22	Selenium (as Se), mg/L, Max	0.05	0.05	–	0.05
23	Nickel (as Ni), mg/L < Max	3.0	3.0	–	5.0
24[2]	–	–	–	–	–
25[2]	–	–	–	–	–
26[2]	–	–	–	–	–

(Contd...)

Sl. No.	Parameter	Standards as per Environment (Protection) Rules, 1993			
		Inland surface water	Public sewers	Land for irriga-tion	Marine coastal areas
27	Cyanide (as CN), mg/L, Max	0.2	2.0	0.2	0.2
28[2]	–	–	–	–	–
29	Fluoride (as F), mg/L, Max	2.0	15	–	15
30	Dissolved phosphates (as P), mg/L, Max	5.0	–	–	–
31[2]	–	–	–	–	–
32	Sulphide (as S), mg/L, Max	2.0	–	–	5.0
33	Phenolic compounds (as C_6H_5OH), mg/L, Max	1.0	5.0	–	5.0
34	Radioactive materials				
(a)	Alpha emitters µc/ml, Max	10^{-7}	10^{-7}	10^{-8}	10^{-7}
(b)	Beta emitters µc/ml, Max	10^{-6}	10^{-8}	10^{-7}	10^{-8}
35	Bioassaytest	90% survival of fish after 96 hours in 100% effluent	90% survival of fish after 96 hours in 100% effluent	90% survival of fish after 96 hours in 100% effluent	90% survival of fish after 96 hours in 100% effluent
36	Manganese (as Mn)	2 mg/L	2 mg/L	–	2 mg/L
37	Iron (as Fe)	3 mg/L	3 mg/L	–	3 mg/L
38	Vanadium (as V)	0.2 mg/L	0.2 mg/L	–	0.2 mg/L
39	Nitrate Nitrogen	10 mg/L	–	–	20 mg/L
40[2]	–	–	–	–	–

Note: All efforts should be made to remove colour and unpleasant odour as far as possible.

1. Schedule VI intestate by Rule 2 (d) of Environment (Protection) Second Amendment Rules, 1993 notified vide G.S.R. 422 (E) dated 19-05-1993, published in the Gazette No. 174 dated 19-05-1993.
2. Omitted by Rule 2 (d) (i) of the Environment (Protection) Third Amendment Rules, 1993 vide Notification No. G.S.R. 801 (E) dated 31-12-1993.

READY REFERENCES

9

GLOSSARY OF TERMS

1. *Absorption* – Assimilation of molecules or other substances into the physical structure of a liquid or solid without chemical reaction.
2. *Acidity* – Theoretically, in water excess of H^+ ions over OH^- ions occurs at a pH below 7. In water analysis excess of H^+ ions that are measurable by titration where pH is less than 4.2 to 4.4, where methyl orange alkalinity disappears.
3. *Alkalinity* – Capacity of water to neutralize acids by its content of bicarbonates, carbonates or hydroxides. By definition, total alkalinity is that which will react with acid as the pH of the sample is reduced to the methyl orange end point—about 4.2. Another significant expression is phenolphthalein alkalinity, which exists above pH 8.2 and is that which reacts with acid as the pH of the sample is reduced to 8.2.
4. *Ambient Monitoring* – Performed to determine existing environmental conditions or contaminant levels in the environment, against which future conditions can be compared.
5. *Amphoteric* – Capable of reacting in water either as a weak acid or as a weak base. For example, aluminium salts hydrolyze in water to produce a compound that may be considered a weak base, $Al(OH_3)$, or a weak acid, H_3AlO_3. A property of certain oxides makes them reactive both with acids and bases. Al_2O_3 is an example.
6. $Al_2O_3 + 3H_2SO_4 \rightarrow Al_2(SO_4)3 + 3H_2O$.
7. $Al_2O_3 + 2NaOH \rightarrow Na_2Al_2O_4 + H_2O$.

8. *Anaerobic* – In the absence of oxygen.
9. *Anion* – A negatively charged ion resulting from dissociation of salts, acid or alkalies in aqueous solution.
10. *Anode* – In electrolysis or electrochemical corrosion, a site where metal goes into solution as a cation leaving behind an equivalent of electrons to be transferred to an opposite electrode, called a cathode.
11. *Aquifer* – Water bearing formation of rock or soil that will yield usable supplies of water. It may be classified as confined or unconfined.
12. *Available Nitrogen* – Amount of nitrogen present as either nitrate or ammonium, forms which can be readily taken up by plants.
13. *Available Water* – The portion of water in soil that can be readily absorbed by plant roots.
14. *Background Level* – Amount of a substance, which occurs naturally in the environment.
15. *Biochemical Oxygen Demand* – Laboratory measurement of the amount of oxygen consumed by microorganisms while decomposing organic matter in a product. BOD levels are indicative of the effect of the waste on fish or other aquatic life, which require oxygen to live.
16. *Biodegradable* – Capable of being broken down (decomposed) by microorganisms.
17. *Buffer* – A substance in solution, which accepts hydrogen ions or hydroxyl ions added to the solution as acids or alkalies, minimizing change in pH.
18. *Carbonate Hardness* – The hardness in water that is caused by bicarbonates and carbonates of calcium and magnesium. If alkalinity exceeds total hardness it is carbonate hardness; if hardness exceeds alkalinity, the carbonate hardness equals the alkalinity.
19. *Catalysis* – Addition of a material (catalyst) that does not take a direct part in a chemical reaction but increases the rate of the reaction.
20. *Cathode* – In electrolysis or electrochemical corrosion, a

site on a surface where cations in solution are neutralized by electrons to become elements that react either on the surface of water or with water to produce a secondary reaction.

21. *Cation* – A positively charged ion resulting from dissociation of molecules in solution.
22. *Chemical Oxygen Demand* – Laboratory measurement of the amount of oxygen used in chemical reactions that occur in water as a result of the addition of wastes. A major objective of conventional wastewater treatment is to reduce the chemical and biochemical oxygen demand.
23. *Chlorination* – Addition of chlorine as a means of disinfecting drinking water or wastewater.
24. *Coagulation* – The neutralization of the charges on colloidal matter.
25. *Condensate* – Water obtained by evaporation and subsequent condensation.
26. *Concentration* – The process of increasing the dissolved solids per unit volume of solution, usually by evaporation of the liquid; also, the amount of material dissolved in a unit volume of solution.
27. *Contaminant* – Any physical, chemical, biological or radiological substance causing an impurity in the environment.
28. *Coordinated Phosphate* – A boiler treatment scheme using phosphate buffers to avoid the presence of hydroxyl alkalinity.
29. *Critical Pressure* – The pressure at the critical temperature above which the fluid no longer has the properties of a liquid, regardless of further increase in pressure.
30. *Decantation* – Process in which a pesticide adheres to a soil particle or some organic material so tightly that it is no longer biologically available.
31. *Denitrification* – Biochemical conversion of nitrate (NO_3) to nitrite (NO_2), ammonia (NH_3) and free nitrogen (N), as in soil by microorganisms.

32. *Demineralization* – A process used to remove minerals from water; however, the term is restricted to ion exchange processes.
33. *Deionization* – A process to remove ions from water.
34. *Desalination* – The removal of inorganic dissolved solids from water.
35. *Dewater* – To separate water from sludge to produce a cake that can be handled as a solid.
36. *Dialysis* – A separation process that depends on differences in diffusion rates of solutes across a permeable membrane.
37. *Dispersant* – A chemical, which causes particulates in a water system to remain in suspension.
38. *Discharge* – Flow of surface water in a stream or the flow of ground water from a spring, ditch or flowing well.
39. *Dissolved Oxygen (DO)* – Oxygen dissolved in water and readily available to fish and other aquatic organisms.
40. *Effluent* – Discharge or emission of a liquid or gas.
41. *Electrolyte* – A substance that dissociates into two or more ions when it dissolves in water.
42. *Elution* – The process of extracting one solid from another.
43. *Elutriation* – The washing of sludge with water to free it of its mother liquor.
44. *Emulsion* – A colloidal dispersion of one liquid in another.
45. *Endothermic* – Absorbing heat.
46. *Equivalent Weight* – The weight in grams of a substance which combines with or displaces one gram of hydrogen; it is usually obtained by dividing the formula weight by the valence.
47. *Exothermic* – Evolving heat.
48. *Filtrate* – The liquid remaining after removal of solids as a cake in the filter.
49. *Flocculation* – The process of agglomerating coagulated particles into settleable flocs, usually of a gelatinous nature.

50. *Flotation* – A process for separating solids from the water by developing froth in a vessel in such a fashion that the solids attach to air particles and float to the surface for collection.
51. *Hardness* – The concentration of calcium and magnesium salts in water. Hardness is a term originally referring to soap-consuming power of water, as such it is sometimes also taken to include iron and manganese. 'Permanent hardness' is the excess of hardness over alkalinity. 'Temporary hardness' is hardness equal to or less than the alkalinity. These are also referred to as 'non-carbonate' or 'carbonate' hardness, respectively.
52. *Heavy Metals* – Metals (elements with high density, malleability and electrical and thermal conductivity) having high specific gravity and high atomic mass, such as lead, cadmium, zinc, copper, silver and mercury. These may be found in the waste stream as part of discarded items such as batteries, lighting fixtures, colorants and inks.
53. *Inorganic Chemicals* – Natural or synthetic chemicals that contain no carbon atom.
54. *Ion Exchange* – A process by which certain undesired ions of given charge are absorbed from solutions within an ion-permeable absorbent, being replaced in the solution by desirable ions of similar charge from the absorbent.
55. *Ionic Strength* – A measure of the strength of a solution based on both the concentrations and valences of the present.
56. *Langelier Index* – Means of expressing the degree of saturation of water as related to calcium carbonate solubility.
57. *Mineral* – Any inorganic or fossilized organic material having definite chemical composition and structure found in a natural state.
58. *Miscibility* – The ability of two liquids, not mutually soluble, to mix.
59. *Mineral Water* – Contains large amounts of dissolved minerals such as calcium, sodium, magnesium and iron.

60. *Mole* – A unit weight or volume of a chemical corresponding to its molecular weight. A mole of water weighs 18 g and its vapour occupies 22.41 at standard temperature and pressure.
61. *Monomer* – A molecule, usually an organic compound, having the ability to join with a number of identical molecules to form a polymer.
62. *Most Probable Number* – Statistical expression for estimating the number of microorganisms in a culture or a volume of waste.
63. *Neutralization* – Most commonly, a chemical reaction that produces a resulting environment that is neither acidic nor alkaline. Also, the addition of a scavenger chemical to an aqueous system in excess concentration to eliminate a corrosive factor, such as dissolved oxygen.
64. *Non-carbonate hardness* – Hardness in water caused by chlorides, sulphates and nitrates of calcium and magnesium.
65. *Nutrient* – Element essential for plant or animal growth. Major nutrients include nitrogen, phosphorus, carbon, oxygen, sulphur and potassium.
66. *Occlusion* – An absorption process by which one solid material adheres to another, sometimes occurring by co-precipitation.
67. *Osmosis* – The passage of water through a permeable membrane separating two solutions of different concentrations; the water passes into the more concentrated solution.
68. *Oxygen Demand* – Materials such as food waste and dead plant or animal tissue that use up dissolved oxygen in the water. Chemical and biochemical oxygen demand (COD and BOD) are measures of the amount of oxygen consumed when a substance degrades.
69. *pH* – A means of expressing hydrogen ion concentration in terms of powers of 10; the negative logarithm of the hydrogen ion concentration.
70. *Polymer* – A chain of organic molecules produced by the joining of primary units called monomers.

71. *Polyphosphate* – Molecularly dehydrated orthophosphate.
72. *Potable* – Suitable for drinking.
73. *Precipitate* – An insoluble reaction product; in an aqueous chemical reaction, usually a crystalline compound that grows in size to become settable.
74. *Reduction* – A chemical reaction in which an element or compound gains electrons, being reduced in positive valence.
75. *Reverse Osmosis* – A process that reverses (by the application of pressure) the flow of water in the natural process of osmosis so that it passes from the more concentrated to the more dilute solution.
76. *Reversion* – The return of molecularly dehydrated phosphate (polyphosphate) to its hydrated origin (orthophosphate).
77. *Receiving Waters* – Water bodies that receive runoff or wastewater discharges, such as rivers, streams, lakes, estuaries and ground water.
78. *Salinity* – Quality of water based on its salt content; sea water contains approximately 18000 parts per million of salt.
79. *Salt Splitting* – The ability of an anion exchanger to convert a salt solution to caustic; the ability of a cation exchanger to convert a salt solution to acid.
80. *Saturation Index* – The relation of calcium carbonate to the pH, alkalinity and hardness of water to determine its scale-forming tendency.
81. *Scale* – The precipitate that forms on surfaces in contact with water as the result of a physical or chemical change.
82. *Scrubber* – Anti-pollution device that uses a liquid or slurry spray to remove acid gases and particulates from flue gases.
83. *Sludge* – Heavy, slimy residue remaining from the treatment of municipal and industrial water and wastewater. Digested sewage sludge remains after decomposition under controlled temperature, pH and mixing in a digester tank.

84. *Slurry* – Water containing a high concentration of suspended solids, usually over 5000 mg/L.
85. *Softening* – The removal of hardness (calcium and magnesium) from water.
86. *Solubility* – Amount of a substance that will dissolve a given amount of different substance, typically, water.
87. *Stoichiometric* – The ratio of chemical substances reacting in water that corresponds to their combining weights in the theoretical chemical reaction.
88. *Surfactant* – A surface-active agent; usually an organic compound, whose molecules contain a hydrophilic group at one end and a lipophilic group at the other.
89. *Turbidity* – A suspension of fine particles that obscures light rays but requires many days for sedimentation because of the small particle size.
90. *Zoning* – Designation by ordinances of areas of land reserved and regulated for different land uses; a type of regulatory ordinance based on a land use plan.

REAGENT SOLUTIONS

Control Preparation

Many of the tests for impurities require the comparison of the colour or the turbidity produced under specified conditions by an impurity ion with the colour or the turbidity produced under similar conditions by a known amount of the impurity. Three types of solutions are used to determine amounts of impurities in reagent chemicals: (1) the blank, (2) the standard and (3) the control.

(1) *Blank* – A solution containing the quantities of solvents and reagents used in the test.

(2) *Standard* – A solution containing the quantities of solvents and reagents used in the test plus an added known amount of the impurity to be determined.

(3) *Control* – A solution containing the quantities of solvents and reagents used in the test plus an added known amount of the impurity to be determined and a known amount of

the reagent chemical being tested. Some of the chemical being tested must be added to the solution because it is known that the chemical interferes with the test.

Throughout this book, the expressions "for the control" or "for the standard" add *X* mg of *Y* ion mean to add the proper aliquot of one of the following solutions. These solutions must be prepared at the time of use or checked often enough to make certain that the tests will not be affected by changes in strength of the standard solution during storage. Calibrated volumetric glassware must be used in preparing these solutions.

Solid Reagent Mixtures

Eriochrome Black T Indicator – Grind 0.2 g of eriochrome black T to a fine powder with 20 g of potassium chloride.

Methylthymol Blue Indicator – Grind 0.2 g of methylthymol blue to a fine powder with 20 g of potassium nitrate.

Murexide Indicator – Grind 0.2 g of murexide to a fine powder with 20 g of potassium nitrate.

Xylenol Orange Indicator – Grind 0.2 g of xylenol orange (either free acid or sodium salt form) to a fine powder with 20 g of potassium nitrate. Alternatively, use a solution of 0.1 g of xylenol orange in 100 ml of alcohol.

Reagent Solutions

Acetic Acid, 1 N – Dilute 57.5 ml of glacial acetic acid with water to 1 L.

Ammoniacal Buffer, pH 10 – Dissolve 180 g of ammonium chloride in 750 ml of freshly opened ammonium hydroxide, and dilute to 1 L with water. (The pH of a 1 + 10 dilution with water should be about 10.)

Ammonia-Cyanide Mixture, Lead-Free – Dissolve 20 g of potassium cyanide in 150 ml of ammonium hydroxide, and dilute with water to 1 L. Remove lead by shaking the solution with small portions of dithizone extraction solution in chloroform until the dithizone retains its original green colour; discard the extraction solution.

Ammonium Acetate-Acetic Acid Buffer Solution – Dissolve

77.1 g of ammonium acetate in water, add 57 ml of glacial acetic acid, and dilute with water to 1 L. (The pH of a 1 + 10 dilution with water should be about 4.5.)

Ammonium Citrate, Lead-Free – Dissolve 40 g of citric acid in 100 ml of water, and make alkaline to phenol red with ammonium hydroxide. Remove lead by shaking the solution with small portions of dithizone extraction solution in chloroform until the dithizone solution retains its original green colour; discard the extraction solution.

Ammonium Hydroxide, 10% NH_3 – Dilute 400 ml of ammonium hydroxide with water to 1 L.

Ammonium Hydroxide, 2.5% NH_3 – Dilute 100 ml of ammonium hydroxide with water to 1 L.

Ammonium Molybdate – Dissolve 5 g of ammonium molybdate tetrahydrate, $(NH_4)_6Mo_7O_{24} \cdot 4H_2O$, in water, and dilute with water to 100 ml. Store in a polyethylene bottle. Discard if a precipitate forms.

Ammonium Molybdate-Nitric Acid Solution – Mix thoroughly 100 g of molybdic acid, 85%, with 240 ml of water, and add 140 ml of ammonium hydroxide. Filter and add 60 ml of nitric acid. Cool and pour, with constant stirring, into a cool mixture of 400 ml of nitric acid and 960 ml of water. Add 0.1 g of ammonium phosphate dissolved in 10 ml of water, allow to stand 24 hour, and filter through glass wool.

Ammonium Molybdate-Sulfuric Acid Solution – Dissolve 50 g of ammonium molybdate tetrahydrate, $(NH_4)_6Mo_7O_{24} \cdot 4H_2O$, in about 500 ml of water, add 27.5 ml of sulfuric acid, and dilute with water to 1 L.

Ammonium Oxalate – Dissolve 35 g of ammonium oxalate monohydrate, $(COONH_4)_2 \cdot H_2O$, in water, and dilute with water to 1 L.

Ammonium Phosphate – Dissolve 130 g of dibasic ammonium phosphate, $(NH_4)_2HPO_4$, in water, and dilute with water to 1 L.

Ammonium Thiocyanate – Dissolve 300 g of ammonium thiocyanate, NH_4SCN, in water, and dilute with water to 1 L.

Aqua Regia - In a fume hood, cautiously mix 5 ml of nitric acid in 15 ml of hydrochloric acid.

Barium Chloride – Dissolve 120 g of barium chloride dihydrate, $BaCl_2 \cdot 2H_2O$, in water, filter, and dilute with water to 1 L.

Barium Chloride, 30% – Dissolve 30 g of barium chloride dihydrate, $BaCl_2 \cdot 2H_2O$, in 80 ml of water, filter, and dilute with water to 100 ml.

Benedict's Solution – Dissolve 173 g of sodium citrate dihydrate and 100 g of anhydrous sodium carbonate, Na_2CO_3, in 800 ml of water. Heat to aid dissolution, filter if necessary, and dilute with water to 850 ml. Dissolve 17.3 g of copper sulfate pentahydrate, $CuSO_4 \cdot 5H_2O$, in 100 ml of water. Add this solution, with constant stirring, to the alkaline citrate solution, and dilute with water to 1 L.

Bromine Water – A saturated aqueous solution of bromine. Add about 10 ml of liquid bromine to 75 ml of water in a 100 ml bottle so that when the mixture is shaken, undissolved bromine remains in a separate phase.

Bromphenol Blue Indicator – Dissolve 0.10 g of the salt form of bromphenol blue in water, and dilute with water to 100 ml (pH 3.0–4.6).

Bromthymol Blue Indicator – Dissolve 0.10 g of bromthymol blue in 100 ml of dilute alcohol (1 + 1), and filter if necessary (pH 6.0–7.6).

Dimethylglyoxime – Dissolve 1 g of dimethylglyoxime in alcohol, and dilute with alcohol to 100 ml.

N, N-Dimethyl-p-phenylenediamine – Add 200 ml of sulfuric acid to approximately 700 ml of water. Cool to room temperature, add 1 g of *N, N*-dimethyl-*p*-phenylenediamine (*p*-aminodimethylaniline) monohydrochloride, and dilute with water to 1 L.

Diphenylamine – Dissolve 10 mg of colourless diphenylamine in 100 ml of sulfuric acid. In a separate beaker, dissolve 2 g of ammonium chloride in 200 ml of water. Cool both solutions in an ice bath, and cautiously add the sulfuric acid solution to the water solution, taking care to keep the resulting solution cold. The solution should be nearly colourless.

Dithizone Extraction Solution – Dissolve 30 mg of dithizone in 1 L of chloroform plus 5 ml of alcohol. Store the solution in a refrigerator.

Dithizone Indicator Solution – Dissolve 25 mg of dithizone in 100 ml of alcohol. Store in a cold place, and use within 2 months.

Dithizone Test Solution - Dissolve 10 mg of dithizone in 1 L of chloroform. Keep the solution in a glass-stoppered, lead-free bottle, protected from light and stored in a refrigerator.

Ferric Ammonium Sulfate Indicator – Dissolve 80 g of clear crystals of ferric ammonium sulfate dodecahydrate, $FeNH_4(SO_4)_2 \cdot 12H_2O$, in water, and dilute with water to 1 L. A few drops of sulfuric acid may be added, if necessary, to clear the solution.

Ferric Chloride – Dissolve 100 g of ferric chloride hexahydrate $FeCl_3 \cdot 6H_2O$, in dilute hydrochloric acid (1 + 99), and dilute with the dilute acid to 1 L.

Ferric Nitrate – Dissolve 17 g of ferric nitrate non-ahydrate, $Fe(NO_3)_3 \cdot 9H_2O$, in 100 ml of water.

Ferric Sulfate – Add 25 ml of sulfuric acid to 125 g of ferric sulfate n-hydrate, $Fe_2(SO_4)_3 \cdot nH_2O$. Add about 700 ml of water, digest on a steam bath to dissolve, cool to room temperature, and dilute with water to 1 L.

Ferroin Indicator, 0.025 M – Dissolve 0.70 g of ferrous sulfate heptahydrate, $FeSO_4 \cdot 7H_2O$ and 1.5 g of 1,10-phenanthroline in 100 ml of water.

Hydrazine Sulfate, 2% – Dissolve 2 g of hydrazine sulfate, $(NH_2)_2 \cdot H_2SO_4$, in water, and dilute with water to 100 ml.

Hydrochloric Acid, 20% HCl – Dilute 470 ml of hydrochloric acid with water to 1 L.

Hydrochloric Acid, 7 M – Dilute hydrochloric acid (1 + 1) with water.

Hydrogen Sulfide Water – Saturate 100 ml of water by bubbling hydrogen sulfide gas for 1 min. This solution must be freshly prepared.

Hydroxylamine Hydrochloride – Dissolve 10 g of hydroxylamine hydrochloride, $NH_2OH \cdot HCl$, in water, and dilute with water to 100 ml.

Hydroxylamine Hydrochloride for Dithizone Test – Dissolve 20 g of hydroxylamine hydrochloride, $NH_2OH \cdot HCl$, in about 65 ml of water and add 0.10 to 0.15 ml of thymol blue indicator solution. Add ammonium hydroxide until a yellow colour appears. Add 5 ml of a 4% solution of sodium diethyldithiocarbamate. Mix thoroughly, and allow to stand for 5 min. Extract with successive portions of chloroform until no yellow colour is developed in the chloroform layer when the extract is shaken with a dilute solution of a copper salt. Add hydrochloric acid until the indicator turns pink, and dilute with water to 100 ml.

Lead Acetate – Dissolve 100 g of lead acetate trihydrate, $(CH_3COO)_2Pb \cdot 3H_2O$, in water. If necessary, add a few drops of acetic acid to clear the solution, and dilute with water to 1 L.

Methyl Orange Indicator – Dissolve 0.10 g of methyl orange in 100 ml of water (pH 3.2 – 4.4).

Methyl Red Indicator – Dissolve 0.10 g of methyl red in 100 ml of alcohol (pH 4.2 – 6.2).

Nessler Reagent – Dissolve 143 g of sodium hydroxide in 700 ml of water. Dissolve 50 g of red mercuric iodide and 40 g of potassium iodide in 200 ml of water. Pour the iodide solution into the hydroxide solution, and dilute with water to 1 L. Allow to settle, and use the clear supernatant liquid. Nessler reagent prepared by any of the recognized methods may be used, but the reagent described reacts promptly and consistently.

Nitric Acid, 10% HNO_3 – Dilute 105 ml of nitric acid with water to 1 L.

Oxalic Acid – Dissolve 40 g of oxalic acid dihydrate, $(COOH)_2 \cdot 2H_2O$, in water, and dilute with water to 1 L.

Phenolphthalein Indicator – Dissolve 1 g of phenolphthalein in 100 ml of alcohol (pH 8.0 – 10.0).

Phenol Red Indicator – Dissolve 0.10 g of phenol red in 100 ml of alcohol, and filter if necessary (pH 6.8 – 8.2).

Potassium Chloride, 2.5% KCl – Dissolve 2.5 g of potassium chloride, KCl, in water, and dilute with water to 100 ml.

Potassium Chromate – Dissolve 10 g of potassium chromate, K_2CrO_4, in water and dilute with water to 100 ml.

Potassium Cyanide, Lead-Free – Dissolve 10 g of potassium cyanide, KCN, in sufficient water to make 20 ml. Remove lead by shaking with portions of dithizone extraction solution. Part of the dithizone remains in the aqueous phase but can be removed, if desired, by shaking with chloroform. Dilute the potassium cyanide solution with water to 100 ml.

Potassium Dichromate – Dissolve 10 g of potassium dichromate, $K_2Cr_2O_7$, in water, and dilute with water to 100 ml.

Potassium Ferricyanide – Dissolve 5 g of potassium ferricyanide, $K_3Fe(CN)_6$, in 100 ml of water. Prepare the solution at the time of use.

Potassium Ferrocyanide – Dissolve 10 g of potassium ferrocyanide trihydrate, $K_4Fe(CN)_6 \cdot 3H_2O$, in 100 ml of water. Prepare the solution at the time of use.

Potassium Hydroxide, 0.5 N in Methanol – Dissolve 34 to 36 g of potassium hydroxide, KOH, in 20 ml of water, and dilute with methanol to 1 L. Allow the solution to stand in a stoppered bottle for 24 hours. Decant the clear supernatant solution into a bottle provided with a tight-fitting stopper.

Potassium Iodide, 10% – Dissolve 10 g of potassium iodide, KI, in water, and dilute with water to 100 ml.

Silver Diethyldithiocarbamate – Dissolve 1 g of silver diethyldithiocarbamate, $(C_2H_5)_2NCS_2Ag$, in 200 ml of freshly distilled pyridine.

Silver Nitrate – Dissolve 17 g of silver nitrate, $AgNO_3$, in 1 L of water. Store in an amber bottle.

Sodium Acetate, 10% – Dissolve 10 g of sodium acetate trihydrate in water, and dilute with water to 100 ml.

Sodium Carbonate, 1% – Dissolve 5.0 g of sodium carbonate, anhydrous, Na_2CO_3, in 500 ml of water. Store in a plastic bottle (10 mg/ml).

Sodium Citrate, 1 M – Dissolve 294 g of sodium citrate dihydrate, $Na_3C_6H_5O_7 \cdot 2H_2O$, in 950 ml of water, and dilute with water to 1 L.

Sodium Cyanide – Dissolve 10 g of sodium cyanide, NaCN, in water, and dilute with water to 100 ml.

Sodium Hydroxide – Dissolve 100 g of sodium hydroxide, NaOH, in water, and dilute with water to 1 L.

Sodium Sulfite – Dissolve 12.5 g of sodium sulfite, Na_2SO_3, in water, and dilute with water to 100 ml. Keep in a tightly closed bottle. For best results, freshly prepared solution should be used.

Stannous Chloride, 40% – Dissolve 40 g of stannous chloride dihydrate, $SnCl_2 \cdot 2H_2O$, in 100 ml of hydrochloric acid. Store this solution in polyethylene or Teflon containers and use within 3 months.

Stannous Chloride, 2% – Dissolve 2 g of stannous chloride dihydrate, $SnCl_2 \cdot 2H_2O$, in hydrochloric acid, and dilute with hydrochloric acid to 100 ml.

Starch Indicator – Mix 1 g of soluble starch with 10 mg of red mercuric iodide and enough cold water to make a thin paste, add 200 ml of boiling water, and boil for 1 min while stirring. Cool before use.

Sulfuric Acid, Chloride and Nitrate-Free – In a hood, gently fume sulfuric acid in a crucible or dish for at least 30 min. Allow to cool and transfer to a tightly capped glass bottle for storage.

Sulfuric Acid 0.5 N – Slowly add 15 ml of sulfuric acid to 750 ml of water, and dilute to 1 L.

Sulfuric Acid, 10% – Slowly add 60 ml of sulfuric acid to 750 ml of water, cool, and dilute with water to 1 L.

STANDARD SOLUTIONS

Acetaldehyde (0.1 mg of CH_3CHO in 1 ml) – Prepare in water by appropriate dilution of an assayed acetaldehyde solution.

Acetone (0.1 mg of $[CH_3]_2CO$ in 1 ml) – Dilute 6.4 ml of acetone with water to 1 L. Dilute 2.0 ml of this solution with water to 100 ml. Prepare the solution at the time of use.

Aluminum (0.01 mg of Al in 1 ml) – Dissolve 0.100 g of metallic aluminum, Al, in 10 ml of dilute hydrochloric acid (1 + 1), and dilute with water to 100 ml. To 10 ml of this solution, add 25 ml of dilute hydrochloric acid (1 + 1), and dilute with water to 1 L.

Ammonium (0.01 mg of NH_4 in 1 ml) – Dissolve 0.296 g of ammonium chloride, NH_4Cl, in water and dilute with water to 100 ml. Dilute 10 ml of this solution with water to 1 L.

Antimony (0.1 mg of Sb in 1 ml) – Dissolve 0.2743 g of antimony potassium tartrate hemihydrate, $KSbOC_4H_4O_6 \cdot 1/2\ H_2O$, in 100 ml of water. Add 100 ml of hydrochloric acid, and dilute with water to 1 L.

Arsenic (0.001 mg of As in 1 ml) – Dissolve 0.132 g of arsenic trioxide, As_2O_3, in 10 ml of 10% sodium hydroxide reagent solution, neutralize with 10% sulfuric acid reagent solution, add an excess of 10 ml, and dilute with water to 1 L. To 10 ml of this solution, add 10 ml of 10% sulfuric acid reagent solution, and dilute with water to 1 L.

Barium (0.1 mg of Ba in 1 ml) – Dissolve 0.178 g of barium chloride dihydrate, $BaCl_2 \cdot 2H_2O$, in water, and dilute with water to 1 L.

Bismuth (0.01 mg of Bi in 1 ml) – Dissolve 0.232 g of bismuth trinitrate pentahydrate, $Bi(NO_3)_3 \cdot 5\ H_2O$, in 10 ml of dilute nitric acid (1 + 9), and dilute with water to 100 ml. Dilute 10 ml of this solution plus 10 ml of nitric acid with water to 1 L.

Bromate (0.1 mg of BrO_3 in 1 ml) – Dissolve 0.131 g of potassium bromate, $KBrO_3$, in water, and dilute with water to 1 L.

Bromide (0.1 mg of Br in 1 ml) – Dissolve 1.49 g of potassium bromide, KBr, in water, and dilute with water to 100 ml. Dilute 10 ml of this solution with water to 1 L.

Cadmium (0.025 mg of Cd in 1 ml) – Dissolve 0.10 g of cadmium chloride 2.5-hydrate, $CdCl_2 \cdot 2\text{-}1/2\ H_2O$, in water, add

1 ml of hydrochloric acid, and dilute with water to 500 ml. To 25 ml of this solution, add 1 ml of hydrochloric acid, and dilute with water to 100 ml.

Calcium (0.1 mg of Ca in 1 ml) – Dissolve 0.250 g of calcium carbonate, $CaCO_3$, in 20 ml of water plus 5 ml of 10% hydrochloric acid reagent solution, and dilute with water to 1 L.

Calcium (0.01 mg of Ca in 1 ml) – Dilute 100 ml of the preceding solution with water to 1 L.

Carbon (4 mg of C in 1 ml) – Dissolve 8.5 g of potassium hydrogen phthalate, $HOCOC_6H_4COOK$, in water, and dilute to 1 L.

Carbonate (0.3 mg of CO_3, 0.2 mg of CO_2, or 0.06 mg of C in 1 ml) – Dissolve 0.53 g of sodium carbonate, Na_2CO_3, in carbon dioxide-free water, and dilute with carbon dioxide-free water to 1 L. Prepare the solution at the time of use.

Chloride (0.01 mg of Cl in 1 ml) – Dissolve 0.165 g of sodium chloride, NaCl, in water, and dilute with water to 100 ml. Dilute 10 ml of this solution with water to 1 L.

Chlorine (0.01 mg of Cl 2 in 1 ml) – Dilute 1.0 ml of a 2.5% sodium hypochlorite, NaOCl, solution with water to 1 L. Correct for any assay not equal to 2.5%. Standardize the sodium hypochlorite solution before use by the following method: Pipette 3 ml into a tared, glass-stoppered flask. Weigh accurately, and add 50 ml of water, 2 g of potassium iodide, and 10 ml of acetic acid. Titrate the liberated iodine with 0.1 N sodium thiosulfate, adding 3 ml of starch indicator solution near the end point. One milliliter of 0.1 N sodium thiosulfate corresponds to 3.723 mg of NaOCl.

Chlorobenzene (0.1 mg of C_6H_5Cl in 1 ml) – Dilute 1.0 ml of chlorobenzene to 100 ml with 2,2,4-trimethylpentane. Dilute 9.0 ml of this solution to 100 ml with 2,2,4-trimethylpentane.

Chromate (0.01 mg of CrO_4 in 1 ml) – Dissolve 1.268 g of potassium dichromate, $K_2Cr_2O_7$, in water, and dilute with water to 1 L. Dilute 1.0 ml of this solution to 100 ml.

Copper Stock Solution (0.1 mg of Cu in 1 ml) – Dissolve 0.393 g of cupric sulfate pentahydrate, $CuSO_4 \cdot 5\,H_2O$, in water, and dilute with water to 1 L.

Copper Standard for Dithizone Test (0.001 mg of Cu in 1 ml) – Dilute 1 ml of the copper stock solution with water to 100 ml. This dilute solution must be prepared immediately before use.

Ferric Iron (0.1 mg of Fe^{3}+ in 1 ml) – Dissolve 0.863 g of ferric ammonium sulfate dodecahydrate, $FeNH_4(SO_4)_2 \cdot 12H_2O$, in water, and dilute with water to 1 L.

Fluoride Stock Solution (1 mg of F in 1 ml) – Dissolve 2.21 g of sodium fluoride, NaF, previously dried at 110°C for 2 hours and dissolve with 200 ml of water in a 400 ml plastic beaker. Transfer to a 1 L volumetric flask, dilute with water to the mark, and store the solution in a plastic bottle.

Fluoride (0.005 mg in 1 ml) – Transfer 5.0 ml of the fluoride stock solution to a 1 L plastic volumetric flask, dilute with water to the mark, and store in a plastic bottle. Prepare the solution at the time of use.

Formaldehyde (0.1 mg of HCHO in 1 ml) – Dilute 2.7 g (2.7 ml) of 37% formaldehyde solution to 1 L with water (prepare freshly as needed). Dilute 10 ml of this solution to 100 ml.

Formaldehyde (0.01 mg of HCHO in 1 ml) – Dilute 10 ml of the preceding solution with water to 100 ml. Prepare the solution at the time of use.

Hydrogen Peroxide (0.1 mg of H_2O_2 in 1 ml) – Dilute 3.0 ml of 30% hydrogen peroxide with water to 100 ml. Dilute 1.0 ml of this solution with water to 100 ml. Prepare the solution at the time of use.

Iodate (0.10 mg of IO_3 in 1 ml) – Dissolve 0.123 g of potassium iodate, KIO_3, in water, and dilute to 1 L.

Iodate (0.01 mg of IO_3 in 1 ml) – Dilute 10 ml of the preceding iodate solution (0.10 mg of IO_3 in 1 ml) to 100 ml.

Iodide (0.01 mg of I in 1 ml) – Dissolve 0.131 g of potassium iodide, KI, in water, and dilute with water to 100 ml. Dilute 10 ml of this solution with water to 1 L.

Iron (0.01 mg of Fe in 1 ml) – Dissolve 0.702 g of ferrous ammonium sulfate hexahydrate, $Fe(NH_4)_2(SO_4)_2 \cdot 6H_2O$, in 10 ml of 10% sulfuric acid reagent solution, and dilute with water to 100 ml. To 10 ml of this solution, add 10 ml of 10% sulfuric acid reagent solution, and dilute with water to 1 L.

Lead Stock Solution (0.1 mg of Pb in 1 ml) – Dissolve 0.160 g of lead nitrate, $Pb(NO_3)_2$, in 100 ml of dilute nitric acid (1 + 99), and dilute with water to 1 L. The solution should be prepared and stored in containers free from lead. Its strength should be checked every few months to determine whether the lead content has changed by reaction with the container.

Lead Standard for Dithizone Test (0.001 mg of Pb in 1 ml) – Dilute 1 ml of the lead stock solution to 100 ml with dilute nitric acid (1 + 99). This solution must be prepared immediately before use.

Lead Standard for Heavy Metals Test (0.01 mg of Pb in 1 ml) – Dilute 10 ml of the lead stock solution to 100 ml with water. This dilute solution must be prepared at the time of use.

Magnesium (0.01 mg of Mg in 1 ml) – Dissolve 1.014 g of clear crystals of magnesium sulfate heptahydrate, $MgSO_4 \cdot 7H_2O$, in water, and dilute with water to 100 ml. Dilute 10 ml of this solution with water to 1 L.

Magnesium (0.002 mg of Mg in 1 ml) – Dilute 100 ml of the preceding solution with water to 500 ml. Prepare the solution at the time of use.

Manganese (0.01 mg of Mn in 1 ml) – Dissolve 3.08 g of manganese sulfate monohydrate, $MnSO_4 \cdot H_2O$, in water, and dilute with water to 1 L. Dilute 10 ml of this solution with water to 1 L.

Mercury (0.05 mg of Hg in 1 ml) – Dissolve 1.35 g of mercuric chloride, $HgCl_2$, in water, add 8 ml of hydrochloric acid, and dilute with water to 1 L. To 50 ml of this solution, add 8 ml of hydrochloric acid, and dilute with water to 1 L.

Methanol (0.1 mg of CH_3OH in 1 ml) – Dilute 5.1 ml of methanol, CH_3OH, with water to 200 ml. Dilute 5.0 ml of this solution with water to 1 L. Prepare the solution at the time of use.

Molybdenum (0.01 mg of Mo in 1 ml) – Dissolve 0.150 g of molybdenum trioxide, MoO_3, in 10 ml of dilute ammonium hydroxide (1 + 9), and dilute with water to 100 ml. Dilute 10 ml of this solution with water to 1 L.

Nickel (0.01 mg of Ni in 1 ml) – Dissolve 0.448 g of nickel sulfate hexahydrate, $NiSO_4 \cdot 6H_2O$, in water, and dilute with water to 100 ml. Dilute 10 ml of this solution with water to 1 L.

Nitrate (0.01 mg of NO_3 in 1 ml) – Dissolve 0.163 g of potassium nitrate, KNO_3, in water, and dilute with water to 100 ml. Dilute 10 ml of this solution with water to 1 L.

Nitrilotriacetic Acid (10 mg of $(HOCOCH_2)_3N$ in 1 ml) – Transfer 1.0 g of nitrilotriacetic acid, $(HOCOCH_2)_3N$, to a 100 ml volumetric flask. Dissolve in 10 ml of 10% potassium hydroxide solution, and dilute with water to volume.

Nitrite (0.01 mg of NO_2 in 1 ml) – Dissolve 0.150 g of sodium nitrite ($NaNO_2$) in water, and dilute with water to 100 ml. Dilute 1.0 ml of this solution with water to 100 ml. This solution should be freshly prepared.

Nitrite (0.001 mg of NO_2 in 1 ml) – Dissolve 0.150 g of sodium nitrite, $NaNO_2$ in water, and dilute with water to 100 ml. Dilute 0.1 ml of this solution with water to 100 ml. This solution must be prepared at the time of use.

Nitrogen (0.01 mg of N in 1 ml) – Dissolve 0.382 g of ammonium chloride, NH_4Cl, in water, and dilute with water to 100 ml. Dilute 10 ml of this solution with water to 1 L.

Phosphate (0.01 mg of PO_4 in 1 ml). Dissolve 0.143 g of monobasic potassium phosphate, KH_2PO_4, in water, and dilute with water to 100 ml. Dilute 10 ml of this solution with water to 1 L.

Potassium (0.01 mg of K in 1 ml) – Dissolve 0.191 g of potassium chloride, KCl, in water, and dilute with water to 1 L. Dilute 100 ml of this solution with water to 1 L.

Selenium (1 μg of Se in 1 ml) – Transfer 0.10 ml of standard (1000 g/g Se, commercially available standard) to a 100 ml volumetric flask, and dilute to the mark with water. Prepare fresh before use.

Silica (0.01 mg of SiO_2 in 1 ml) – Dissolve 0.473 g of sodium silicate, $Na_2SiO_3 \cdot 9H_2O$, in 100 ml of water in a platinum or polyethylene dish. Dilute 10 ml of this solution (polyethylene graduate) with water to 1 L in a polyethylene bottle.

Silver (0.1 mg of Ag in 1 ml) – Dissolve 0.157 g of silver nitrate, $AgNO_3$, in water, and dilute with water to 1 L.

Sodium (0.01 mg of Na in 1 ml) – Dissolve 0.254 g of sodium chloride, NaCl, in water, and dilute with water to 1 L. Dilute 100 ml of this solution with water to 1 L.

Strontium Stock Solution (1 mg of Sr in 1 ml) – Dissolve 0.242 g of strontium nitrate, $Sr(NO_3)_2$, in water, and dilute with water to 100 ml.

Strontium (0.1 mg of Sr in 1 ml) – Dilute 10 ml of the strontium stock solution with water to 100 ml.

Strontium (0.01 mg of Sr in 1 ml) – Dilute 10 ml of the strontium stock solution with water to 1 L.

Sulfate (0.01 mg of SO_4 in 1 ml) – Dissolve 0.148 g of anhydrous sodium sulfate, Na_2SO_4, in water, and dilute with water to 100 ml. Dilute 10 ml of this solution with water to 1 L.

Sulfide (0.01 mg of S in 1 ml) – Dissolve 0.75 g of sodium sulfide nonahydrate, $Na_2S \cdot 9H_2O$, in water, and dilute with water to 100 ml. Dilute 10 ml of this solution with water to 1 L. This solution must be prepared immediately before use.

Tin (0.05 mg of Sn in 1 ml) – Dissolve 0.100 g of metallic tin (Sn) in 10 ml of dilute hydrochloric acid (1 + 1), and dilute with water to 100 ml. Dilute 5 ml of this solution with dilute hydrochloric acid (1 + 9) to 100 ml. This solution must be prepared immediately before use.

Titanium (0.1 mg of Ti in 1 ml) – Dissolve 0.739 g of potassium titanyl oxalate dihydrate, $K_2TiO(C_2O_4)_2 \cdot 2H_2O$, in water, and dilute with water to 1 L.

Zinc Stock Solution (0.1 mg of Zn in 1 ml) – Dissolve 0.124 g of zinc oxide, ZnO, in 10 ml of dilute sulfuric acid (1 + 9), and dilute with water to 1 L.

Zinc Standard for Dithizone Tests (0.001 mg of Zn in 1 ml) – Dilute 1 ml of the zinc stock solution with water to 100 ml. This dilute solution must be prepared immediately before use.

VOLUMETRIC SOLUTIONS: PREPARATION AND STANDARDIZATION

General Information

The concentrations of volumetric solutions usually are expressed as N, normality (the number of gram equivalent weights in each litre of solution), although concentration sometimes is expressed as M, molarity (the number of gram molecular weights in each liter of solution).

The accuracy of many analytical procedures is dependent on the manner in which such solutions are prepared, standardized and stored. The directions that follow describe the preparation of these solutions and their standardization against primary standards or against already-standardized solutions. Alternatively, in cases where suitable primary standard chemicals are available, volumetric solutions may be prepared by dissolving accurately weighed portions of these substances to make an accurately known volume of solution. All volumetric solutions, of course, must be thoroughly mixed as part of their preparation. Stronger or weaker solutions than those described are prepared and standardized in the same general manner, using proportional amounts of reagents and standards. Lower strengths frequently may be prepared by accurately diluting a stronger solution. However, when necessary because of the accuracy requirements of the analysis being performed, volumetric solutions prepared in this manner should be standardized before use against a primary standard or by comparison with an appropriate volumetric solution of known strength.

It is desirable to standardize a solution in such a way that the end point is observed at the same pH value (or oxidation-reduction potential) anticipated during subsequent use. For example, a sodium hydroxide solution found to be 0.1000 N when standardized against potassium hydrogen phthalate to phenolphthalein (pH 8.5) may behave as though 0.1002 N when used for titrating a strong acid to methyl red (pH 5). Only a small part of this difference is due to the NaOH required to bring pure water from pH 5 to 8.5. In this case, the error can be avoided by titrating the strong acid to phenolphthalein (pH 8.5), the same indicator that was used in standardizing the sodium hydroxide.

Storage

Glass containers are suitable for the storage of most volumetric solutions. However, polyolefin containers are recommended for alkaline solutions. Volumetric solutions are stable for varying lengths of time, depending on their chemical nature and their concentration. Dilute solutions are likely to be less stable than those that are 0.1 N or stronger. If there is any doubt about the reliability of a solution, it should be restandardized at the time of use.

Temperature Considerations

If possible, volumetric solutions should be prepared, standardized, and used at 25° C. If a titration is carried out at a temperature different from that at which the solution was standardized, a temperature correction may be needed, depending on the accuracy requirement of the analysis being performed. If the temperature of use is higher than the temperature of standardization, the correction is to be subtracted from the standardization value; if the temperature of use is lower than the temperature of standardization, the correction is to be added. For guidance with respect to temperature corrections, consider that a 5°C temperature change will alter the normalities of solutions approximately as follows: For aqueous solutions 0.1 N or less, by 1 part in 1000; 0.5 N, by 1.2 parts in 1000; and 1 N, by 1.4 parts in 1000. For non-aqueous solutions, based on the expansion coefficients of the solvents, by 5.4 parts in 1000 for glacial acetic acid; 5.5 parts in 1000 for dioxane; and 6.2 parts in 1000 for methanol.

Errors caused by temperature differences, as well as by improper drainage of burettes or pipettes, can be avoided if measurements are made on a weight basis. With a sensitive direct-reading balance and the use of squeeze bottles, titrations by weight have become very practical and precise.

Correction Factors

It is not necessary that volumetric solutions have the identical normalities (or molarities) indicated in this section, or as specified in many of the standardization and assay calculations in this book. It is necessary, however, that the exact value be known, because if it is different from the nominal value specified, a correction factor will have to be applied. Thus, if a calculation is based on an exactly 0.1 N volumetric solution, and the solution actually used is 0.1008 N, its volume must be multiplied by a factor of 1.008 to obtain the corrected volume of 0.1 N solution to use in the calculation. Similarly, if the actual normality is 0.0984 N, the factor is 0.984.

Replication

Because the results obtained by titrations depend on the reliability of the volumetric solutions used, it is imperative that the latter be standardized at least in duplicate, with particular care, and preferably by experienced analysts. Duplicate standardizations for solutions from 0.1 N to 1 N should agree at least to within 2 parts in 1000. Duplicates for 0.05 N solutions may differ by as much as 10 parts in 1000. If deviations are greater than indicated, the determinations should be repeated until the criteria are met.

Volumetric Solutions

Acetic Acid, 1 N

Add 61 g (58.1 ml) of glacial acetic acid to sufficient water to make 1 L, and mix thoroughly. Standardize as follows: Measure accurately 40 ml of the solution into a 250-ml conical flask, add 0.10 ml of phenolphthalein indicator solution, and titrate with 1 N sodium hydroxide volumetric solution to a permanent pink colour.

EDTA, 0.1 M

Dissolve 37.22 g of $Na_2EDTA \cdot 2\,H_2O$ in 500 ml of water in a 1 L volumetric flask, dilute to mark, and mix thoroughly. Standardize as follows: Weigh accurately 0.40 g of calcium carbonate, chelometric standard, transfer to a 400 ml beaker, and add water. Cover the beaker with a watch glass, and introduce 4 ml of hydrochloric acid (1 + 1) from a pipette inserted between the lip of the beaker and the edge of the watch glass. Swirl the contents of the beaker to dissolve the calcium carbonate. Wash down the sides of the beaker and the watch glass with water, and dilute to 200 ml. While stirring, add from a 50 ml burette about 30 ml of EDTA standard solution. Adjust the solution to pH 12–13 with 10% sodium hydroxide and 300 mg of hydroxy naphthol blue indicator, and continue titration with the EDTA standard solution to a blue end point.

Ferrous Ammonium Sulfate, 0.1 N

Dissolve 40 g of ferrous ammonium sulfate hexahydrate in 200 ml of 25% sulfuric acid, dilute to 1 L with water, and mix thoroughly. On each day of use, standardize as follows: Measure accurately 40 ml of the solution into a 250 ml conical flask, add 0.1 ml of 1,10-phenanthroline reagent solution, and titrate with 0.1 N ceric ammonium sulfate volumetric solution to the change from pink to pale blue.

Hydrochloric Acid, 1 N

Dilute 85 ml of hydrochloric acid to 1 L, and mix thoroughly. Standardize as follows: Weigh accurately about 2.2 g of sodium carbonate, alkalimetric standard, that previously has been heated at 285°C for 2 hours. Dissolve in 100 ml of water, and add 0.1 ml of methyl red indicator solution. Add the acid slowly from a burette, with stirring, until the solution becomes faintly pink. Heat the solution to boiling, cool, and again titrate until the solution becomes faintly pink. Repeat this procedure until the faint colour is no longer discharged on further boiling.

Iodine, 0.1 N

Place approximately 40 g of potassium iodide and 10 ml of water in a large, glass-stoppered weighing bottle. Mix the contents by swirling; allow to come to room temperature, and then weigh accurately. Add approximately 12.7 g of assayed iodine, previously weighed on a rough balance, and reweigh the stoppered bottle and contents to obtain the exact weight of the iodine added. Mix and transfer quantitatively to a 1 L volumetric flask, dilute to the mark, and mix thoroughly. For approximate work, calculate the normality from the weight and assay value of the iodine taken (atomic weight = 126.90). For more exact work, standardize as follows: Measure accurately 40 ml of 0.1 N arsenious acid volumetric solution into a 250 ml conical flask. Add 2 g of sodium bicarbonate dissolved in 20 ml of water, and titrate with the iodine solution until within about 2 ml of the anticipated equivalence point. Then add 3 ml of starch indicator solution, and continue the titration to the first permanent blue tinge.

Oxalic Acid 0.1 N

Dissolve 6.5 g of oxalic acid dihydrate in 200 ml of water, and dilute to 1000 ml in a volumetric flask. Mix well. Measure accurately 40 ml of the solution in a 250 ml conical flask, add 50 ml of water and 7 ml of sulfuric acid and slowly with stirring add 30 ml of 0.1 N potassium permanganate volumetric solution. Heat the solution to 70°C and continue the titration until the pink colour persists for 30 s.

Potassium Dichromate, 0.1 N

Weigh exactly 4.903 g of potassium dichromate, NIST Standard Reference Material, previously dried for 4 hours at 120°C, transfer to a 1 L volumetric flask, dilute to volume, and mix thoroughly.

Potassium Hydroxide, Methanolic, 0.1 N

Dissolve 6.8 g of potassium hydroxide in a minimum amount of water (about 5 ml), dilute to 1 L with methanol, and mix thoroughly. Allow to stand in a container protected from carbon dioxide for 24 hours. Carefully decant the clear solution, leaving any residue behind, into a suitable container, mix well, and store protected from carbon dioxide. Standardize as follows: Weigh accurately about 0.85 g of potassium hydrogen phthalate, Acidimetric Standard, previously lightly crushed and dried for 2 hours at 120°C. Dissolve in 100 ml of carbon dioxide-free water, add 0.15 ml of phenolphthalein indicator solution, and titrate with the methanolic potassium hydroxide solution to a permanent faint pink colour.

Potassium Iodate, 0.05 M

Weigh exactly 10.700 g of potassium iodate, previously dried at 110°C to constant weight, transfer to a 1 L volumetric flask, dilute to volume, and mix thoroughly.

Potassium Permanganate, 0.1 N

Dissolve 3.3 g of potassium permanganate in 1 L of water in a 1500 ml conical flask, heat to boiling, and boil gently for 15 min. Allow to cool, stopper, and keep in the dark for 48 hours. Then filter through a fine-porosity sintered-glass filter, and place in a glass-stoppered amber bottle. Standardize as follows: Weigh accurately 0.24-0.28 g of sodium oxalate, NIST Standard Reference Material, prepared for use as directed in the applicable NIST certificate, transfer to a 500 ml conical flask containing 250 ml of water and 7 ml of sulfuric acid, and heat to 70°C. Titrate immediately with the permanganate solution to a pink colour that persists for 15 s. The temperature at the end of the titration should not be less than 60°C.

Potassium Thiocyanate, 0.1 N

Weigh exactly 9.7 g of potassium thiocyanate, previously dried for 2 hours at 110°C, transfer to a 1 L volumetric flask, dilute to volume, and mix thoroughly. Standardize as follows: Measure accurately 40 ml of 0.1 N silver nitrate volumetric solution into a 500 ml conical flask and add 100 ml of water, 1 ml of nitric acid, and 2 ml of ferric ammonium sulfate indicator solution. Titrate with the thiocyanate solution, with agitation, to a permanent light pinkish-brown colour of the supernatant solution.

Silver Nitrate, 0.1 N

Weigh exactly 16.987 g of silver nitrate, previously dried for 1 hour at 100°C, transfer to a 1 L volumetric flask, dilute to volume, and mix thoroughly. Standardize as follows: Weigh accurately about 0.33 g of potassium chloride, previously dried for 2 hours at 110°C, place in a 250 ml beaker, and dissolve in 50 ml of water and 1 ml of nitric acid. Pipette 50 ml of the silver nitrate solution into the beaker, slowly, and with agitation. Heat to boiling, cool in the dark, and filter, washing the precipitate thoroughly with 1% nitric acid. To the filtrate, add 2 ml of ferric ammonium sulfate indicator solution, and titrate the excess silver nitrate with 0.1 N potassium thiocyanate volumetric solution, with agitation, to a permanent light pinkish-brown colour of the supernatant solution.

Sodium Hydroxide, 1 N

Dissolve 162 g of sodium hydroxide in 150 ml of carbon dioxide-free water, cool the solution to room temperature, and filter through a suitable filter, such as hardened filter paper. (*Note:* A reagent-grade 50% sodium hydroxide solution may be used in place of the solution prepared in this way). Prepare a 1 N solution by diluting 54.5 ml of the concentrated solution to 1 L with carbon dioxide-free water. Mix thoroughly, and store in a tight polyolefin container. Standardize as follows: Weigh accurately about 8.5 g of potassium hydrogen phthalate, Acidimetric Standard, previously lightly crushed and dried for 2 hours at 120°C. Dissolve in 100 ml of carbon dioxide-free water, add 0.15 ml of phenolphthalein indicator solution, and titrate with the sodium hydroxide solution to a permanent faint pink colour.

Sodium Thiosulfate, 0.1 N

Weigh accurately about 210 mg of NIST current standard reference material potassium dichromate, previously crushed and dried at 120°C for 4 hours. Dissolve in 100 ml of water in a glass-stoppered iodine flask. Swirl to dissolve the sample, remove the stopper, and quickly add 3 g of potassium iodide, 2 g of sodium bicarbonate, and 5 ml of hydrochloric acid. Insert the stopper, swirl slightly to release excess carbon dioxide, cover the stopper with water, and allow to stand in dark for 10 min. Rinse the stopper and the inner walls of the flask with water and titrate the liberated iodine with the sodium thiosulfate until solution becomes faintly yellow in colour. Add 3 ml of starch indicator solution and continue the titration to the disappearance of the blue colour. Restandardize the solution frequently.

Sulfuric Acid, 1 N

Add slowly (use caution), with stirring, 30 ml of sulfuric acid to about 500 ml of water. Allow the mixture to cool to room temperature, dilute to 1 L, and mix thoroughly. Standardize against sodium carbonate, Alkalimetric Standard, as directed for hydrochloric acid, 1 N.

TESTING PROCEDURE AT A GLANCE

Analysis	Definition	Method
Acidity – total	Acidity phenolphthalein Reported as $CaCO_3$	Titration with standard base to phenolphthalein end point
Acidity-free mineral	Acidity to methyl orange Reported as $CaCO_3$	Titration with standard base to methyl orange end point, or potentiometric to pH 4.5
Alkalinity – total	Alkalinity to methyl orange. Reported as $CaCO_3$	Titration with standard acid to methyl orange end point, or potentiometric to pH 4.5
Alkalinity – hydroxide	Alkalinity to phenolphthalein after precipitation of carbonate Reported as $CaCO_3$	Precipitation of carbonate with $BaCl_2$. Titration with standard acid to phenolphthalein end point.
Alkalinity – phenolphthalein	Alkalinity to phenolphthalein Reported as $CaCO_3$	Titration with standard acid to phenolphthalein end point.
Aluminium (Al) – total	Soluble and insoluble aluminium	Atomic absorption spectroscopy
Aluminium (Al) - soluble	Soluble aluminium	Filtration – atomic absorption spectroscopy
Ammonia (NH_3)	Evolvable ammonia nitrogen	Distillation at pH 9.5 followed by Nesselerization or titration with standard acid
Antimony (Sb) – total	Soluble and insoluble antimony	Atomic absorption spectroscopy
Arsenic (As) – total	Soluble and insoluble arsenic	Atomic absorption spectroscopy
Barium (Ba) – total	Soluble and insoluble barium	Atomic absorption spectroscopy
Beryllium (Be) – total	Soluble and insoluble beryllium	Atomic absorption spectroscopy
Biochemical oxygen demand (BOD)	Biochemical oxygen demand	Dilution – 5 day incubation – dissolved oxygen determination
Bismuth (Bi) – total	Soluble and insoluble bismuth	Atomic absorption spectroscopy
Boron (B)	Soluble and insoluble boron	Colorimetric (circumin) or mannitol titration
Bromide (Br)	Bromide ion concentration	Conversion to bromate titration
Cadmium (Cd) – total	Soluble and insoluble cadmium	Atomic absorption spectroscopy

Analysis	Definition	Method
Calcium (Ca) – total	Soluble and insoluble calcium	Atomic absorption spectroscopy
Calcium (Ca) – soluble	Soluble calcium	Filtration – atomic absorption
Cesium (Cs) – total	Soluble and insoluble cesium	Atomic absorption spectroscopy
Chloride (Cl)	Soluble chloride ion concentration	Titration with silver nitrate – chromate indicator
Chromium (Cr) – total	Soluble and insoluble chromium	Atomic absorption spectroscopy
Chromium (Cr^{+6}) – hexavalent	Hexavalent chromium	Colorimetric (diphenylcarbazide) or titration with thiosulfate
Cobalt (Co) – total	Soluble and insoluble cobalt	Atomic absorption spectroscopy
Chemical oxygen demand (COD)	Determination of organic and oxidizable inorganic material	Oxidation with potassium dichromate – titration with ferrous ammonium sulfate
Conductivity	Determination of specific conductance – ambient temperature	Conductivity meter
Copper (Cu) – soluble	Soluble copper	Filtration – atomic absorption spectroscopy
Cyanide (CN) – free and combined	Free and combined cyanide	Distillation – colorimetric (pyridine barbituric acid) or titration with silver nitrate
Cyanide (CN) – free	Free cyanide	Distillation – colorimetric (pyridine barbituric acid) or titration with silver nitrate
Fluoride (F) – free and combined	Free and combined fluoride ion concentration	Distillation – ion – selective
Fluoride (F) – free	Free fluoride ion concentration	Ion selective electrode
Hardness – total	Hardness due to calcium and magnesium Reported as $CaCO_3$	Titration with EDTA using Erichrome black T indicator
Hardness – Calcium	Hardness due to calcium ions Reported as $CaCO_3$	Titration with EDTA using Muroxide indicator
Gold (Au) – total	Soluble and insoluble gold	Atomic absorption spectroscopy
Iodide (I)	Iodide ion concentration	Conversion to iodate – titration with sodium thiosulfate

Analysis	Definition	Method
Iron (Fe) – total	Soluble and insoluble iron	Atomic absorption spectroscopy
Iron (Fe) – soluble	Soluble iron	Filtration – atomic absorption spectroscopy
Iron (Fe) – total	Soluble and insoluble iron	Colorimetric method
Lead (Pb) – total	Soluble and insoluble lead	Atomic absorption spectroscopy
Lithium (Li) – total	Soluble and insoluble lithium	Atomic absorption spectroscopy
Magnesium (Mg) – total	Soluble and insoluble magnesium	Atomic absorption spectroscopy
Magnesium (Mg) – soluble	Soluble magnesium	Filtration – atomic absorption spectroscopy
Manganese (Mn) – total	Soluble and insoluble manganese	Atomic absorption spectroscopy
Mercury (Hg) – total	Soluble and insoluble mercury	Flameless atomic absorption spectroscopy (cold vapour technique)
Molybdenum (Mo) – total	Soluble and insoluble molybdenum	Atomic absorption spectroscopy
Nickel (Ni) – total	Soluble and insoluble nickel	Atomic absorption spectroscopy
Nitrate (NO_3)	Nitrate ion concentration	Colorimetric method
Nitrite (NO_2)	Nitrite ion concentration	Colorimetric method
Nitrogen (N) – Kjeldahl	Total free and combined ammonia nitrogen	Kjeldahl digestion – distillation – Nesselerization or titration with standard acid
Nitrogen (N) – organic	Total combined ammonia nitrogen	Evolution of free ammonia – Kjeldahl digestion – distillation – Nesselerization or titration with standard acid
Oil and grease – hexane	Hexane extractable – non-volatile at 70°C	Acidification – liquid – liquid extraction with Freon gravimetric determination
pH	Measurement of hydrogen ion activity in aqueous solution	pH meter
Phenols	Phenols reacting with 4–amino antipyrine	Distillation – colorimetric (4–amino – antipyrine)
Phosphorus (P) – total	Total organic and inorganic phosphorus	Oxidation with per sulfate reversion – colorimetric

Analysis	Definition	Method
Phosphorus (P) – total inorganic	Soluble and insoluble ortho and poly phosphate	Reversion in acid – colorimetric
Phosphorus (P) – soluble inorganic	Soluble ortho and polyphosphate	Filtration – reversion – colorimetric
Phosphorus (P) – orhto	Soluble and insoluble phosphate	Colorimetric
Platinum (pt) – total	Soluble and insoluble platinum	Atomic absorption spectroscopy
Potassium (K) – total	Soluble and insoluble potassium	Atomic absorption spectroscopy
Selenium (Se) – total	Soluble and insoluble selenium	Atomic absorption spectroscopy – flameless (graphite furnace) or flame (hydride generation)
Silica (SiO_2)	Molybdate reactive silica	Colorimetric (ammonium molybdate with 1-amino-2-naphthol-4-sulfonic acid reduction)
Silver (Ag) – total	Soluble and insoluble silver	Atomic absorption spectroscopy
Sodium (Na) – total	Soluble and insoluble sodium	Atomic absorption spectroscopy
Solids – total	Total filterable and non-filterable residue – non-volatile at 180°C	Gravimetric determination – dried 180°C
Solids – total dissolved	Total filterable residue – non-volatile at 180°C	Millipore filtration – gravimetric determination on filtrate dried at 180°C
Solids – total fixed	Total residue remaining after ignition at 550°C	Gravimetric determination – ignition at 550°C
Solids – total suspended	Total non-filterable residue – non-volatile at 105°C	Millipore filtration – gravimetric determination – dried at 105°C
Solids – volatile suspended	Total non-filterable residue volatile at 550°C	Millipore filtration – gravimetric determination – dried at 550°C
Solids – total volatile	Total residue volatile at 550°C	Difference between total solids and total fixed solids
Solids – settleable	Settleable solids at 5 min and 1 hr	Imhoff cone
Strontium (Sr) – total	Soluble and insoluble strontium	Atomic absorption spectroscopy
Sulphate (SO_4)	Soluble sulphate	Turbidimetric

Analysis	Definition	Method
Sulfide (S)	Sulfide ion concentration	Evolution – iodometric titration or colorimetric (methylene blue)
Surfactants – anionic	Methylene blue active substances	Colorimetric (methylene blue dye and chloroform extraction)
Thallium (Tl) – total	Soluble and insoluble thallium	Atomic absorption spectroscopy
Thiosulphate	Thiosulphate ion concentration	Iodometric
Tin (Sn) – total	Soluble and insoluble tin	Atomic absorption spectroscopy
Titanium (Ti) – total	Soluble and insoluble titanium	Atomic absorption spectroscopy
Turbidity	Light scatter reported in nephelometric turbidity units	Nephelometric
Vanadium	Soluble and insoluble vanadium	Atomic absorption spectroscopy
Zinc (Zn) – total	Soluble and insoluble zinc	Atomic absorption spectroscopy
Zinc (Zn) – soluble	Soluble zinc spectroscopy	Filtration – atomic absorption
Zirconium (Zr) – total	Soluble and insoluble zirconium	Atomic absorption spectroscopy

FEW OTHER WATER-RELATED STANDARDS OF BIS

Terminology

IS 7022 (Pt 1): 1973	Glossary of terms relating to water, sewage and industrial effluent, Part 1
IS 7022 (Pt 2): 1973	Glossary of terms relating to water, sewage and industrial effluent, Part 2
IS 10446: 1983	Glossary of terms for water supply and sanitation

Methods of sampling and analysis – Sewage and industrial effluents

IS 2488 (Pt 1): 1966	Methods of sampling and test for industrial effluents, Part 1
IS 2488 (Pt 2): 1966	Methods of sampling and test for industrial effluents, Part 2
IS 2488 (Pt 3): 1966	Methods of sampling and test for industrial effluents, Part 3
IS 2488 (Pt 4): 1966	Methods of sampling and test for industrial effluents, Part 4
IS 2488 (Pt 5): 1966	Methods of sampling and test for industrial effluents, Part 5
IS 4733: 1971	Methods of sampling and test for sewage effluents
IS 6582: 1971	Bio-assay methods for evaluation of acute toxicity of industrial effluents and wastewater

Treatment for disposal of industrial effluents

IS 4903: 1979	Guide for treatment and disposal of effluents of cane sugar in industry
IS 5061 (Pt 1): 1978	Guide for treatment and disposal of effluents of pulp, paper and board industry, Part 1 – For mills with chemical recovery systems
IS 5183: 1977	Guide for treatment and disposal of effluents of tanning industry

IS 7453: 1974	Guide for treatment of effluents of electroplating industry
IS 7967: 1976	Criteria for controlling pollution of marine coastal areas
IS 8032: 1976	Guide for treatment and disposal of distillery effluents
IS 8073: 1976	Guide for treatment and disposal of steel plant effluents
IS 8682: 1977	Guide for treatment of effluents of dairy industry
IS 9427: 1980	Code of practice for operating and maintenance of deionizing columns
IS 9508: 1980	Guide for treatment and disposal of effluents of cotton and synthetic textile industry
IS 9509: 1980	Guide for treatment and disposal of effluents of viscose rayon industry
IS 9841: 1981	Guide for treatment and disposal of effluents of fertilizer industry
IS 10044: 1981	Guide for treatment and disposal of effluents of petroleum refinery industry
IS 10495: 1983	Guide for treatment and disposal of effluents of wool processing industry

UNITS OF MEASUREMENT

1 milligram per liter (mg/L) = 1 parts per million (ppm) = 1000 parts per billion (ppb)

1 microgram per liter (µg/L)= 1 nanogram per milliliter (ng/ml) = 1 part per billion (ppb)

1 nanogram per liter (ng/L) = 1 part per trillion (ppt) = 1000 parts per quadrillion (ppq)

1 picogram per liter (pg/L) = 1 part per quadrillion (ppq)

1 grain per gallon (gpg) = 117.1 milligrams per liter (mg/L)

ACCREDITATION OF LABORATORIES

Laboratory accreditation is the formal recognition, authorization and registration of a laboratory that has demonstrated its capability, competence and credibility to carry out specific test or types of tests claimed by the laboratory. Accreditation of laboratories creates a transparent situation in the world of quality assurance and is a powerful tool in developing and establishing confidence and credibility between parties in the market. The accredited laboratory is authorized to issue calibration/test reports and reports of chemical analysis which are recognized and accepted internationally.

Under Section 51/52 of the Water Act, the Central/State Government may establish a Central/State Laboratory, or specify any Laboratory/and State Laboratory or institute as a Central/ State Water Laboratory to carry out analysis of water and wastewater samples. Under Section 53 of the Water Act, the Central/State Government may appoint a Government Analyst for analysis of water and wastewater samples sent for analysis to any laboratory established or specified under the Water Act. Similar provisions are there under Section 12 and 13 of the Environment (Protection) Act, 1986 for recognition of laboratories or institutes as Environmental Laboratories to carry out functions entrusted to an environmental laboratory, and appointment of a Government Analyst through Official Gazette Notification.

A laboratory seeking accreditation must be able to demonstrate that it is meeting all the requirements of National Accreditation Board for Testing and Calibration Laboratories (NABL) accreditation criteria Doc. 101 (1994). NABL Doc. 101 is consistent with the provisions of ISO/IEC – Guide 25 and European Standards EN 45001. ISO/IEC – Guide 25 has been amended and the new standard is ISO – 17025. After adoption of ISO – 17025 standard, the laboratories will be given a time limit to update their quality to new norms.

WATER POLLUTION—EXISTING LEGAL FRAMEWORK

Water pollution is becoming an acute problem in many parts of India. Most of the rivers are polluted by the discharge of industrial effluents and sewage into them. The main source of water pollution in India is sewage, which comprises 90% of pollutants and only 10% comes from industry.

The professed aim is to restore and maintain waters at various places to such qualities as are needed for their best use. The Indian legal system provides four major sources of law for addressing water pollution problems:

- A comprehensive scheme of administrative regulation through the permit system of Water Act, 1974
- Provisions of the Environment (Protection) Act, 1986 relating to water quality
- Public nuisance actions against polluters, including municipalities charged with controlling water pollution
- And the common law of right of riparian owners to unpolluted water.

Though sufficient protection has been provided by the law of the land, laws alone are not sufficient to prevent pollution. Public participation also has to play an active role. With our population, illiteracy and shrinking resources, how far we can stretch our legal system to offer a desirable level of environmental protection is debatable.

INDEX